A Lawyer

A Memoir
Ronald L. Ruiz

ISBN: 1-4751-1950-X
ISBN-13: 9781475119503

To Randy and Stephanie —

Enjoy

Ron Ruiz

Other works by Ronald L. Ruiz
Happy Birthday Jesús
Giuseppe Rocco
The Big Bear

Praise for other works by Ronald L. Ruiz

Happy Birthday Jesús
- "The novel succeeds... because of the relentless nature with which Ruiz forces us to see what he sees." — *San Francisco Chronicle*
- "A talented, painstaking, and intelligent writer." — *The Houston Post*
- "Savage and searing... A rare degree of intensity... His narrator's voice is convincingly authentic... What might otherwise be merely shocking is written with such burning conviction, and with such obvious dead-on accuracy, that it casts a dazzling light... [Ruiz] knows his characters intimately, and he renders them on the page so vividly that only a reader with a heart of stone could ever forget them." –Alan Ryan, San *Jose Mercury News*
- "Undeniable raw power and genuine feeling for the downtrodden... Riveting... Frighteningly real." — *New York Newsday*
- "Powerful... important and illuminating." — *Houston Chronicle*
- "A Novel on a Mission: ... gripping... thrusts us vividly into the consciousness of those members of our society who may become the ruin of all of us... Ruiz's novel has earned an important place in our literature for the courage to shock us from our complacency." — Gerald Nicosia, *Los Angeles Times*
- "There's no redemption here for anybody... You can agree or not, but you won't be the same after reading this book." — Carolyn See, *The Washington Post*

Giuseppe Rocco
- Winner of the 1998 Premio Aztlán Award
- "A talented, painstaking and intelligent writer."– *The Houston Post*
- "Ruiz is at his best in describing the beauty and transformation of the countryside around the city of San Jose beginning in the 1950's. He also has a deep understanding of the nomadic lives of Mexican workers in labor camps and cheap motels." — *Independent Publisher*

The Big Bear
- "A notably different courtroom drama in which a young Mexican-American battles overwhelming odds to become a lawyer, then a good lawyer, and finally-sadly enough-a successful one... Ruiz... creates a warts-and-all protagonist for his third outing...: you may not always like Gabby, but you'll probably find yourself rooting for him." — *Kirkus Reviews*

For Amanda, who taught me love, and without whose help this book would not have been possible.

Chapter 1

When I think back to the 38 years I spent as a lawyer and try to settle on the path that led me there, I have only to look as far back as my grandparents. Beyond them I have no history, which for this purpose is just as well.

Jose Ruiz, a Tarascan Indian, said that he rode to the United States border on a white horse from his native Michoacán, Mexico, paid a dollar, crossed, and never looked back. He was a short, stout, dark, strong, thick-necked man who settled many disagreements with violence. My father used to say that he had seen "the old man" fight many a man. He liked to tell how "the old man" would stalk his opponent, often taking many blows before he could grab that opponent with two hands and then lift him and then throw him at whatever was closest. As a boy, that image often filled me with awe. On the other hand, not awesome at all, was the fact that he often beat my grandmother. It was his blows that probably crippled her, and which bred in her a deep hatred for "the old man."

He was a shrewd man who soon found a way out of the oppressive labor and slave wages that Mexican immigrants worked under in those days on California's agricultural fields. He became a labor contractor. He was quick to learn that, despite his limited English and youth, he could sell the services of other immigrants to white growers who spoke no Spanish. He and the grower would agree upon a price. Then he would recruit and transport eager immigrant workers to and from a given ranch. The grower would pay Jose for his crew's labor and Jose in turn would pay the workers after he deducted his transportation costs, the meals that his wife, Soledad, had provided for them, shelter that he often gave them, even in his own open backyard, and his time. Before long, Jose Ruiz was one of the wealthiest Mexicans in the Fresno area. He bought a large truck, a family car, and one of the few homes owned by a Mexican in Malaga, a small hamlet outside of Fresno.

They say that Jose Ruiz liked to drink which was no doubt true. But he could not have liked the misery it caused him and his family. The more money he made, the more he drank. When the family heard the big truck pull up at the end of the work day, everyone in the house, especially Soledad, knew to stay out of his way. He would have already been drinking and the silent, seemingly deserted house would soon take him out into the back yard to continue drinking under one of Malaga's lone trees. After a while, he would go directly to the tree with his jug rather than stop at the house. Many a night, he slept under that tree and many a night Soledad tried to coax one of the boys to go out and sleep with him. It was not his safety that she was concerned about, but rather the large sums of money that he always carried in his pockets. Many nights there were workers sleeping in the back yard sheds or chicken coops or in the open air, and few could have missed his lavish display, once he was drunk, of the money he carried.

It was not the years of drinking that did Jose Ruiz in but rather arthritis that crippled him. By the time their children were grown and gone, he had squandered thousands in his drunkenness and they moved to Fresno where Soledad cared for Welfare kids to support them. The few times I visited them on Callisch Street, my grandfather was nowhere in sight. Years later, my father bought them a house in San Jose. There I did see him when I visited. He was sitting, sleeping, living on a worn couch in the bare, attached garage with a dog. My grandmother lived in the house. The only contact she had with Jose Ruiz was when she limped to the kitchen door that opened onto the garage with a plate of food three times a day. Then she would open the door and bark, "Jose!" and set the plate down next to the dog's bowl on the garage step. How Jose Ruiz got to the step from the couch, I don't know.

I visited my grandfather as he lay dying in the hospital. We were not close and I really did not know the man. On one level, I admired him for refusing to be just another Mexican immigrant. I thought he paid a price for that and I wondered if he thought so, too. We traded pleasantries. He seemed glad to have a visitor. He became animated near the end of our visit when I asked him to say something in his native Tarascan. Out came the harsh, clipped, guttural sounds, words that I didn't and would never understand. He spoke them loudly and clearly and with pride, so far from the mountains where he had first heard and learned them.

Years later, I became involved in Caesar Chavez's struggle to improve the working and living conditions of farmworkers in California. Hated even more than the growers by Caesar and his union, were the Mexican labor contractors who had so callously taken advantage of their own. I often thought of the abuses that my grandfather must have inflicted on the needy, even more naive farm-workers of his day. I never mentioned my grandfather to anyone in the labor movement. But I didn't hate him.

The racism that existed against Mexicans when I was growing up as a boy in Fresno in the 1940's and 50's was a major force in shaping me. Still, it had to have been worse for my father's and grandfather's generations. My father and I never talked about it. He never broached the subject. But there is an incident that remains firm in my mind that spoke for him.

He and I are in one of the better department stores in Fresno, one that most Mexicans don't shop in. But then, he is well-dressed. I'm eleven or twelve. The saleslady is writing up a sales slip. She appears to be well-meaning enough.

"Will that be all, Mr. Rue-ez?"

"That's Reese." The Spanish pronunciation is Rrueece.

"Reese?"

"Yes."

"R-e-e-s-e?"

"That's right."

"I'm sorry. Let me erase that, Mr. Reese."

The woman is more respectful now, deferential even. He's no longer a Mexican. I'm embarrassed. My father stands firm, upright in his snappy clothes.

"Here you are, Mr. Reese," handing him a sales slip bearing his new sur-name.

From that day on, whenever anyone said to me, "Is that Rue-ez?" I nodded or said, "Yes."

Leo Ruiz was born to Soledad and Jose Ruiz in 1915, the second of five sons and two daughters. There is a photograph of him and his younger brother, Joe, taken by a street photographer in San Francisco, probably in the mid1940's. He is wearing an expensive, conservative, grey tweed suit with a grey fedora hat, a black shirt buttoned at the collar and black wing-tipped shoes. Joe is similarly dressed in clothes most likely selected by his older brother. The look on Leo's face is one of determination and confidence. His long stride adds the same dimension. Where he is going only he knows. For sure he has gone far, far from Malaga, that dusty little hamlet of lean-to shacks with rusty, corrugated tin roofs, erected catch-as catch-can by and for the Mexican farmworkers. He looks to be a handsome, ambitious, energetic, intelligent young man in his late twenties, even though he has had but a fourth-grade education. Had he been the son of a wealthy, white, established family, there is no telling what he might have already been. Instead, he has long since learned to live by his wits and take everything he can by doing so.

He liked to tell how, as a boy, he was the only one of the boys who was willing to sleep next to his drunken father under the tree in their Malaga backyard. How he had to be careful to cloak his willingness so that his brothers wouldn't suspect that there was something to be gained from it. How taking enough blankets to keep warm and hide what he was about to do, he would seemingly, reluctantly go out there with "the old man" to spend the night. There he would pinch and kick "the old man" to make sure that he wouldn't come out of his drunken stupor while he took "the old man's" money out of his pocket and peeled off just enough so that no one would ever suspect what he had done. Then he would sleep until daybreak and wake "the old man" before returning to the house and his bed.

He went to school only until he had learned to add, subtract, multiply and read some. Then he could do what no one else in the family or any of the farmworkers could do. He became his father's paymaster when he was 12. There it was easy to siphon off money from his father and the workers without being detected.

He was the only one of four sons who didn't become a prize-fighter. "Are you kidding? Go in that ring and get my head knocked off! For what? For chump-change?" As it turned out, he got part of the chump-change anyway without ever stepping into the ring. He became each of his brother's managers.

Slight of build at 5'6" and 130 pounds, he began carrying a gun before he was thirty. He carried one for some thirty years. A gun was always in his car, next to his bed, within reach whenever he was "working," or if necessary, on his person. He often told of the look in men's eyes when he pulled out his gun, of the instant respect and control it gave him in any situation. He never spoke of shooting anyone, but he was quick to brandish it whenever he felt threatened or even intimidated.

Leo and his older brother, Eddie, became an accomplished singing duet. They sang at Mexican fiestas, dances and parties. Leo was the lead singer and Eddie accompanied him on the guitar. Leo's voice was strong, good. So good that they became the first Mexican singers in the valley to make a recording. As 17 and 16-year-olds, they drove the family car to San Francisco for the occasion.

Then they were even more popular among the Mexican communities in the Central Valley. Less than a year later, Leo left the duet. He was restless. There was always something better, had to be something better over the next horizon. He used to say that he could never go to movies, hated being in school, because he was too worried thinking about what might be happening, what he might be missing outside. Even when he was hanging out at Fernie's Pool Hall in Chinatown as a youngster, he said he would take breaks between games and go out on the street, walk around Chinatown to make sure he wasn't missing anything.

Why he married my mother, he at 20 and she at 19, remains a mystery to me. She was neither glamorous nor beautiful nor white, as all but one of his six wives were that followed. The fact that she was pregnant with me and had been thrown out of her mother's household and was living in the Ruiz household no doubt had much to do it. Their marriage was over three years and three children later. But it was really over long before that.

My earliest memory of Leo is of him taking me to San Francisco when I was 5 or 6 years old. World War II had begun. He took me to Playland at the Beach and bought me, dressed me and paraded me around in an Army suit. I remember the positive responses we got from people. Ironic indeed. Leo had just gotten out of the Army, after boot camp, with an honorable discharge and a lifetime pension for a physical disability. Often he boasted how he had outwitted the Army doctors by taking pills that had been smuggled onto the base, by eating soap and feigning dizziness.

The next time I remember seeing Leo was when my mother took me to a fancy bar where he was working as a bartender. She sat me on a bar stool for all to see as he worked. He was not making the court-ordered child support payments and she meant to embarrass him. It didn't and by the time I was 10, she was sending me downtown to his lawyer's office to see if the monthly $50 payment for the support of three children was there. After a while, the lawyer's secretary would just shake her head when I opened the door and she saw me. We didn't speak. There was nothing to say. How I hated going up to that office every month. My mother must have hated it even more.

It wasn't that Leo Ruiz had no money, because before I was 12, I had seen him driving around Chinatown in a brand new Cadillac. My mother said he had two Cadillacs. What I didn't tell her was that when I saw him there was, what I thought and believed at the time, a gorgeous, beautiful white woman sitting as close to him as she could. I knew that would just make her angrier. Nor did I tell her that I had seen his kid brother, my uncle Gilbert, driving a new convertible with the top down with two beautiful (they were all beautiful to me then) white women, one in the front and one in the back, their long blonde hair flapping and flying in the wind. (Later, Gilbert would tell me that he used to drive around Chinatown like that by the hour because it so infuriated the white cops to see him with those white women.) Not long after I had seen Gilbert and his blondes, my mother told me that people had seen Gilbert driving around Chinatown with two white pigs in a new car that Leo had bought him.

Still, he wasn't paying the $50 a month court-ordered support payment, which was making our lives more difficult. I couldn't understand it. He wasn't denying paternity, nor was he ashamed of me as I found out once I got my paper route. I was 12 then. Part of my route included Chinatown and one of my business customers in Chinatown was the Valley Rooms.

The Valley Rooms was one of Fresno's two whorehouses and it intrigued me. It was located on the second floor of a two-story building. The entrance was a set of steep stairs that went up from the street through a narrow, dark passageway to a door that would only be opened after you had announced yourself and a sliding peep hole had verified your announcement. The third and fourth stairs up from the street were wired to set off a buzzer to let the girls know that someone was coming up. Once I knew that, I devised a way to get up to the door without stepping on those stairs. I loved pounding on that door unannounced and yelling out, "Collecting for the Bee!" and hearing the commotion that followed inside. But after a few such entries, the girls had a surprise for me. One day as I stepped inside, one of them said, "Look, ladies, it's Leo's boy!" Then several scantily clad women came out and "Oowed" and "Ahhed" at me. From then on, that's how they greeted me every month when I went upstairs collecting for the Bee.

Some men donate millions to institutions of higher learning and have buildings built and named after them. Some bishops and cardinals have huge, elaborate churches constructed as monuments to themselves. As soon as he was wealthy enough, Leo Ruiz had a pool hall built in Malaga.

I don't know what Malaga looks like now but I clearly remember what it looked like then. It was still the same dirty, dusty village of shacks and lean-to's constructed by the poorest of Mexicans. One of Malaga's few permanent structures was an old, small wood-framed building near Highway 99 that served as its only store. Next to that store, Leo built his pool hall. It was made of newly painted stucco and glass, and solid wood doors. There was nothing else like it in Malaga. It had three pool tables, benches, a bar that served beer and soft drinks, an office and a toilet. At that time, neither Leo nor any of his family lived in Malaga. A young couple ran it for him. He visited the pool hall at unannounced times, usually on Saturdays and Sundays when the place was busy. He enjoyed the respect and tributes that were paid to him whenever he entered, both verbally and with looks. He carried his gun on those visits and brandished it several times, especially at the beginning, threatening to blow one wild-eyed youngster's head off if he didn't shape up or if he had to talk to him again.

He also bought a ranch with his new money. As far as anyone could tell, he was the first Mexican to own a ranch in the Central Valley. It was a small ranch: 40 acres of grapes and apricots. He moved his parents and two young siblings into the ranch's red farm house. He put his father in charge of raising the grapes and apricots. "Give the 'old man' something to do." He had an old barn leveled and had an apartment built for himself some 75 yards from the house. He had developed a penchant for apartments: no maintenance, great mobility, one wasn't tied down to it like a house, and they were always new and cheap enough so that he could have several in different places. But the ranch apartment was different. He owned it and he had it built to his specifications. It was a white, two-story stucco structure with a garage and storage downstairs and two large rooms, a small kitchen which he never used and a bathroom upstairs. One entered the apartment through the front room which had a curved bar on one side with a full stock of whiskeys and wines behind it. There were sofas and tables and dark drapes covering all the windows. The room was dark, day or night, unless one turned on the lights. By this time Leo was "working" nights and sleeping days. The bedroom had a large bed, dressers and mirrors everywhere. It too was dark. There was no telling when he would be at the ranch. When he was there he slept, occasionally with a woman, had a meal with his mother, and left. He never visited the fields except during a few weeks of the harvest season. Then he made it a point to walk the fields with his father for ten or fifteen minutes, dressed in what he called his "safari outfit" (like clothes you could once buy at The Banana Republic). Those walks had the purpose of making it clear to the migrant workers who the owner (*el dueño*) was and who the real boss (*el mero jefe*) was.

Leo loved his mother. She may have been the only woman he ever loved. Proof of it was that he trusted her with his money and no one else. Soledad Ruiz was a small, slight woman who still dressed as the Mexican women in her *rancho* dressed: dresses and skirts that came down to their feet, that billowed out over several undergarments. Leo told me that there were times when he was carrying "lots of money," so much money that he was afraid that the police might stop and search him or that he might be robbed. For those situations, Soledad had sewn pockets and belts onto her undergarments and the backsides of her skirts. For days and sometimes weeks, that little, old, crippled woman carried his money around with her, with no one the wiser, until Leo felt it was safe to move it. I never asked him, and he never said where all the money had come from.

There were some things I thought better not to ask about. I never asked about his drug habit either even though he told of an occasion when he was going to have to surrender to the police but was strung out. He was afraid of what might happen, what he might say if he turned himself in in that condition. So he went up to a cabin in the mountains alone and kicked "cold turkey." He usually told this story when he was scoffing at some miserable addict who couldn't or wouldn't "kick." Beyond that, there was nothing more ever said about his addiction.

Soledad must have loved me, not like she loved Leo, but loved me nevertheless. I must have been 9 years old one day at St. Alphonsus School. The school took up an entire square block in west Fresno. The classrooms were in a two-story building that stood on one corner of the block. The rest of the block was an open field with basketball courts, a volleyball court, two baseball diamonds, a slide and exercise bars. The lunch period was an hour long. It took me two or three minutes to eat my lunch and I usually spent the rest of the hour running around the fields. That day when I was at the far end of the field near the fence, a Cadillac honked. I looked up and saw Leo behind the wheel. He parked and I went to the fence and he rolled down the window and said, "She wants to see you." I looked at the back seat and there was my grandmother, smiling, her head just above the window, with my Aunt Emily sitting behind her holding her up. I hadn't seen my grandmother in several years. "She's been real sick. We've been at the doctor's all morning. She kept saying she wanted to see you. Talk to her." I didn't say anything. I didn't know what to say. She didn't say anything either. She just smiled for several minutes. Then Leo drove off.

When the subject of Leo's two Cadillacs came up at home, I would ask my mother what kind of work he did to have that kind of money. She would say,

"Your father's a bad man, mi'ijo, a bad man." I knew she was hurt and that she hated him. What I didn't know then was that she still loved him. What neither of us knew, or could have known, was how "bad" he really was.

In the late 1940's, a Colonel White, the head of the state's drug enforcement task force, announced a breakthrough in a major narcotics traffic ring that spanned from Los Angeles to San Francisco. Several arrests had been made and trial was to begin in a few months. The Fresno Bee gave the case front page coverage. On the eve of trial, a man by the name of Abe Davidian was shot in the head several times as he lay sleeping in his mother's home in Fresno. He died instantly. Davidian was Colonel White's prime witness in the narcotics case. Without him, the State had no case. The F.B.I. had hidden Davidian and his wife, Marie, pending trial, at a dude ranch outside of Phoenix. He was to stay there until the trial began, but Davidian apparently tired of the boredom and secrecy and went to Fresno to visit his mother. It was then and there that he was murdered. The F.B.I and state officials questioned Davidian's wife who had left Phoenix sometime before he did. They also questioned Leo Ruiz, with whom Marie Davidian was then living. "They had us in there for three days and three nights. The feds and the state. They came at us from every which way. I got to hand it to that woman. She really held her mutt. They got nothing out of her and they didn't get anything out of me, either. Of course, I got a hold of Matt Goldstein right away. Want a lawyer? Get a Jew. They finally let him in and then they had to let us go after three days and three nights." Those are my father's words as best as I can remember them.

Just after my fifteenth birthday I ran away from my mother's house and made my way to San Jose where Leo was living with Jean, a white woman who was a waitress in a local restaurant. Why Jean was with him, what she got from him, I never understood. I lived with Leo for five months. It was one of the more important educations of my life.

Leo did not have a job when I arrived, which did not surprise me. But he was "working."

Given the Cadillac, the apartments, the good food and drink, he had to be "working." Most nights he'd leave the apartment around ten or eleven. I don't know when he returned but it had to have been late because he always slept until about noon. Sometimes he would be gone for a few days or even a week. Where he went or what he did was never discussed at first. The most I knew then was what Jean told me. "Your Dad's gonna be gone for a few days." From what I had heard from my mother and my aunts, I assumed it was something illegal. Once Speed Hunsaker became comfortable around me, it was clear that they were gambling.

Speed Hunsaker was a sixty or seventy-year old German Jew, who came to the apartment two or three times a week. He would arrive around 3:00, stay for dinner, and then stay until he left with Leo around ten at night. He was a spry, bald old man with tufts of white hair above his ears who liked to walk back and forth across the front room and into the dining room, talking as he paced. Except for a pot belly, he was in good physical condition, lean and firm everywhere, even around that belly. He had a long full nose and bulbous grey eyes that he would close as he nodded to himself, certain that what he had just said was correct. He wore black dress slacks that he belted above his belly, soft black leather high-tops and a white dress shirt. As he paced and talked, Leo sat where he always sat, at one end of the couch, not listening, not hearing, his eyes distant, his intertwined thumbs twitching around each other in his lap, his jaw tight in anticipation of what was to come but seldom came, or when it did, was never enough. In the kitchen, Jean had to be thinking what she would say to me the next morning, "That old man is driving me crazy." But he was Leo's friend and associate. So what could she say? What dared she say?

Leo must have bragged to Speed, as he did to some of his "old rounder" friends, that I was "real smart in school," that I wanted to go to college. So early on, from the second or third day we were together, Speed started in on me as he paced. "Alright Ronnie, if you're so smart, what's the capital of Germany?"

"Berlin."

"That's a real easy one. Anyone should know that, even kids in grammar school should know that. If you're so smart who drafted and signed the Declaration of Independence?"

"Thomas Jefferson, John Adams...uh...uh."

"Come on. Come on. If you're so smart, that should be on the tip of your tongue, pop right out of your head. If you're so smart, when and where was the Battle of Bull Run fought?"

On and on it went at least once or twice a week, with Leo sitting there with a smirk on his face, half-amused by the silliness without leaving the more serious things he was considering.

After a while I guessed correctly that Speed didn't know the answers to many of the questions he posed either and any answer would do, would have him close those bulbous grey eyes as he nodded, and sometime before dinner say, "Pretty smart boy you got there, Leo."

Jean was a terrific cook. But at the dinner table, Speed invariably compared a dish that she had prepared to a similar but better one he had had in a fine restaurant as far away as the east coast. She had said enough to me about Speed's quips that caused me to look over at her as Speed went on, watch her lower her head and bite her lip and occasionally look at Leo. If Leo had heard anything, it hadn't registered. What was about to happen somewhere else, at some other time, was always consuming him.

After a few weeks and after Jean had gone to work, they talked openly around me about their gambling. How Speed would go up to Eureka three days before Leo and sit in on a game they had heard about. Leo would then go up as a total stranger and sit in on the game the day before pay day and again on pay day. They had to be careful not to be seen talking to each other or acknowledging each other in any way. There would be hell to pay if anyone connected them. Another time they discussed the game the Armenians had going in Fresno, but backed away from it because Leo was afraid that someone might know him there. Often they had discussions about what had happened the night before. One day Speed was very upset, claiming that Leo had slipped or almost slipped and left the other players with a suspicion that they were together. He was almost certain that they hadn't heard the last of it. When Speed went to the bathroom, Leo said to me, "You know he's the one who really fucked it up, not me. He's not what he used to be anymore. He's getting old. In his day, he was one of the best. Now he gets rattled, nervous, scared. I don't know how much longer I want to run with him."

Leo had another apartment across town which he used whenever Marie was in town. He had told me much about Marie before I met her. He had a respect for her that I had never seen him have for another woman. He always said that she was good to him and often repeated that for those three days and three nights, "She really held her mutt." He loved to tell about the time that she had come "home" and said, "Honey, I brought you something."

"What?"

"It's there in the suitcase."

He went to the bed where the suitcase was lying.

"Open it."

"Why, what's in it?"

"Open it."

He opened the suitcase and almost fell over. The suitcase was filled with money. Twenty, fifty and hundred dollar bills. Full.

"It's all yours, sweetheart. I knew you'd like it."

Marie was the Madam of a Nevada whorehouse. "She's French," Leo was always reminding me. He was as proud of that as he was of the fact that she had her own whorehouse. Marie was French-American but what Leo meant was that she wasn't some Oakiefied, mongrel, white bitch which was the best any other Mexican could do. To me, she was a complete surprise. She was quiet, not a quietness born of timidity or shyness but rather of a certitude that she need only speak when she had something to say. Her favorite pastime seemed to be sewing. She would sit in the room, needle and thread and a garment in her hand, listening mostly to my father and occasionally saying something, all the time sewing. She was a handsome woman, though not strikingly beautiful, in her late thirties or early forties. It was her dignity that spoke to me, much more than anything she ever said, wore or looked like. Her face was long and narrow and her complexion was a pale white, yet soft and warm. She wore no makeup when I was around, and her round green eyes seemed to take in everything. Her voice was soft yet firm.

At 15, I was very excited about meeting this queen of sex. I'm sure I imagined that she would at least let me have a glimpse of what had to be a well-preserved body or titillate me with stories about her whores and their customers. That was not to be. Marie turned out to be as straight-laced and dignified as any woman I had ever met.

I never saw Leo so much as kiss Marie on the cheek. But then I only saw her four or five times, and that was for an hour or two in an afternoon. I'm sure Leo saw her more often than that when she came to town. He would tell Jean that he "had to take care of some things" and be gone for a night or several days.

There were some evenings, after Jean left for work and Marie wasn't in town, that Leo would drive us to his other apartment. Once there, we would sit in the front room and he would play recordings of the music he loved. Usually we sat there for two or three hours as the room gradually darkened and then was completely dark. With one exception, all the musicians were black: Count

Basie, Duke Ellington, Jimmie Lunceford, Lionel Hampton, Billy Holiday, Dinah Washington, Sarah Vaughn, Ella Fitzgerald and the blind English pianist, George Shearing. He had seen most of those artists in Los Angeles and every so often he would talk about where and when he had seen and heard them.

It was the first time I had heard that music, and I liked it. Little did I know then how much I would grow to like it. Later, Leo owned a bar in San Jose and his juke box played only Mexican *rancheras* which usually told of a man losing his woman to another man, to drink or some other weakness. His Mexican patrons played the juke box constantly. The more they drank, the more they seemed to relate to those sad songs. Leo had traveled leagues beyond those *rancheras*. How this man from Malaga had acquired a taste and appreciation for world-renowned and respected musicians like Ellington and Basie, Lady Day and Ella Fitzgerald has always fascinated me.

As we sat there, Leo was as relaxed as I ever saw him. Instead of sitting wondering, worrying, anticipating what was to come, he was enjoying that music. He wore a dazed, thoughtful, sometimes regretful look as he listened and perhaps revisited the past. At times he would shake his head, "tsk" or "hmph" to himself. He was not yet 40 but sometimes the look seemed to say that life had already passed him by.

After the five months I lived with Leo, I saw Marie only once more. I was a junior in college and the Brother Prefect came to my room and told me that my father was outside and wanted to see me. He was parked in front of my dorm in his latest Cadillac. Marie was sitting next to him. He got out of the car when he saw me and came toward me. His flashy Las Vegas clothes, his loud manner and his showy car embarrassed me. Others were watching. I went back to the car with him. Marie looked at me with those round green eyes and said, "Hello, Ronnie." Her hair was redder than before, she was wearing make-up and her skirt was well up on her thighs, so much so that I didn't want her to get out of the car. "We were just in the neighborhood, just passing through and thought we'd stop by and say hello." My father never quit. St. Mary's College was located far back in the Contra Costa County hills. There was no "just in the neighborhood," no "just passing through." You were either going to or coming from the college if you were on the road that led to the college. We visited there next to the Cadillac with Leo and Marie sitting in it and me standing outside it. I'm sure they saw and felt my awkwardness and embarrassment. Our visit didn't last long.

When he visited me at St Mary's, Leo had already moved to Las Vegas and was married to another woman. What he was doing with Marie in northern California, I never knew.

After that I only saw Leo once every two years or so. No matter what woman he was living with then, I always asked about Marie. When I did, it was as if I had struck a nerve. He would pause, stop everything he was saying or doing, think anew and tell me that she was still calling him from time to time, asking him to join her in northern Nevada where she was still making a lot of money. Once he said that she had actually gone to the Tropicana in Las Vegas where he was the manager of the Keno Department and shown him her new Mercedes roadster, complete with doors that swung upward over the car's cab, begging him to go with her, promising that they could be "real happy" together. Happy or not, he was too ensconced in the life he had and needed in Las Vegas.

Leo's move to Las Vegas was precipitated by a relationship he had developed with a man I'll call Tony. Leo told me that at one time Tony controlled all the gambling and prostitution in three California counties. Once the casino boom began in Las Vegas, Tony bought one of the old downtown gambling casinos. Leo had gained Tony's confidence and served pretty much as his right hand man. "He's as smart as anyone you're ever gonna meet. He doesn't say much. He just watches. You know, in California he used to sit alone in one of his bars, way down at the end of the bar where it was pretty dark, with a drink, two at the most, and just watched the people as he nursed his drink. He does the same thing here. Damnedest thing I ever seen. But he's rich and powerful." He was more than that.

Tony was a white-haired, blue-eyed, tanned Italian whom I met in Las Vegas and later came to know in Mexico, where he lived for several years with his wife, an ex-showgirl. Part of that time he spent at his hotel near Mexico's west coast. He fished in the Pacific once or twice a week using a little motor launch. He walked every day and ate all his meals in his restaurant. But what he did mostly was read. He read literature, history, politics, economics and more. I was in my early twenties then and couldn't understand how Tony had stooped to such a close relationship with Leo. One day I made some snide remark about Leo and Tony turned, angry and scolded me. "He's your father, Goddammit! He's your father!"

The last time I asked Leo about Marie, he was nearing 70 and she had to be in her 60's. He said that she had called a year or so back and said that she had a pet store in Santa Fe and they could still have a good life together. She knew of his many wives, but that didn't matter. But it was too late. He was losing his eyesight from glaucoma and was afraid to move.

Chapter 2

It is late February or early March in 1935. The trees behind them are leafless. They are on the grass. He is in shirt sleeves and her arms are bare. They are in Roeding Park. A Japanese cone bridge spanning a make-believe creek looms behind them. He is kneeling on his left knee. His right knee juts up and around her right side. She is sitting on the grass between his legs, her back pressed against him. His right arm is wrapped across her breast, his open hand resting on the side of her left breast. Her right hand is clutching his arm. She is 18 and he is 19. They are lovers. She is smiling. In all the years I knew her, I never saw her happier than I see her in this photo. He is the love of her life. Despite all the misery, hardship and agony he put her through, Leo was, is and will always be the love of Lucy's life.

I turn to December, 1998 for what is to me irrefutable proof of that love. Leo is dead. His coffin is resting on wooden slats awaiting his last journey into the pit below him. When I arrive at the cemetery, some are already there, standing, sitting, waiting for the priest's arrival. The first row under the awning at the grave site has been reserved for family members. As I move past people to that first row, I am shocked to see: my mother, Lucy, already sitting in the first row, less than three feet from the coffin. Even more shocked, hurt and embarrassed am I to see sitting next to her, my stepfather and Lucy's husband for more than 50 years, Andrew. Andrew is as good and decent a man as I have ever known. He is the father of Lucy's last child, my half-brother, Steven. He was always more of a father to my sisters and me than Leo could ever have dreamed of being. I feel anger. What the hell is she doing here? Worse, how could she have dragged that poor man here? After a few moments, what she is doing here is readily apparent: she is grieving. She is mourning, mournful.

Later at a family reception, she is there with Leo's surviving siblings: Eddie, Emily and Irene. These are people who over the years she has scorned and at times said she hated. Now she grieves with them. As Andrew watches.

Whatever success I've had in my life, I owe to my mother. Mom was a difficult person, endured and even hated by one of those closest to her. But with each passing year, I love, respect and admire her more. On the other hand Lucy was clearly Jesusita's daughter. Grandma was as tough, difficult, complex, and disciplined as anyone.

In 1915, Mercedes and Jesusita Arriaga left their home in Jerez, Zacatecas, fleeing the ravages of the Mexican Revolution. They took their son and two daughters and whatever they could carry and headed northward to the United States. A year later they arrived in Chihuahua where Lucy, my mother, was born. It was another year before the family waded across the Rio Grande in the dead of the night, carrying their few possessions in a sheet and a blanket. They made their way to Douglas, Arizona, where my grandfather worked in a copper mine for three years. It was hard work for a man who had been a saddle maker and a trumpet player, unaccustomed to manual labor. But there was no other way. Josephine, their fourth daughter, was born in Douglas. They heard that the wages and living conditions were better in California and moved to Fresno, where Mercedes went to work laying track for the Southern Pacific Railroad. It wasn't long before the blistering summer heat and the biting winter cold took their toll on Mercedes. He caught pneumonia in his second year on the track and died. He left Jesusita with five children, ages 12 to 3.

Many years later, I asked my grandmother, "When my grandfather died and you had all those little kids, why didn't you go back to Mexico?" She didn't hesitate, didn't have to give it a second thought. "When I lived in Mexico, I had maids. I was not going to return to Mexico as a maid." She was a fiercely proud woman.

It was that pride and incredible self-discipline, strength and courage that carried her and those five children up and down California's Central Valley and along its central coast for six years, thinning, picking, harvesting everything from plums to row crops, from the first days of April to mid-November, under horrendous conditions before they returned to Fresno for five months. They slept under fruit boxes and fruit trays, and when there were none, under trees or vines or bushes. After working from sun-up to sun-down, she and Rudolf, the boy, dug pits and gathered rocks and wood to build fires to cook on. They dug other pits for their human waste. Leaves were their toilet paper. There were never any stores around and refrigeration was not even a dream. So they ate mainly beans and tortillas and whatever fruits and vegetables they were harvesting. Water came from the ranch house, which to Lucy always seemed a mile away. In the beginning, she was too young to work in the field, so it was her job to fetch the water, a jug at a time. She also had to pull Josephine around in a fruit box with an attached rope to keep them near wherever the others might be working.

Throughout those seven months in the *campo*, Jesusita spent as little money as possible. She kept her money, money that would be needed to get them through the winter months when there was no work, tied and hidden under her clothes. Returning to Fresno, they took whatever lodgings were available: first a garage, then a room, then rooms, improving year by year until they were finally able to rent a house. The pattern continued until Rudolph, at 18, got a year-round job with a milk company and Lupe, the oldest daughter, was hired by a local department store. Jesusita and the three younger girls continued following the crops until Jesusita got a "steady" job cleaning in an office building at night. About that time Elvira, the second daughter, contracted tuberculosis and died.

Jesusita was a holy woman, attending the 6 o'clock mass and receiving Holy Communion daily. She organized the Guadalupana Society which cleaned and prepared the altar every Saturday for Sunday masses. By the time I was 6 years old, she had made me an altar boy. There were mornings when I went to the 6 o'clock mass with her. She prayed that I would become a *sacerdote* (priest); she said that nothing would make her happier. There were times when I saw her crawl on her hands and knees, dressed in black, from the vestibule to the altar railing in a show of her unworthiness, begging for God's forgiveness. Yet I never saw her go to Confession. But then no one expected her to confess. Confess what? She was a holy woman. A woman close to God. Holy indeed. What the congregation did not see, but what I saw, was what went on in her home.

One by one, Jesusita's children married and left. She began supporting herself by caring for Welfare children: Mexican kids who were either orphans, or had been abandoned by their parents, or had been taken from their parents by the court and, in some cases, who were juvenile delinquents. Grandma was strict with those kids. She was strict with everybody. The punishments she meted out for transgressions as slight as not answering her quickly enough, or spilling something, or not making the bed the way she had instructed, were open and frequent; accepted as part of everyday life in her house.

I can still see Pifi or her sister Nena being led into the pantry, terrified. Grandma is behind, belt in hand. The belt has not yet been used, but we all know it is coming. She leads either or both of the girls into the pantry. There the girl kneels on two bricks and Grandma puts a half-brick in each upraised hand. "I'll be listening," she says and closes the door behind her. She posts herself at the door and as soon as a brick drops, she springs into the pantry. The slap of the belt and the cries of the girl follow.

She had a special punishment for my friend, Phillip. By sliding a railing in front of a cot in one of the bedrooms, she would make what looked like a big crib. Then she would bring Phillip into that bedroom and order him to strip. We would all be watching. She had a towel that she used as his diaper, fastening it on each side with huge safety pins. Once he was diapered, he would turn and go to his crib, without a word or motion from her, head down and shoulders drooping. He would get into his crib facing us, which was the only direction he was allowed to face, while she got his bottle ready. He would lie there, sad-eyed, like a beaten dog. When she returned, it was with his bottle, a quart-sized milk bottle filled with water and covered by a huge rubber nipple. She would shove it through the railing and he would take it to his mouth with both hands and begin sucking. Compliant? No. She had the belt with her and all the kids said that nothing hurt worse than that belt on bare skin. "You want to act like a baby!" she'd shout. "Then you'll be treated like a baby! Some day you might start acting like a man!" She would stalk out, leaving us to stare at Phillip. Not that you had to be in the room to see him, because the door was kept open so that anyone passing could see him. Phillip was 13 when he ran away.

Then they were gone, all of them: Grandma, Phillip, and all the kids, without a word of goodbye. Mom said that Grandma had decided to move to San Francisco to be near Uncle Rudolf, and Phillip and all the kids had gone back to the Welfare Department. Mom had always resented the special love Grandma had for Rudolf, so her move made sense to me. But I missed the other kids.

The summer after my first year in college, I found a job in San Francisco and arranged to stay there with Grandma and her sister, Carmelita. Again, I saw a side of Grandma that few knew. The two older women lived in a flat in a grey, grimy alley in a low industrial area just south of Market Street. Their flat was one of six in a three story building. It was long, dark and narrow with two bedrooms, a living room, kitchen and bathroom. It had six windows: two in the front bedroom facing the alley, two in the kitchen overlooking a small block of cement that they called the backyard but which was never used by anyone, and two in an air-shaft that let in more darkness than light, day or night. Grandma had the front bedroom. Next to that was Carmelita's bedroom with one of the air-shaft windows, followed by the bathroom and a living room with my couch and the other air-shaft window.

The sisters worked in a small, sweat-shop sweater factory adjacent to the city's then "skid row." They spoke very little English and the owner of the factory spoke only Chinese. How they communicated I never knew, but they worked there for several years, even though after many a payday, they complained that "*El Chino*" had cheated them.

They lived frugally. They managed with the barest of necessities. In the two bedrooms each had a single bed, a dresser and a chair; the living room had a red couch and the kitchen had a table and four chairs and a small radio that was never played. It was 1958. Black and white television had probably made its way into some of the neighbors' flats, but not theirs. Their food consisted mainly of beans, rice, eggs, squash and tortillas.

My first impression was that they wore the same clothes, day in and day out: dark, usually black, cotton skirts and blouses and black overcoats to cover everything whenever they went out. They wore sweaters in the flat during San Francisco's cool summer days and probably more sweaters during the winter. They had an abundance of sweaters. "*El Chino*" couldn't watch them every minute of every day. When I asked Carmelita how the little gas heater in the living room worked, she said she didn't know because they had never used it.

Carmelita made it clear that she was saving every penny she could for her eventual return to Mexico, where she would live out the rest of her days. Grandma didn't say, but I assumed that because her children and their families were in California, she would be staying and was saving toward the day that she would be living alone. Despite her frugality, Grandma had been writing to Mom and my aunts for years asking that they send her five or ten dollars because she couldn't make ends meet.

I saw very little of the women while I was living there. Mornings we were busy getting ready for work. When I returned in the evenings, they had already eaten and each was in her own room with the door closed. Fridays after work, I hitch-hiked to Fresno and then back again on Sundays, sometimes arriving after they had gone to bed. Carmelita was pleasant with me but I seldom knocked on her door. Some evenings I knocked on Grandma's door, wanting to make some sort of contact.

One evening when I knocked, I found her sitting by the windows overlooking the alley, reading. I had never seen her read anything before.

"What are you doing?"

"I'm reading."

"What are you reading?"

"A book called *Don Quijote de la Mancha*."

"What's it about?"

"It's about a man, a knight, who rides his horse around the countryside in Spain trying to do good acts."

It would be at least a year before I heard of the book in college, and many more before I appreciated its importance. Years later, especially after I had visited Jerez and realized that there probably wasn't even an elementary school when she was living there, I would think back to that evening and wonder how my grandmother had come to be reading *Don Quixote de la Mancha*.

A few weeks later, I knocked on Grandma's door one Thursday evening. There was no answer. I knocked again. Still no answer. I hadn't heard anyone go out, and she never went out at night that I knew of. Concerned, I opened the door. She wasn't there. I went to the other side of the bed to be sure. No. I went to the closet and was about to open it, when Carmelita said, "She's not there."

"Where is she?"

"She went to the opera."

"To the opera?"

"Yes."

"What opera?"

"The one she always goes to."

"When did she go?"

"About 20 minutes ago."

"I didn't hear her go out."

"I didn't hear her either and I'm right there."

"To the opera?"

"She goes every Thursday night except when they're not playing."

"Where's the opera?"

"I don't know. She says it's in the center of town somewhere. She says it's in a big, beautiful building with lots of lights and a big stage."

"Is it free?"

"Oh no, no."

"How much does it cost?"

"I don't know, but it must cost a lot because she never has any money."

"It can't cost that much?"

"Well, besides paying to get in, she saves her money to buy fancy clothes and shoes and hats. You haven't seen her when she's all dressed-up in her opera clothes. You wouldn't recognize her."

"I didn't know she liked music so much,"

"She doesn't. She doesn't. We have that little radio in the kitchen. Have you ever heard her play it? Not once."

"Why does she go then?"

"It's the people. She wants to be like them."

"The people?"

"The people that go there. She says they're all rich and beautiful. She wants to be like them. That's why she saves her money. To buy fancy clothes like they have. And she won't wear the same dress or shoes or hat too many times. Because she says that then they will think that she has no money. So she keeps buying fancy new clothes and shoes and hats that she wears only a few times. Because she says the fashions change, so she has to buy more new clothes."

"She goes there all the time?"

"Every Thursday except when the opera's on vacation."

"How does she talk to these people? She doesn't speak much English."

"She doesn't talk to them. She's so light-skinned, you know, that she says they all think she's from Europe some place. She's never told then she's a Mexican because what would they think of her if she said that? She says that all she's ever had to do is nod or shake her head or say yes or no or smile. That's been enough.... You should see her before she goes. She's so excited. And when she comes home, she's so happy."

"How does she get there?"

"She walks."

"Walks? This is a dangerous neighborhood."

"That's what I try to tell her, but she walks anyway."

"How does she get home?"

"She walks too."

"What time does she get home?"

"Usually between 10:30 and 11:00."

"And she's not scared?"

"No, she always laughs at me whenever I try to warn her. So I don't say anything anymore. She always tells me that nothing has ever happened to her after all these years, so why should she be scared now?"

The following Thursday after dinner, I crouched behind the wall next to the hall. When I heard the front door lock click, I jumped in the hallway. "Grandma!"

She stopped and turned in the open doorway. Carmelita was right. I would not have recognized her. There she stood in black high-heels, dark stockings, and a multi-layered black hat with netting that hung just below her eyes and a fine black coat that I had never seen before. She looked at me for a moment, an imperious look, and then, without a word, stepped out onto the landing, closing the door behind her.

She died a few years later and was buried in her fine opera clothes.

Almost fifty years later, just before her own death, my mother said to me, out of the blue, "I think I should tell you that the reason your grandmother left Fresno and went to San Francisco was that the District Attorney had threatened to send her to prison for what she had been doing to those Welfare kids she was taking care of, if she didn't leave town."

Aside from hearing about the hardships the family endured in the California agricultural fields and the bleak days of the Great Depression, I know very little about Mom's early life. I know that she reached the eleventh grade but never completed it, presumably because she went to work. She never spoke to me about what had to be one of the bigger events in her life: her pregnancy with me. What I know of it, I learned from others.

When it came to her children, Jesusita, like most parents, had her pecking order. Rudolf was her king, Lupe her princess. Elvira had died and Josephine was her baby. Lucy was at the bottom of that totem pole. For Jesusita, sex outside of marriage was a mortal sin which made the offending woman a whore in this life and an eternal resident of hell in the next. There were no exceptions and no excuses. She had made this abundantly clear to her daughters. So when Lucy at 19 turned up pregnant with me, when she could no longer hide it, Jesusita was outraged. Not only had Lucy offended God, but she had ravaged Jesusita's reputation in the community; and for Jesusita, nothing mattered more. Revered by her peers as a holy woman, she was about to become a laughing stock.

"Out! Get out of my house! Now! Before I beat you and your sin to death! And don't you ever set foot in here again! You're no daughter of mine! You're a disgrace!"

Lucy left with only the clothes on her back, walked out into Fresno's scorching heat, not knowing where she was going or how she would get there, knowing only that she had to reach Leo. He came for her just before dark and drove to his parents' home in Malaga where he and his three brothers and two sisters lived. Gossip said that there was already another pregnant girl living there. The two-bedroom house that had seemed palatial when Jose Ruiz bought it some 20 years before was now badly worn. It still had no running water and the outhouse in the back yard was in constant use. Lucy and Leo shared one of the bedrooms with Leo's three brothers and the other pregnant girl. Fresno was five miles away and accessible only by car but not everyone had a car.

Lucy was miserable. Living in Malaga in the middle of nowhere, confined to a house that was bursting with people, wearing whatever discarded clothes fit her as I swelled in her belly, her situation, their situation, had to have affected Leo. He got his first steady job at the Valley Bedding Company, a mattress factory in Fresno. In those days a man married the woman he had impregnated, thereby making her an honorable woman. It was the right thing to do and Leo must have been reminded of his obligation on all sides. So Leo married Lucy in a simple civil ceremony with only one of his brothers and one of his sisters in attendance as his best man and Lucy's matron of honor.

They moved to Fresno, to a tiny grey house in an alley behind a poultry processing plant. In the years that followed, Mom would often say when we passed that alley, "That's where you were born," or "That was your first house," or "That's where we were living when you were born." The alley was between "E" and "F" streets bordered by Merced and Tuolomne streets. Merced was the street we walked down to get to downtown Fresno. The house itself was no more than a third of a block down the alley. But the house's exterior was so depressing that I never went into the alley to examine it.

The house had to be a dejecting sight for Mom as well. Her memories of it must have been horrendous. Sometime after my sister Eleanor was born, Leo and his brother Eddie began singing and playing at bars and clubs, and at weddings and parties on the weekends. He initially told Mom that it was to earn the extra money that we needed. It wasn't long before those weekend jobs took up the entire weekend, until there were no earnings to show for them, and instead, some of his weekly paychecks were being spent on them. When Mom protested, Leo beat her, beat her into fear and submission, which gave him a free rein.

Payday was Friday at Valley Bedding and Mom said that Leo was spending so much on the weekends that by Thursday, there was nothing to eat in the house. One week it got so bad that Mom took Eleanor and me to Jesusita's house two blocks away so that we could eat. She hadn't been there since she had been thrown out three years before.

Grandma greeted us at the door. "What do you want?' she said coldly, sternly.

"I wanted you to meet your grandchildren."

"They're nothing to me and will never be anything to me as long as that man is their father."

"I've told them all about you. I've told them that you're their grandmother and they want to meet you."

"Stop! Do you take me for a fool? The little one in your arms wouldn't understand any of that, and I doubt that he can understand much more."

"Can we come in?"

Grandma paused, looked away and then unlatched the screen door and said, "Come in."

Mom said that I went into the kitchen and stood next to some of the Welfare kids watching them eat their lunch of rice and beans.

"Can he eat?" Mom said.

"What's the matter, doesn't that man of yours make enough money to feed his own kids? You sure picked a good one."

Grandma hated Leo. He was the son-in-law who had blemished her reputation. He was a Malaga Mexican. Only the poorest and filthiest of Mexicans lived in Malaga where there was no running water or toilets, and for some, there was no electricity. They never bathed. How could they? If you were in a Mexican store, you knew who the Malaga Mexicans were. They stank and none of them ever went to church. Was it any wonder that they were poor and lived in filth? The father of that clan was a mean drunk, known in every bar for throwing his money around, womanizing and beating anyone he thought had gotten in his way. None of his six children had ever held a steady job, although she had heard that Leo was working.

"Is your husband still working?"

"Yes."

"Sit down then and let the children eat."

It wasn't long before we were there again. Mom tried a different approach. "Things have been slow at Leo's job and his paycheck doesn't go very far. Can we have something to eat?"

"Please, I'm not an idiot. It's all over town how your husband and his brother have one big party every weekend with lots of women, music and liquor. Money never seems to be short for him. Does it?"

Mom said that it took all she had to keep from crying. But she was afraid that if she did, we might not eat. While she was feeding Eleanor, Grandma saw what Mom was afraid she might see.

"You're pregnant again. Are you out of your mind? How could you want anything more to do with that man?"

If her mother only knew what it was like to be beaten by your husband, she thought.

Mom said there were other times when Grandma let us eat and she would sit cold and imperious, watching us, as if she enjoyed seeing our hunger.

Then Marian was born. By then, Leo was in the habit of taking his Friday paycheck and not coming home until Monday morning to change his clothes with little or no money left. Mom was in the hospital for four days after Marian was born and Leo did not go to the hospital once to visit them. Once home, Mom found his sporty new dress clothes hanging in the closet with lipstick smeared on the shirts. She took a pair of scissors and cut his entire new wardrobe into long strips of ribbons. Leo gave her the beating of her life and left. We had no money or food. We went to Grandma's again. Once there, Mom asked if we could stay, that she, we, couldn't go back. When Grandma saw Mom's condition, there was no turning us away, not even by Grandma.

But there was no place to put us. Grandma had six Welfare kids living with her in a two-bedroom house. Kids slept everywhere. If the Welfare woman came and found four more people living there, she might take the six and Grandma's livelihood away from her. Finally, it was decided that the basement would be our room. This was no modern basement. You entered it in the backyard by lifting a set of wooden planks up and over the hole that dropped down into a dirt basement. Grandma had shelving and canned fruit jars down there so that the floor at least had to be packed. I was almost five then and one of my earliest, most unforgettable memories is standing outside that open descent, staring at the dirt walls, knowing that we would be sleeping down there.

I don't know how long we slept in Grandma's basement, but it had to have been several months. My next memory is always the same. Suddenly we are at another place, another house.

It is night and the only light in the room is from candles casting big shadows on the wall. There is a bed in the room and my sisters are already asleep in the bed. Mom is guiding me to the bed. Then she blows out the candles and all four of us are in the bed. Once again, she has managed to keep us together.

War is raging in Europe. America's involvement seems imminent. There is an ongoing buildup of the armed forces. Men are volunteering for the service. There is something of a conscription. There's a scarcity of manual labor. Mom had gotten a job at Valley Bedding. She is doing Leo's work. He left months ago. At five-foot-one and a hundred and twenty pounds, she is doing a man's job. She is making mattresses and toting them from place to place. Welfare as we know it today didn't exist then. Welfare was for orphans and abandoned children. Unlike Leo, Mom didn't abandon us. With her second paycheck she rented a one-bedroom house whose backyard abutted Grandma's. She worked 9 hours a day, Monday through Friday and from 8:00 to 1:00 on Saturdays. She fed, bathed and clothed us. We had no car. So all our food and whatever else we needed had to be bought and carried on foot by Mom.

Mom hired Lala, our next door neighbor's grandmother, to watch over us while she worked. Lala was a dried-up, shriveled-up old woman in her 80's who had trouble hearing and seeing. She dressed in black: long, full, plain, black skirts down to her shoe tops and loose black blouses. A large, wooden rosary dangled from her waist. But for the fact that she didn't wear a habit and that her grey/black hair hung in a single braid below her waist, she could have passed for a nun. Her work consisted of walking across the six-foot slab of cement that separated the two houses once or twice in the morning and afternoon to see "how we were doing," and to sit with us at noon while we ate the sandwiches and drank the milk that Mom had left for our lunch. In those days, there wasn't a Spanish equivalent for Ronald or Ronnie, so Lala just settled on "Brine" which she croaked out in a funny and at times ghastly manner. Mom didn't pay her much, but then she didn't do much and Mom didn't have much to pay her with.

As September neared, Mom decided that I would be going to St. Alphonsus School as a first-grader when the school year began.

"But I'm only five, Mom. You have to be six to be in the first grade. Everybody knows that."

"Well, from now on, you're six."

"How could that be?"

"Because I said so. That's how."

"Why can't I go to Columbia School. It's way closer and all the kids at Grandma's go there."

"Because I said you're going to St. Alphonsus. That's why."

"Why?"

"Because I said so. That's why."

That was all the reason or reasoning Mom ever had or needed. But then, that was all the reason and reasoning Grandma had ever needed.

A week before school started, Mom quizzed me every day. "How old are you?"

"Six."

When were you born?"

"May 2."

"What year?'

"1935.... Right?"

"Right."

Grandma was ecstatic. I was her first grandchild, her first child, to enroll in a Catholic school. She was so proud. And she was also so sure that this was a sign from God that I would be the first priest in the family. I became her favorite grandchild. If not then, for sure the following year when I became an altar boy and began serving Mass.

Lala had to be happy too that I was starting school. I'm sure she had reported to Mom that I never obeyed her, that I laughed at her, that I ran from her whenever she tried to talk to me, and that I wasn't very nice to my sisters.

Mom did our wash on Friday night because she only had to work half a day on Saturday. The washing machine and wash trays were located in a small, screened-off back porch which faced our back yard, contiguous with Grandma's back yard. It was on one of those Friday nights that I was awakened by a commotion on the back porch. I got out of bed and went to the back door, but it was locked. The yelling continued. I ran out the front door and around to the back yard. What I saw was Mom standing beside the washing machine being beaten by Grandma and my Aunt Lupe. Grandma had something in her hand and was hitting Mom with it. Lupe was pulling on Mom's hair and hitting her too. They were yelling about what a disgrace Mom was to the family: first a divorced woman and now going out with men. Everybody in town was talking about her. Had she no shame? I started crying and screaming, "Leave my mother alone! Leave her alone! Stop hitting her!" My Aunt Marie came out of the house and tried to take hold of me. I ran from her, crying and screaming. When Aunt Lupe saw me, they stopped and left. I went to the back porch. Mom was hunched over the washing machine crying. I didn't know how to comfort her. She was all we had. Would they ever stop hating her?

Afterwards, I was sick in bed for more than a week. I had a fever, was weak and couldn't get out of bed. We never went to doctors because they cost too much. But after a week, Mom got scared and took me to a doctor. He could find nothing wrong with me. Of course, we didn't mention the beating. Aunt Lupe was my godmother. After we went to the doctor, she sent me presents. I didn't want her presents. Mom was our everything. She was our family.

When Grandma moved to San Francisco, we moved into her bigger, nicer house. Then with little regard for the Catholic Church and Grandma, for the family's reputation, for what her siblings thought, Mom partied. She and her friends worked long, hard hours six days a week and on Saturday nights they partied with an abandon. It was the only time I saw Mom let loose, and it lasted only until she met Andrew.

Of all her children, Grandma held Mom in her lowest esteem. On the other hand, Grandma was not Mom's favorite person either. Yet in some ways, Mom became the exact image and likeness of Jesusita, more so than any of her other children. Perhaps it was Mom's life circumstances that created this anomaly. Like Grandma, Mom had to struggle and persevere against incredible odds to keep her family together, to survive. They became strict disciplinarians. Their way was the only way. Their way had brought them survival. In the process, they became incapable of seeing other ways. Incorporated in their way was the use of violence. Mom had seen and felt it used often; she had learned it well. In Mom's family we all had our chores and expected mode of behavior. Mom worked hard and obeyed all the rules and expected us to do the same. Step out of line and there would be whippings with sticks and belts. For several years, I bore the brunt of those whippings, often receiving them daily, because, I always thought, Mom was determined that being the only boy, I wasn't going to be another Rudolf, another family favorite. How I resented my Uncle Rudolf in those days, even though I hardly knew him.

Eventually, Andrew came into our lives. A wonderful man. Mom ruled him too. Together they worked. He, like my grandfather, didn't speak English and so worked as a common laborer on highway construction up and down the Central Valley in its blistering heat and bitter cold. She in fruit packing sheds and plants. All the money, every cent, went to and through Mom. Every dime was important. On Saturdays and Sundays, I shined shoes outside our two neighborhood bars. Sometimes I made as much as eight dollars. (Eighty shoe shines!) Every one of those dimes went to Mom. That was always understood. She saved and scrimped and bargained and shopped and saved some more. Not in vain. We were one of the first Mexican families that I knew of to move into a house that we were *buying*. It was not much of a house but it was "ours." A few years later, she made an even bigger leap, something none of us expected. She sold the first house and made a big down payment on the house of her dreams: a big, sparkling new house with a huge bay window in a new tract on the edge of expanding Fresno.

We were out of the barrio. Across the street lived a young doctor and his wife; behind us lived a successful young businessman and his family. There wasn't another Mexican in sight. I didn't believe we belonged there. Sadly, that came true. After a year and a half, no matter how much she scrimped, she couldn't make the house payments. They lost everything. Mom was heartbroken. We moved to an older neighborhood in North Fresno to a house that was worn and small. We were still out of the barrio, but Mom was crankier than ever.

Mom's iron hand, her determination to control us, to make us into her likeness and image, when most of the time she seemed miserable, had repercussions. I ran away from home. Marian followed a few years later. Then Eleanor left. Worse, for many years, until Marian's death, Mom had to live with Marian's open, bitter, and vocal hatred of her.

The seeds for my running away were planted in the summer following my freshman year in high school. I was 14 and Mom decided that I was old enough to work full time that summer, to learn what it was to work and contribute to the family fund. She found me a job in a packing shed cutting fruit. After three days, the foreman laid me off. He told Mom that I wasn't keeping up with the other workers. Mom was angry. She said that I had deliberately set out to be fired, that I was lazy and didn't want to work, that I was intent on being just like Rudolf. Throughout the following school year, she often mentioned my faux pas and promised me that I would work full time the next summer. But summer arrived and she had not been able to get me a job. The first morning after my high school sophomore year, she was angry. She vowed that she'd get me a job soon, but in the meantime, she ordered me to clear all the weeds along our back fence. I was angry too. Without a word, I went out to the back fence with a hoe in hand and began hoeing in the early morning Fresno heat. A few minutes later, I decided that I didn't need Mom or that hoeing. It was then that I jumped over the fence and ran away from home.

During my high school years, Mom seemed miserable and seldom happy. But then one night, I saw that like Jesusita, Mom had her own deep secret. After five months of living with Leo, I had called her, to ask her if I could come home. Yes, she said. Two days later, Leo and I arrived in Fresno after dark. Andrew was working nights. At the house, I went to the door and Leo remained in the car. I didn't know what to expect when I knocked. Mom answered. She was dressed-up and made-up and went right past me out to the car. I didn't talk to her until the next morning because after three hours, I went to bed and she was still in the car with Leo.

Then, just after they were married, Lucy took Andrew down to the bar where Leo was working. When Leo went over to them and asked them what they would like to drink, she said, "Leo, this is my husband. This is my new husband."

I didn't see Mom much once I left for college. Over the last ten years of her life, I called her almost every Sunday night. They were not fun calls. More often than not, I dreaded them. They were long dirges of how hard and unfair life was. After all her work, discipline, sacrifice and strength, she had come to this: a tired, miserable, afraid, moaning old woman. One of her hardest blows had been Marian's public hatred of her. Despite her harshness and short-comings, and there were many, I couldn't hate her. She had done so much for me.

I loved her. One thing in particular has always stood out in my mind: the time she woke me in the middle of the night and changed my life.

I was 13. I had just finished the first week of my freshman year at Edison High School in West Fresno where, at that time, all the *niggers* and *spics* went to school. It was not a problem for me. I was where I was expected to be. "Ronald," she said. She always used the full name she had given me when the matter was, in her mind, serious. "You're not going to Edison anymore. You're going to San Joaquin Memorial."

"What?"

"You heard me. You're going to Memorial, not Edison."

"Why? I don't want to go there. Who's going to pay for it? How am I going to get there? It's way on the other side of town."

"You're going there and that's it." That was Mom. That night she changed my life forever. I will always be grateful. But for her, I couldn't or wouldn't be writing any of this.

Just before I left for Berkeley and the University of California's School of Law, I went to see Leo's old attorney, Matt Goldstein. He had become a judge in Fresno and had counseled me one day four years before when I left for college. I had returned no doubt to boast, brag about not only going to Boalt Hall, but going there on a scholarship. Court was in session and his bailiff approached him on the bench and whispered that I wanted to see him. He looked over at me and nodded. He was gracious and kind in his chambers. The thing I remember most, in fact the only thing I remember and will always remember about that meeting, are these words: "You know, they were not educated, but you come from a very intelligent mother and father."

Chapter 3

It was 1943 and Fresno was still a very arid place. Temperatures often reached 100 degrees by the first day of May and continued on into September. But it was a dry, bearable heat, though hot nonetheless. In that summer on Sunday evenings, I bathed in wash-trays in a screened-off back porch. The water was cold but welcomed. It must have been around eight o'clock. The sun was red in the west. There was a speedway on the edge of West Fresno where midget race cars raced on those summer Sunday nights. The drone of the small cars rose and fell as they maneuvered turns and straight-aways. As I sat in the water, I knew that Sunday was the end of the week, the sky's redness said it was the end of the day and the droning emphasized that everything came and went. Everything would end, especially me. And the thought terrified me.

But religion gave me succor. I had been taught that there was a life hereafter, one that went on for eternity where there would be Everlasting Happiness. But there was a price to pay. The nuns had taught me that I was born to know, love and serve God in this life and to be happy with Him forever in the next. But I had to be good. Because if I sinned I would go to Hell forever and ever. There were two kinds of sins: a venial sin and a mortal sin. Both could be absolved and I could be put in the State of Grace if I confessed them to a priest, felt genuinely sorry that I had committed them, and vowed that I would never commit them again. If I was in the State of Grace when I died, I would go to Heaven and be happy with God forever. On the other hand, if I died with a venial sin, a lesser offense, on my soul, I would have to burn in Purgatory for a while, depending on the number and gravity of those venial sins, before the Gates of Heaven would be opened for me. But if I died with a mortal sin on my soul, as defined by the nuns and the Catechism and the priests, I would spend Eternity burning in the blazing, hottest fires of Hell. More often than not, I was convinced that I would die in mortal sin, especially after I was 13 and was masturbating, which was not only a mortal sin but which some priests said could lead to insanity. Once in Hell, the only relief I would be able to give myself, I thought, was to volunteer to be one of Satan's helpers. In that way, I could tend to the fires and poke all the other poor bastards into the fire, keeping them in the hottest flames while I burned to a lesser degree on the side in that darkness.

It would be several years later in college before I ran into that old Roman philosopher, Lucretius, who for the first time in anything I had heard or read said, you live this life and when you die it's over. Final, end! None of this here-after stuff. It's not so remarkable then, that from those early college years in my Great Books studies, one of the few figures that I remember is old Lucretius. All I can remember about *The Iliad* and *The Odyssey* is that one was about a war and the other about a voyage.

I don't remember how race crept into my life but it had to be at a very early age. We lived in that part of West Fresno where only "Messicuns and niggers" lived. There was plenty of racism in that little section of Fresno. I can remember women telling me to be careful of niggers because they were mean, evil people who would kidnap, beat and kill you if you weren't careful. To this day I can still see me walking alone to a nearby bakery. I couldn't have been more than five. All of a sudden, I see this big, black nigger man walking toward me on the sidewalk and I don't know what to do. If I turn and run, he'll for sure catch me. If I keep walking toward him, he'll catch me sooner. I stop and wait. I'm about to cry. He comes and looks down at me. I scoot off to the side. He sees how scared I am. He smiles and says something like, "How you doin', little fella?" and walks by.

I don't remember anyone telling me about the other racism. I first became aware of it without words. There was no need for words. It was everywhere. A few of "the others" lived nearby but most of them lived in another part of West Fresno near the school and the church and on the other side of Kearney Bou-levard. Their homes were big beautiful things, in some cases two-stories, with beautiful lawns and lovely trees. We never went there. We didn't belong there. No one ever said that. They didn't have to. I knew that. To the east of us were the Southern Pacific railroad tracks, then downtown and beyond that, where all the rest of them lived; to me then, a sea of them, although at the time Fresno's population hovered around 50,000. When my Aunt Lupe and Uncle Raymond moved to the Eastside, as far as I knew, they were the first Mexicans there. But Raymond was white-skinned with green eyes. His family came from the state of Jalisco in Mexico to which many of Maximilian's French army had fled. My cousins were light-skinned and the few times I went over there to play, I could feel all the neighbors staring at me. I didn't belong there. I knew that then. Fifty years later when I revisited Bend Avenue, I was embarrassed by my early shame. My cousins' house was very small, modest and worn. The neighborhood now was the home of lower income whites and some Mexicans.

Once I started school, the racism was no longer unspoken. St. Alphonsus Grammar School enrollment consisted mainly of whites, some Mexicans and a few blacks. There I heard the words spic, greaser, grease-ball, cholo and dirty Messicuns for the first time. Birthday parties in those fine homes around Kearney Boulevard were constantly talked about at school before each occasion. I was never invited. I never expected to be. I was ashamed of everything: the beans and tortilla tacos that were brought by us to school for lunch (although today there seems to be a taqueria on every corner in Fresno), my mother ("Mom, if you're going to the school play, please dress-up, please look pretty."), but mostly about myself.

How I despised my brown skin. How I dreamed and longed to be born again, but this time with blond hair and blue eyes. Everywhere I looked, billboards, magazines, stores, movies, everything beautiful and fine was white. Everything ugly, dirty and poor was brown, Mexican. Yet it wasn't too many years later that I began wondering what it would be like to have been born black, born a nigger. I remember the 1968 Olympics in Mexico City when two black American track stars, Tommy Smith and Juan Carlos, stood on the victory podium and raised their black fists in protest as the Star Spangled Banner played. I thought then how lucky I had been not to have been born black, because had I been, I probably would have done more than that. I probably would have gone out into the street with a machine gun.

I graduated from St. Alphonsus' eighth grade and went on to San Joaquin Memorial High School on the other side of town. It was run by the Christian Brothers, a Catholic teaching order to whom I am forever grateful. But not before I spent my first week of high school at Edison High in West Fresno. The only other option would have been Memorial which, being a private school, could take me even though I lived out of the district. I didn't want to go to Memorial. All the Catholic white kids in town were going there but only a few Mexicans.

We didn't have much money and I expected to go Edison. I wanted to go to Edison where all the dirty Mexicans and niggers went. I would be comfortable there. But Mom intervened -how she persevered for all those years, where she got the strength, wisdom and courage, I'll never know- and I went to Memorial instead.

My first year at Memorial was not the panacea Mom thought it would be. Brother Albert, "Black Al" as all the students called him because of his five o'clock shadow, took one look at my brown skin and determined on that first day that I wasn't college material. He put me in the Freshman B section where all the Mexican students were and not in the Freshman A section where all the college-bound whites were. I was not allowed to study Algebra, but rather had to take Basic Mathematics. I couldn't take Latin and I refused to take Spanish: by this time I was no longer eating beans and I would be damned if I would regress further by studying Spanish. I was assigned to the Wood Shop and the "Manual Arts Program" to help prepare me, like all the other Mexican students, for the skills I would need to financially support myself for the rest of my life once I graduated from high school. In spite of "Black Al" I was elected class president and received A's in every course I took. When I returned for my sophomore year, we had a new principal, Brother Ignatius, and I pleaded with him to put me in the Sophomore A class, telling him that I wanted to go to college. Now I wonder if it was college I wanted, or if I just wanted to get away from all the other Mexican kids, to get away from so clearly being a Mexican. Brother Ignatius granted my request but I had to take Algebra I and II simultaneously as well as Latin I and II that year.

Religion and race as I knew them at St. Alphonsus were the same when I started high school, but it wasn't long before they appeared in a new form having to do with sex and girls. Sex was driving me crazy. Wet dreams were common. I was masturbating constantly. Always the objects of my dreams and fantasies during my masturbating were beautiful, luscious white girls, girls that I could never have but girls that I lusted after relentlessly. Never Mexican girls. I never found anything beautiful, much less sexually appealing, in Mexican girls; it was always white girls. When we moved to Vagedes Avenue and Mom's dream house, the doctor's wife across the street and the businessman's wife behind us used Eleanor as a babysitter. They marveled at my sister's beauty. Eleanor was beautiful. But I couldn't see it. I thought those white women were lying, looking down on us poor dirty Mexicans, throwing us a few crumbs to make themselves feel good and superior. Because everything Mexican was ugly. Now 60 years later and living near a high school in a Mexican community, I can see the beauty of the Mexican girls that I pass on the street every day, and at times marvel at how marred and scarred I once was.

From time to time, Sally Oaxaca still seeps back into my mind. Sally sat across from me in the eighth grade. I was 12 and she was anywhere from 16 to 18 and a full grown woman. She had to be the poorest of the poor. She came to school in the shreds of *huaraches*. Her cotton dresses were threadbare, printless and stained. Her big, brown legs were caked with grime. And she stank. God Almighty, how she stank. There I sat, next to her, knowing that every white kid in the class was smelling her and tying me to her. Some days I couldn't stand the stench, couldn't stand her big, sad, cow eyes and would whisper loud enough so that the white kids could hear, "Sally, take a bath! You stink! You smell like rotten piss! Aren't you ashamed? Take a bath before I puke!" Wherever you are, Sally, I hope you've long forgotten me. If I knew that, maybe I could finally forget you.

Racism left its heavy, ugly mark on me early on. By the time I was six, I knew that I didn't belong, that I wasn't wanted in white society and that "me and my people" were dumb, dirty excuses for human beings worthy of working only in the fields or on the most menial jobs in town. That conviction sent me on an almost life-long mission to prove white people wrong, at least as to me. I was obsessed, driven to proving them wrong in my case. But no matter what I accomplished, it never seemed to be enough. No matter what level of society I excelled in, there were still many in that level who wouldn't accept me, or another, higher level that I needed to be accepted in. Late in life, I began to understand that most people, regardless of their race or background or their position in society, were also driven by their fears of failure and inadequacy. Too often, the most successful had the biggest fears and the deepest feelings of inadequacy, and consequently were the most driven.

Ironically, in light of the recent revelations of the sexual perversions in the priesthood and the whole-scale attempts to cover them up, the priests weighed-in heavily on sex at student retreats. We boys, with our masturbation, were going straight to Hell and before we got there, probably to an insane asylum. Of course, I was convinced that I jacked-off more than anybody in the school. Going to Confession was a nightmare.

"How many times?"

"I can't remember, Father."

"Surely you haven't forgotten? How many times since your last Confession?"

"Sometimes once."

"Every day?"

"Yes, Father."

"More than once?"

"Yes, Father."

"How many times?"

"Sometimes two and three times."

"A day!"

"Yes, Father."

"Young man, you have a very serious problem. Do you realize that you're risking Eternity?"

"I know, Father."

"You know and still you keep committing this horrible sin of self-abuse, not once but two and three times a day?"

"Yes, Father."

"How can I be sure that you are sincerely promising not to commit this sin again? If you're not, I can't forgive you these sins and you must know that you're on the steps of Hell!"

"Yes, Father."

"Do you sincerely promise me that you won't ever masturbate again?"

"Yes, Father," knowing full-well somewhere, maybe down in the tips of my toes, that sometime after Holy Communion tomorrow, I would do it again. Knowing too that I would have to go to a different priest the next time I went to Confession, even if it meant taking the bus across town.

And then too, there were the movies. I loved movies and had risen past cowboys and Indians, past Doris Day and Rock Hudson, over war movies where the Americans were always the infinite good guys, and somehow had stumbled onto some masterpieces. Tennessee Williams *The Glass Menagerie* fascinated me. Arthur Miller's *Death of a Salesman* and his Willie Loman captivated me. Then there was Marlon Brando and *A Streetcar Named Desire*. But the Catholic Church's censorship panel had declared *Streetcar* obscene and immoral and not to be seen under pain of mortal sin. So there I sat in church that morning after that infallible pronouncement, wondering if I could risk eternal damnation. What if I were struck dead by God in the theater? A week passed. *Streetcar* wasn't going to be playing much longer. I wanted to see it. I finally decided to see it and go to Confession as soon as I could afterwards, somehow willing to risk that I wouldn't be struck dead in the theater. I didn't dare tell Mom that I was about to see that movie, that I was about to commit a mortal sin. I was already sure she suspected me of masturbating. I told her instead that I was going to see a movie that I had already seen, but one she didn't know I had seen. That Sunday afternoon I hung around the corner of the Warner's Theater until I was positive that no one who knew me, or knew anyone in my family, would see me. Then I rushed to the ticket window and inside. Wow! Brando screaming up the staircase, "Stella! Stelllaaah! Stelllaaah!" Blanche lying in bed as Stanley approaches, sure to rape her. I saw the movie twice and somehow avoided God's wrath.

Near the end of my high school senior year, because of my grades, I was one of four students that the Brothers took on four successive Saturdays to visit college campuses in the Bay Area. Mom didn't like the idea but she didn't say anything because whatever the priests, Brothers or nuns supported was not to be challenged. She saw no need for me to go to college. Trade unions were now beginning to accept young Mexicans out of high school into their apprenticeship programs. In her eyes, if I became an electrician, I would be a supreme success. As an electrician, I could make more money that she had ever dreamed a Mexican could make. By then there had been a dramatic change in the household dynamics once I returned from my run-away episode with Leo. By then, I was much bigger and stronger than Mom. But that didn't stop her. A few days after my return, I must have offended her because she came at me with the belt. She was going to beat me again, but I grabbed her cocked arm, twisted it back, went face to face with her, my fist clenched, and said, "You hit me with that strap and I'm going to knock you across this room." She screamed, "Andrew! Andrew! Come! He's going to hit me! He's going to hit me!" I'm not proud of that moment but she never hit me or even tried to hit me again.

So two Brothers took us first to Stanford, then to Berkeley and the University of California, followed by the Jesuits' Santa Clara University, and lastly to their own small liberal arts college, St. Mary's, 30 miles east of Oakland in the Contra Costa County foothills. This was 1953 and I had never seen anything like Stanford's bucolic campus. I had seen plenty of ranches when I had picked grapes and figs and apricots and plums, but never anything like "The Farm" at Stanford. The place reeked of rich white money and wealthy white students. Berkeley was another white world and it scared me, as did the university's sprawling campus. Santa Clara, in my mind, was an alternative for rich, white Catholics and even though it was far cheaper than Stanford, it was still well beyond my means. St. Mary's was small and seemed remote, and since dropping its football program, had suffered a severe drop in its all-male enrollment. It was by far the least expensive of the four institutions, a "poor man's college" to me even then. But those funds too were out of my reach. Fresno State was something of an option but I viewed it as a teacher's college and teachers didn't make much money. Besides, whoever heard of a Fresno State graduate who had accomplished anything? Further, it had a reputation then of being a college where all the white kids who couldn't get into the better universities went, and I wasn't about to hang out with lesser whites.

Just before graduation, the Brothers offered me a full academic scholarship to St. Mary's that would be good for four years so long as I maintained a certain grade point average. As for my room and board they said they would put me to work on campus to pay for that. Wonderful! Little did I know then that I would have to work weekends and nights to take care of my other financial needs.

The day I announced to Mom and Dad that I was going to St. Mary's, there was complete, absolute silence in the kitchen. Dad looked down at his plate. I don't know what he was thinking but I knew that he knew what Mom was thinking. I stood there waiting. Finally she said, "I don't see why you have to go to college. You can stay here in Fresno and get into one of those apprentice programs and become an electrician and make more money than Andrew and me ever will." I shot back, "Because I don't want to be a peon like the two of you!" I have never forgiven myself for those words. They of all people didn't deserve them.

I went off to St. Mary's and the realization came nowhere near measuring up to my summer-long expectations. That first week at St. Mary's I was miserable. I was one of three Mexicans in my class and I did everything I could to stay as far away from the others as possible, even though I was too scared to try to talk to the white students. The college seemed buried in the foothills without any other signs of life in sight, except for cows. The closest village was seven miles away. I had no car and saw no possibility of ever having one, so I was doomed to be imprisoned there for four, long years. The job the Brothers gave me was working in the kitchen serving breakfast, lunch and dinner in a white jacket to white students. After each meal, I ate not in the dining hall like all the other students, but back in the kitchen with a crop of old, broken white men, ex-winos and some winos still, who did menial jobs on campus for little more than their room and board. This was obviously their last stop and that week, I was convinced that it would be mine too. I avoided my white roommate, never speaking to him and, at night, in bed, hid my tears from him. I just wanted to be home in God-forsaken Fresno. I just wanted to be out of St. Mary's.

Friday after class, I hitch-hiked the 170 miles back to Fresno. It was dark when I got home. Mom and Dad were shocked to see me. I cried big tears and sobbed, "I'm not going back! I'm not going back! I'm staying here! I'm staying home!" "Why?" "Because I'm homesick, that's why! I miss all of you, that's why! I want to be here with you, that's why!"

Mom said nothing. But on Sunday morning after Mass, she came to my room and said, "Ronald, you're going back. You have to go back. Andrew will drive you back after lunch." That's all she said. But once again, she had risen to incredible heights. Dad drove me back. A rough, tough Brother Ralph, the dormitories disciplinarian, by chance happened to meet us as we drove up. My abrupt departure had been awkward to say the least. No doubt Brother Ralph, in all his years at St. Mary's, had seen his share of sorry, similar incidents. He was kind, thoughtful and above all, helpful. I was at St. Mary's to stay.

By the time I had selected St. Mary's, I knew I wanted to be a lawyer. But I said that to no one for fear of being ridiculed. *A MEXICAN LAWYER!* Who ever heard of such a thing? But I was convinced that being a lawyer would lift me out of poverty and being a Mexican. The college tours I went on strengthened my determination to be a lawyer. Two of the other boys on the tour, one the son of a lawyer, talked openly about becoming lawyers. My grades had been better than theirs and, I thought, if they could do it, so could I. By then, I was certain that I had discovered the formula for success in all human endeavors: hard work and discipline.

The practice of law was the only profession I had been exposed to. Matt Goldstein had been Leo's answer to so many of his and his brothers' legal problems. Mom would read aloud from the Fresno Bee's society page about events that Matt Goldstein and his wife had attended. He was the only person in Fresno's high society that she had ever met. Every year during the Christmas season, we drove to Christmas Tree Lane. It was where all the rich people lived and all the trees and houses were beautifully lighted and decorated. And each year

Mom pointed to the same beautiful house and said, "That's where Matt Goldstein lives."

And Matt Goldstein also represented Leo regarding child support. It was to his office that Mom sent me every month to pick up the child support he was supposed to be paying. As much as I hated going up to Matt Goldstein's office to be told by his secretary that Leo's lousy fifty bucks weren't there, still even her office was the most luxurious room I had ever been in; and after each rejection I loved to sneak off to the stairwell. Because Matt Goldstein's office was on the eighth floor, the highest floor in the tallest building in Fresno, and from the stairwell there was a magnificent view of Fresno and the Central Valley that I never tired of. Then too, I could almost say that I knew Matt Goldstein; a few times when I arrived, he had been standing at his secretary's desk and had looked at me and said, "Hello there, young man."

The week before I left for St. Mary's I went up, unannounced, to see Matt Goldstein. It had been some time since Mom had stopped hoping for Leo's child support and the secretary did not recognize me. "Can I help you?" I loathed those words. For years, every time I walked into a downtown store, a white saleslady would say, "Can I help you?" when I knew that what she was really saying was, "Get out of here you dirty little Mexican! We both know you don't have any money."

"I would like to see Mr. Goldstein, if I could."

"Do you have an appointment?"

My shoulders slumped: a new way of saying, "Can I help you?" "No, I don't. But Mr. Goldstein was my father's lawyer. His name is Leo Ruiz and I'm his son. And I'm going to college to study to be a lawyer and I would like to ask Mr. Goldstein for advice on how to do it.... I won't take long."

She thought for a few moments, not shaking her head like she always did. She sighed and stood and went into his office and closed the door behind her. I held my breath. I knew what the answer would be and each moment I became more embarrassed. I should never have come. I didn't belong there.

But when she returned she said, "Mr. Goldstein will see you now."

It was a gorgeous room. Polished wood everywhere. Beautiful rugs. Glass-encased book shelves with leather bound books. Books everywhere. He sat behind a huge desk. "What can I do for you, young man?" he said softly, graciously.

I told him that I was going to college on a scholarship to study to be a lawyer and rambled on about my good grades and how I knew that if one worked hard, studied hard, he could reach his goal.

He listened, watched, nodded encouragingly and after a while asked, "And what's your major going to be?"

I looked at him, puzzled.

"I mean, what's your main course of study going to be?"

"Political science," parroting what the boys on those trips had said.

"Political science? Why Political science?"

"Because I want to be a lawyer."

What he said next, I didn't understand at the time, but it was something I've always remembered.

"Nonsense. Get yourself an education. Educate yourself. Forget about being a lawyer. Educate yourself and becoming a lawyer will take care of itself. Major in English. Study literature. Get to know Shakespeare. I'm a lawyer now and I've been a lawyer for many years. When I was your age in New York and went to college, I majored in English. I studied literature. I learned to appreciate Shakespeare. Those studies opened up a whole new world for me and they will for you too."

I left Matt Goldstein's office floating on a cloud. But I was perplexed too. What was wrong with political science? Weren't most politicians lawyers? Get an education? I was going to college. Wasn't that an education? Study English? I already knew English. The one day that Brother Matthew had read something from Shakespeare in class, I had almost fallen asleep. Study literature? Four years of days like that Christmas vacation in the Fresno County Library reading Wuthering Heights, the first novel I had ever read, because it was required for me to graduate from high school. No way. Yet what a splendid introduction this had unknowingly been to Brother Robert.

Brother Sixtus Robert. He was at most five feet tall, bald and bespectacled. Students called him "The Penguin" and at a distance, he did resemble a penguin. Under his black cassock, his big belly seemed to begin just under his neck and extend down to his toes. His teaching order's white, stiffly-starched, medieval collar hung several inches down in front of his cassock. He seemed ageless: there was little change in the physical appearance of the man that I first met in 1957 and the man I last saw in 1994. He always chuckled before he laughed, and his clear brown eyes twinkled whenever he liked a concept, or was amused by it, or thought it was downright funny.

In my mind, he single-handedly breathed life into a college that had been depleted financially and academically. He brought Mortimer Adler's Great Books Program at the University of Chicago and instilled it as the mainstay of St. Mary's Liberal Arts Program. This meant that for four years, liberal arts students would read and discuss the Great Books beginning with *The Iliad* and *The Odyssey* and classics down through the centuries to modern times. It also meant that I, in Matt Goldstein's words, got an education. It many ways this little Christian Brother was my father figure. He was my main classics professor who, over four years, led endless hours of round-table discussions about The Great Books. Fortuitously, he was also my dorm prefect in my freshman year, which meant that he lived down the hall from me. He took an interest in me (and others to be sure) from the beginning and I lapped it up like a puppy dog. I wanted only to please him. I trudged through books that were often boring and I vigorously participated in classroom discussions that I sometimes thought were silly or beyond me, always to make sure that he didn't lose interest in me.

Sometimes on weekends when the dorm was empty, he would invite me into his room and give me juice and snacks and read to me. Most of what he read I didn't understand then, but I was interested anyway. It felt so good to be invited there. After my freshman year, he was no longer my dorm prefect and I didn't see as much of him. But I continued to confide in him over the four years, revealing some of my deepest fears and secrets.

At the end of my first semester there was an 18-day break during which I went home to Fresno. Before leaving St. Mary's, I went to Brother Robert's room and asked him what I should read during that semester break. He gave me Fyodor Dostoevsky's *Crime and Punishment,* saying that he thought I could relate to the book. I had never heard of Dostoevsky or the book, but it was to have more of an impact on me than any other book I have ever read. I have read it three times. The first time, the book was over one hundred years old. The last time, six years ago, it was 150 years old. It is the most powerful book I have ever read.

Relate to it, I did. I was 17 in February of 1954 and the perennial, winter, tule fog that curses California's Central Valley was just beginning to lift. Those days, as I sat and lay reading *Crime and Punishment* in my parents' backyard, are still very clear to me. Raskolnikov, a poor, destitute, tormented student lays in his squalid room thinking about the old, miserly, greedy, money-lending land-lady that he despises. "Kill her and take her money....For one life thousands of lives saved from decay and degeneration. One death and a hundred lives—that's simple arithmetic. And what, when weighed on the scale of things, does the life of this consumptive old woman mean? No more than the life of a louse or a beetle....." He brutally murders the old woman. What follows is his mental and physical punishment. After reading *Crime and Punishment*, it occurred to me for the first time that I wanted to be a writer, forgetting for those few moments that I had to be a lawyer.

In spite of Brother Robert, my need to rid myself of everything Mexican and all it's attendant feelings of inadequacy was greater than ever. My formula for success swung into high gear, several notches above what it had been in high school: the competition was keener. I studied day and night and as the final exams approached and arrived, sometimes all night. Those academic walls were the key to my future success. I was not interested in knowledge, I was interested in grades. Grades were what would get me into a prestigious law school.

For four years I had been consistently on the scholastic honor roll. I had been class president and class representative to the student council. I had run for student body president and lost. I could now openly say that not only did I plan to go to law school but I was also applying to law schools for scholarships. The only question seemed to be which law school would I choose? An English professor had encouraged me to go to the University of Chicago and earn a Ph.D. in English. He was certain I could be granted a scholarship there and was fond of saying, "You'd be a wonder at the university. The first Mexican-American intellectual." I wasn't interested in becoming a teacher or an intellectual. I wanted to be a lawyer. I wanted money. I wanted to climb into the white world.

What a rude awakening I was in for during those last days at St. Mary's. One night I walked into a room in the senior dorm looking for someone or something. There were ten or more guys in the room. One was the student body president; most of the others belonged to the so-called "in-group" of the senior class. One in particular was a little white guy from San Francisco's Mission District, fittingly for and ironically for what was about to happen, the city's Latino neighborhood. His name was Ken Stange. I don't remember many names from that class, but his I'll never forget. The group had probably been drinking and was having a boisterous meeting when I entered. No sooner had I closed the door when Stange began shouting. "What the fuck do you want here, you fucking spic! Who invited your filthy, fucking, Mexican brown ass in here anyway!" There was laughter all around. It may have been uncomfortable laughter, but I didn't think so at the time. "You're nothing but a dirty, grease-ball cholo and don't you ever forget it!" I stood frozen, not daring to leave and yet not wanting to stay, maybe hoping that it was all said in jest, that it would stop and they would all apologize. "Get your fucking greaser ass out of here before I kick it out!" More laughter. I left.

Finally, in my last semester, I had to deal with the existence of God in a way that I had never done before. I was aware of God even before I started kindergarten. My grandmother had made sure of that. Once in Catholic schools, He was everywhere. He was the reason for our being: to know, love and serve Him in this life and to be happy with Him forever in the next life. Even Lucretius' musing that there was no afterlife had not put a dent in His existence for me. The Brothers Karamazov had questioned His existence in a way that was troublesome. When one of the brothers tells of seeing soldiers throwing infants to hungry dogs and cries, "Where is your God!" that got my attention, that made me think of God and human suffering. But not nearly enough to doubt His existence. In those last months, God's existence took on an even greater importance because of a recurring thought. Given God's existence, wouldn't the best thing I could do with my life be to devote it completely to Him by becoming a priest? For months I ran from that question and its answer. I tried to block it out of my mind, but it kept returning. Finally, the irrefutable YES answer just wouldn't leave.

I began visiting the college's chaplain. He was a Marianist priest, the only priest on campus, and in no way connected with the Christian Brothers. He lived alone in quarters behind the chapel. My visits with him were usually late at night after I had finished studying. He had been a priest for many years and what struck me most about him was his solitary life. He was a lonely man. His quarters reeked of loneliness. And it was clear to me that he used alcohol to get him through many a night. I had usually been too busy to be lonely. But there were nights on weekends when the dorm was empty and I could study no more, that loneliness crept in and I longed for a relationship with a girl. I had never had one. I had always denied myself one, convinced that it would thwart my long-range plans. There would be plenty of time for a relationship, with a white girl preferably, once I climbed into the white world. My visits with the priest became more painful, taunting. I watched him carefully, scoured him for any human weakness, and finding almost as many as I chose to find, connected all of them to the loneliness of his solitary life. The thought of an endless life of loneliness for me was unbearable. For the first time, I turned my back on God.

Chapter 4

In 1957, Boalt Hall, the law school at the University of California in Berkeley, ranked third scholastically behind Harvard and Michigan. It was situated in a big, new, impressive building. Its faculty was replete with renowned legal scholars. In my first year, Dean Prosser used his own textbook on Torts, Professor Louisell taught from his text on Civil Procedure, and Professor Barret's treatise on Pleadings was our text. The law school attracted students from all over the country.

When I arrived, I was overwhelmed. It didn't help that in a student body of 300 plus, there were but three Mexican-American students. I put my success formula, hard work and discipline, into overdrive. For the first two months, I studied for what seemed like every waking minute. On Friday, Saturday and Sunday nights, I was one of the few law students in the law library and one of the very few who stayed until it closed. But my formula wasn't working. I didn't understand much of what I was reading and I understood even less of what was going on in class. When called on, I would sputter unintelligently, usually not understanding the question, let alone having any idea of what my answer should be. A blank look of silence was my answer, to the dismay of the professor. By the third month, I was packing T.S. Eliot's poems in my briefcase, and every hour or so when my brain felt like cotton, I would leave the library with my book of poems and find some private space to read a poem or more until I felt ready for another hour of study. I'm not at all sure that I turned to those poems out of a love of literature. More likely it was a matter of trying desperately to prove to myself that I wasn't a moron, or worse, just another dumb Mexican.

Our textbooks were a collection of cases written by appellate courts and the U.S. Supreme Court setting down various legal principles. By studying the facts of each case as set out by the court, and then following the court's reasoning, one should have been able to see how and why a particular rule of law had been arrived at by the court. But there were so many cases, thousands of sets of facts, reasonings and rules of law, that I was lost. By Thanksgiving, I was certain that come January and the exams, I would fail. Dean Prosser's opening day remarks plagued me: "Look to the right and left of you. One or both of them sitting there won't be with you when this class graduates three years from now."

The professors had warned us against using the law summaries that were available in campus bookstores. "Use those, and you will never have a sound, reasoning, legal mind." Panicked, I went to the bookstores after the Thanksgiving holiday and bought a Gilbert's Law Summary for each of my courses. What the summaries did was to lay down the rules of law in each course in a few sentences, telling which facts did and did not apply. For me, each summary said in 30 or 40 pages what a textbook didn't say in over 400 pages. All through December, I memorized my summaries. I passed my January exams with C's, well down in the class standings. But I was still in law school and there were a remarkable number who weren't.

When I returned for the second semester, I was determined to abandon the summaries and develop a "sound, reasoning, legal mind." However, I'm a slow reader and the assignments in the second semester were even more voluminous than they had been in the first. I could spend an hour reading a case and still not have the facts straight enough to follow the court's reasoning, nor know what proposition of law the case stood for. Every day, the number of cases assigned could be as high as 20. On the other hand, it would take me five minutes to locate and read a case in the summary and learn what rule of law it represented and what type of facts applied or didn't apply. Of course, as I labored over a text, the summary was within arm's reach. Still, the use of a textbook was of no help to me when I was called on in class. I was still a babbling idiot and the professors called on me less and less, either because they pitied me or didn't want to waste class time, certain that it wouldn't be long until I dropped by the wayside. After a month, I returned to the Gilberts summaries and at the end of the semester my grades improved to a C+, raising me a few notches in the bottom of my class. During the summer, I returned to San Jose and its canneries where I had worked during some of my college years. I worked twelve hours a day, six days a week, stockpiling money for the coming school year. When I wasn't working or sleeping, I was reading. Faulkner was a wonder to me. The Existentialist Movement was big in Europe and I read some of their fiction and treatises. During those months, the study of law seemed absurd. For the first time it occurred to me that if that was what it took to become a lawyer, then maybe I didn't want to be a lawyer. The life of a writer, writing the great

American novel, seemed so much more appealing. How little I knew about life as a writer.

I returned to Berkeley and Boalt Hall in the first days of September. By mid-October, I was gone. In the first September week I had purchased all the Gilbert summaries for my second year courses. I was no longer willing to spend those torturous hours bent over casebooks. The study of law seemed a glorified fraud. Literature had unfolded a new world for me. I was no longer isolated and uniquely suffering. My experiences, my feelings, my emotions had been experienced from time immemorial. That was comforting and I wanted to join the ranks of those great men who had written about life and living because I felt I had so much to say and add. It seemed so easily attainable then. As I look back on my last law school days at Berkeley, I'm amazed at how I was able to completely keep out of my consciousness then something that had to be deeply affecting me: the fact that I had failed to scale that elite law school's wall. My formula for success hadn't worked. As hard as I had tried, I had not been able to learn the law. I was at the bottom of my class. I was being ignored, tolerated, by my professors and the serious, able students. I hadn't made it in that white world. I was still very much a Mexican from Fresno.

The day I left Boalt Hall, I went to St. Mary's looking for Brother Robert. I needed to explain to him why I was leaving law school. I tried to give him what I thought would be ample justification. The study of the law was dry, boring, unintellectual. It was light years removed from the Great Books. I needed to be a writer, write the Great American Novel. He listened and for a long time said nothing. Finally he said, "Depending upon what you now do, your leaving may turn out to be a very good thing."

Over the next two and a half years, I did many things in different places as I wrote and read. I coached youth sports in Fresno. I made ice cream in Seattle. I worked in a bank in San Francisco. I painted fences in Las Vegas. I worked in a liquor store and delivered liquor in San Francisco. What I wrote was at best therapeutic, an outpouring of autobiographical misery and self-pity. My self-deception came to an end when I arrived at Villa Montalvo.

Villa Montalvo had been the retreat and summer home of State Senator James Phelan. It is a palatial mansion located in the forested foothills of the Santa Cruz Mountains between Los Gatos and Saratoga. In his will, Senator Phelan asked that Villa Montalvo become a place for the development of the arts, a place where artists, writers and scholars could take up residency while they worked. In 1960, under the guise of being a struggling young writer, I entered into an agreement with the Montalvo management to work on the grounds as an assistant to the gardener for four hours a day in exchange for a small apartment there and access to the grounds. It was by far the best living situation I had had since I left law school. The setting was wonderful: isolated, tranquil, beautiful everywhere you turned. The ideal place to write.

A visiting scholar in residency at Montalvo then was an English professor from a Midwestern university. He was living there with his wife and two young daughters. They befriended me. I visited with them in their apartment, they included me in their Montalvo activities and I baby-sat for them on weekends. The wife took an interest in my writing and I marketed myself well: a sensitive young man who had fled the callous halls of law school to pursue a yearning and passion for the life of a struggling writer. Nor did I miss any opportunity to stoke her interest in a budding Mexican-American intellectual, a rarity then. Every afternoon after my work on the grounds, I would go to my apartment to write, so I said, regardless of whether I wrote or not. She began asking what I was writing about. I said it was about a Mexican-American boy growing up in California's Central Valley. Soon she was asking if she could read some of my work. I put her off saying it was a work in progress. She continued asking and every time she asked, my self-importance grew. So much so that at times I began thinking of myself as the most important writer who had ever set foot on Montalvo. She kept asking. Weeks later, I proudly handed her a packet saying something like, "It's far from finished but I'll let you see what I have. But remember, it's a first draft." She was grateful and excited and as I turned and walked away, my self-importance swelled with every step.

I waited for her response, waiting for what was sure to be overwhelming praise and encouragement. I knew that once she read it, she would go to Montalvo's management and demand that they immediately move me to one of the larger apartments reserved for accomplished writers, artists and scholars, and insist too that they make me stop working on the grounds and begin giving me the same stipend they gave their respected guests.

Four, then five days passed. She should have read it by then. But I hadn't seen her and I was too proud to go to their apartment and ask. A week passed and there was no sign of her or them. I told myself that they had probably gone to visit her parents who lived nearby. Now I was reluctant to go near their apartment. Near the end of the following week, she came to where I was hoeing weeds along an endless driveway and said, "I think I should return this to you." I looked up; the packet was almost touching me. As I reached for it, she turned and left.

I left work and snuck back into my apartment. The manuscript was in the exact same condition it had been when I gave it to her. There were no markings, no folded corners, no rumpled pages. Had she even read it? Probably not. Maybe it was her husband. He had to be jealous of all the attention she had been giving me. I went over my last contacts with him and yes, he had been acting strangely. He had probably forbidden her reading it. That made sense.

Still, their apartment was no more than 50 yards from mine and now they were never out and about as they used to be. I reacted by not passing by their apartment anymore, which was the quickest way to the old carriage house where the gardening tools were kept. Instead, I began walking down the road to the great lawn in front of the mansion and then up the exit road to the carriage house, twice the distance. A few days later, the husband drove past me while I was working alongside the road without honking and waving as he always did. That confirmed my suspicions. Then one day as I was returning from town and when I came into view of the apartments, I saw her walking down the road toward me. As soon as she saw me, she stopped, turned and went back. That upset me; it had to be her husband. A few days later, I came out of my apartment and saw her in front of her apartment playing with her little girls. When she saw me, she went inside with them. Clearly, they were avoiding me. I began thinking that if this continued, maybe I would have to leave Montalvo.

The next morning as I was taking my tools from the carriage house, she came up behind me and said, "Ron, I have something to say to you, something that needs to be said." Her look was calm and steady. "I want to be frank because I think that is best. Your manuscript, the packet you gave me last week, I read it. It was not very good.... In fact, I was shocked at how poorly it was written. I don't mean to hurt you, but I think I will be doing you more harm by not telling you. I have read a great deal. As I've told you, I have a Masters in Contemporary American Literature. Writing is not what you think it is. However much you may want to be a writer, not everybody can be one. It takes a certain talent, a certain skill and knowledge. I didn't see any of that in what you showed me. Most of us think we have a story to tell and some of us think we could write a great novel. But that's a far step from reality. You're young yet. You have your whole life in front of you. Go back to law school. You were able enough, as you told us, to earn a scholarship at one of the best law schools in the country. Go back. Become the good lawyer I'm sure you're capable of becoming. Writing is just not for you. I say this in all sincerity and in your best interest."

I left Montalvo that night, taking my few possessions with me without a word to anyone.

I returned to San Francisco and rented a studio apartment which at one time had been part of a garage. I wandered about the city looking for a job, finally finding one as a night clerk at a motel near the Tenderloin. That year was a low point in my life: I had failed as a law student, lost a scholarship at a prestigious law school, gone off to write the great American novel only to be told almost three years later that I was an abysmal failure as a writer. Now the only job I could find to support myself was as a night clerk working from midnight to eight in the morning in a dingy motel next to one of the worst districts in San Francisco. For many weeks after I had finished making the daily bookkeeping entries at the motel, I would sit from 2 until 8 staring off into space. I couldn't bring myself to write anything, not even a postcard. Slowly I began reading again, not novels, but a biography, a little each night until after several months I had worked my way through Joseph Blotner's two volumes on the life of William Faulkner. But I had no desire to ever write again, and each time I thought of my pompous attempt, I was filled with shame.

It was then, in 1961, that I met my first wife, the first relationship I had with a woman. In two months she was pregnant; she was carrying my child. My father had abandoned me before I knew him and I was determined not to repeat the same offense. We were married when she was four months pregnant. Years later as a lawyer, when I saw some of the dreadful things that happened to children and adults in the courts, I would often think that people should be required to take an exam and obtain a license before they could marry and have children. If such an exam had been required of me before I was about to be married and have children, I would have flunked badly. I was a terrible husband and not much better as a father. The only good things to come out of that marriage were four children who were undoubtedly affected by an absent, preoccupied and driven father.

Once married, I got the only job I could find to support a family: selling life insurance in San Jose for one of the major insurance companies in America. Those companies were eager for new salesmen. New salesmen meant new sales to all of the new salesmen's friends, relatives and acquaintances. What the company offered me was a guaranteed monthly salary for one year so long as I met a minimum number of monthly sales. After a year, I was on my own: no sales, no income. I found a niche selling life insurance to city employees through a payroll deduction plan that the company had with the City of San Jose. I would post myself outside the various city plants and yards and wait for the workers to come out to pitch them and I met with them and their wives in their homes at night and on the weekends. "If something were to happen to you tonight, God forbid, and you had no life insurance, what would happen to your wife and kids?... Think of it. And think too that you can pay for that protection every month without feeling it. It'll automatically come out of your paycheck once a month. You'll never see it and you'll never miss it. And your family will be protected."

I was miserable. I hated what I was doing. I didn't believe in life insurance. If what I was selling to these hard-working men was purely for their benefit, then how was it that my corporation was one of the biggest, richest corporations in America? But how else was I going to support my family? In a way, my dilemma was self-solving. After ten months, I had pretty much written all the insurance I could on San Jose City employees, and I had already approached the few other folks I knew in San Jose. In two months I would have no salary.

Breakfast at Tiffany's is as memorable a movie as any in my life, even though there is very little I can tell you about it. I was sitting behind the wheel in my little Chevrolet on a Saturday night at the Tropicana Motor Drive-In Movie Theater on Alum Rock Avenue in East San Jose. I had hit rock bottom. As beautiful Audrey Hepburn strolled in and out of wondrous Tiffany's on the giant screen, my wife was putting her hair up in rollers and our baby was fidgeting and letting out little cries in her crib on the back seat. I had failed at everything. My formula for success was a joke. I was sitting in a drive-in movie on a Saturday night with my wife and child in the poorest part of San Jose. In two months I wouldn't even be able to afford that and more children were bound to come. My life seemed over. What had I done wrong? All my life-long hard work for nothing! Where was I going to get my next job? I was suited for nothing. I had always shunned manual skills. I wasn't even qualified to teach in an elementary school. I would never sell anything for anyone again. I couldn't. And I had dropped out of law school. All that was left for me was a life as a day laborer, like my stepfather had been, working on construction sites. I would never last there. I was too small, too slight of build. Not even suicide was an option. Suicide was a mortal sin and I would be sentencing myself to the eternal flames of Hell, and Hell was the only thing worse than my life then. Meanwhile, Audrey Hepburn pranced around that huge screen in brilliant colors in glorious, wondrous Manhattan. But I was so preoccupied with my fears that I have never known what that movie was about.

That night I slept little, resenting my wife who was sleeping soundly next to me and our baby who was occasionally gurgling in her bassinette. Sometime during the night it occurred to me that even though I had recklessly left Boalt Hall in my second year, my first year credits might be transferable, acceptable to a more plebeian law school. If so, I could be a lawyer in two years. My mind began spinning: two years and a lawyer! During my various stays in San Francisco, I had learned that there were three law schools in the city that catered to part-time students who were fully employed. And I would have to work. But those were four-year programs, the classes being taught at night after the workday. However the law school at the University of San Francisco not only had a four-year program, but also a regular three-year day program which meant that if it accepted my first year units, I could be a lawyer in two years.

Within two months, in September of 1962, I was enrolled as a law student at the University of San Francisco with a full-time job as a night clerk at an upscale motel on Franklin Street. I worked from midnight to eight in the morning, and from there I went to classes at the university until noon. That night job did not afford me the free time the previous one had. The bookkeeping was lengthier, the switchboard was busier, and given this motel's proximity to a huge hotel nearby, as well as its design and location, the foot traffic was greater. I averaged just two or three hours of free time a night which I used to study. But the pay was better, enough to support us. I rented a two-room apartment on Golden Gate Park's Panhandle, close enough so that I could walk up the hill to the university and also catch a bus for a five-minute ride to work. When I came home from class, I slept on the floor in a long, narrow, closeted space that had once held a Murphy bed. I got up around 5:30 and then showered, shaved and ate, after which I went downstairs to the apartment's basement to study in one of its lockers. Near eleven, I went upstairs, changed clothes and left for work. On the weekends, I slept and studied as much as I could. It was not much of a life for the three of us. That didn't matter to me. I was clawing my way up out of what was a seemingly bottomless pit.

There were few pretensions at the University of San Francisco's Law School. The faculty was extremely proud of its passing rate on the State Bar examinations. They made that very clear: passing the State Bar was the bottom line. There was no philosophy of the law, no developing sound, reasoning, legal minds. Pass the Bar. That was it. I had my faithful Gilbert's summaries in tow from the beginning but I was still having difficulties. It had been five plus years since I had completed my first-year studies and those courses were a foundation for what was to follow. I had forgotten what I had learned that first year. But then, I used to ask myself: how can you forget something you never knew? So I was constantly referring back to my first year summaries. There were other differences in the class formats at U.S.F. Roll was taken and one's absence could affect one's grade or even enrollment; and we were told that class performance could play a part in our semester grades. So I always made sure that I sat in the very last row nearest the door, so that I could sneak out of class once roll was taken. I passed all my classes over those two years with a C or a C+ grade.

But the Bar examination was a different matter. It was a three-day ordeal that had over the years caused mental and physical casualties. The summer after graduation, a two-month Bar Review Course was held in a great auditorium with 500 plus law students attending from around the country. The review texts were almost too heavy to carry. I failed my first Bar examination. The bulk of the questions over those three days had to do with the first-year courses, and by then it had been seven years since I and my Gilbert summaries had taken those courses.

Even though I had been doubtful about passing, the reality was still a blow. I had climbed so close to the edge of that hole only to be slammed back down. Self pity, desperation and despair set in. For days I wallowed in them, determined to try no more. That was momentary. The next Bar exam was in February. I had to take it. I had no choice. It meant almost another year of the shabby family life we were living, but that was not a consideration.

I had heard of a Bar review course that was taken by law students who had failed the Bar examination. It was given by Judge Bussey, a black man, who for many years had been the sole lawyer in the black Fillmore district until he had been appointed to the bench. He was a tall, elegant man, bald and bespectacled who spoke slowly, clearly and precisely. He taught his course in a little office in the Fillmore every week night for two months. He told us from the beginning that no one needed to be a genius to pass the Bar exam. Then he said that if we learned the basic principles of the law in each subject and then followed his method, he could almost guarantee that we, the failed ones, would pass the Bar.

The Bar examination at that time consisted of numerous essay questions that had to be answered over a three-day period. Judge Bussey told us that the law hadn't changed much over the past 25 years and neither had the questions on the Bar examination. Yes, the facts in the questions had changed but not what the examiners were looking for. "You learn the basic law on your own and I'll teach you how to answer those questions." Every night for two months, for three hours each night, we studied, answered and discussed our answers to hundreds of old Bar exam questions. During the day and on weekends I memorized my Gilberts summaries. By the end of Judge Bussey's course, I was able to take any past Bar exam question and spot the issues, discuss the applicable law and come to a conclusion on either side of an issue.

The February 1965 Bar examination was held in an auditorium atop San Francisco's Nob Hill. At the end of the third day, I sailed down that hill supremely confident that I had passed. And I did, thanks to Judge Bussey.

A few days after the exam, I was at St. Mary's again visiting with Brother Robert, telling him that I expected to be sworn in as a lawyer in a few months. Oakland sits across the Bay from San Francisco in Alameda County. A job as a Deputy District Attorney in Alameda County was highly sought after by recent law school graduates, including some from Boalt Hall. At that time, the District Attorney for Alameda County for some 35 years had been Frank Coakley, a graduate of St. Mary's who was reputedly still very loyal to the college. I asked Brother Robert if he could help me get a job in Mr. Coakley's office. He said he would see what he could do. A week later I received a call telling me that I had an interview with Mr. Coakley.

I went to Frank Coakley's office in Oakland. He was a grumpy old man who looked steadily at me as he questioned me and took notes on a yellow legal tablet with a yellow pencil. He asked me about my family and my background. Then he asked me about my experience at St. Mary's and some of the Brothers. Luckily, I knew one of the older Brothers that he was still very friendly with. The interview lasted some 20 minutes. There wasn't a single question about the law or about my legal schooling. At the conclusion, he said, "Well, young man, you come highly recommended by the Brothers and I'm sure you'll make a fine lawyer. I'm going to hire you. You can start working here next Monday as an investigator in my Family Support Division in West Oakland. As soon as you pass the Bar, you'll be sworn in as one of my deputies and assigned to misdemeanor cases in the Oakland Municipal Court."

I was ecstatic. My hard work and discipline had finally paid off. All those days of sleeping on that hardwood floor where the Murphy bed once stood, of walking around by the end of the week like a sleep-deprived zombie, of constantly pounding myself with a mantra that this was my only hope, my only way out, had come to an end. Nothing could stop me now. In my mind, no one had ever worked as hard as I had, had suffered as much as I had, to get through law school and the Bar exam. The world was mine for the taking. All I had to do was apply my formula, and there was no one better at that than me.

In those days, my image of the most successful, famous, richest of lawyers was a trial lawyer. I had pursued a job as a Deputy District Attorney because it would put me in court every day in front of more juries in a year than 99% of the lawyers in the country would ever *see*. I was not a good public speaker and had always shied away from speaking in public. But the Murphy bed closet had taught me that I could overcome anything. In my calculations, I had decided, even before I was sworn in as a Deputy District Attorney, that I would be in that office no more than a year. That's all I would need to gain the trial experience that would lead me to fame and fortune.

Once I was a deputy, I worked morning, noon, night and weekends. There wasn't any family life. That wasn't a consideration. I was on my way to finally prove that I wasn't a Mexican, or at least not just another dirty, little Mexican. I worked harder than anyone in the office. At one point, while reviewing one of my cases with my supervisor, I off-handedly said that I had been working on that case since four o'clock that morning. He paused, pulled away, waited until I looked at him, and said, "Ron, these are just misdemeanor cases. No one has to be working that hard on any of these cases." All the cases I tried that year were in fact petty crimes, misdemeanors that generally warranted a sentence of straight probation or seldom more than 90 days in the county jail. But to me then, they might just as well have been death penalty homicides.

I had been in the office just three days when I got my first jury trial. A 60-year-old drunk who had no fewer than 40 prior arrests for drunkenness was demanding a jury trial on a charge of being drunk in public. My total trial experience to that point had been watching my colleagues try cases for two days. When I was handed the poor old drunk's case, I was terrified. Riding down the elevator to the courtroom, I wasn't sure what I should say or if I could even speak once I got there. But when the trial began there was a vocal eruption from within me that was outrageous, inadmissible, prejudicial and incredibly inappropriate. The Public Defender literally tired of standing and objecting. The judge admonished me time and again. But I got every piece of nastiness in that pathetic man's life before the jury, no matter how inadmissible it might have been.

"Mr. Jones, isn't it true that since 1940 you've been arrested 41times for being drunk in public?"

"Objection!"

"Objection sustained."

"That's a damn lie. I've only..."

"Please Mr. Jones, you need not answer the question. The objection has been sustained."

"Yes, but that so-called District Attorney is one big liar. I've only been arrested 36 times since 1940."

"Mr. Ruiz, I've warned you," the judge interrupted, "and I'm not going to warn you again. Those questions are completely inappropriate and inadmissible and the jury is instructed to disregard not only the answer to the question but the question itself, because it is highly improper."

But how do you un-ring the bell? The jury deliberated 15 minutes, just moments longer than it took to pick a foreman. I was ecstatic. Victories were beginning to abound. The judge reported me to my supervisors, but from what I could gather, my supervisors were pleased: they had a real pistol on their hands.

I volunteered for anything and everything: traffic cases, court trials, jury trials, anything that would put me in court pleading my case. There was one week that I remember well. I started a jury trial on Monday morning, got a conviction late Tuesday, and started a second jury trial on Wednesday. I argued that case to the jury late Thursday and the judge asked the jury to return the following morning to begin their deliberations. Friday morning, I began selecting my third jury that week even as my second jury deliberated. I remember reading the third case file for the first time as I rode down the elevator to start that trial. Of course, it wasn't long before I was scorning colleagues who left early on Friday afternoons, taking the back stairs out of the building.

The Oakland Municipal Court was located on the edge of West Oakland. West Oakland was a city within a city. In some two square miles, all those old houses, buildings and businesses were by and for blacks. There was not a white face to be seen except for the two in the police car that patrolled there daily. Oakland's first black judge, Alan Broussard, who later became the first black member of the California Supreme Court, was then one of nine judges sitting in the Oakland Municipal Court. On the few occasions I had personal contact with him, he was thoughtful, kind and considerate. But in his court, in his department, he had his hands full. The courtroom was always full of black people: lawyers, the defendants, their families, friends and spectators. And those people, all of them, expected more, wanted more, their eyes demanded more from their first black judge. He was one of them. He knew where they had come from. He knew what they had been through. Time and again, I saw the discomfort on Alan Broussard's face as he backed away uneasily, but as gently as he could, from their expectations, expectations that the law and his position, his oath of office forbade.

On one Monday morning in Judge Broussard's courtroom among that crowd of black lawyers and people, there stood Clint White, without a doubt the best trial lawyer I ever had the privilege of watching try a case in my 30-plus years of practicing law. If you hadn't noticed him when you first walked into that courtroom, I guarantee you would the moment he spoke. His was a deep, strong, baritone voice that controlled everything around him. His enunciation was sharp, perfect, without a trace of the jargon that I so often heard from blacks. He had gone to Stanford on an athletic scholarship in days when that was a rarity. He was a tall, powerfully built man, and though he had put on weight and was big around the waist, he was still very much physically imposing. He was ebony black. Black as he was, and as dark as his eyes were, you could clearly see his intensity and strength of purpose in those eyes. When he got emotional or angry in the courtroom, it was like thunder booming down on you. During those times, I was sure you could see red inside his nostrils, like fire. He was a handsome man. How much of that was due to his strength and power I have often wondered. And he was always tastefully, impeccably dressed.

When I first joined the office, Clint White was a frequent topic of conversation among my white colleagues. No matter what was said about him, there was always respect for his abilities as a trial lawyer. Even though he had intimidated and humiliated some in court, the respect was still there. Whenever I had a free moment and heard that he was trying a case in the building, I would hurry to whatever department he was in to watch him.

The first time I saw him try a case in court, he was cross examining a police officer. He paced slowly, ponderously around the courtroom, sometimes seemingly deep in thought between questions, one hand in his pants pocket, his suit coat pushed back exposing the expansive white of his shirt covering that great chest and stomach. When he paced about the courtroom, he paced wherever he pleased, places where I never saw another lawyer step. He owned the courtroom. Every inch of it belonged to him and his awesome ability, especially when he was cross examining a witness or arguing his case to a jury. On that occasion, he had the officer stumbling badly. His voice got louder and louder. He wasn't shouting. He didn't need to shout. He simply raised the volume, the tone of that incredible voice. The officer kept glancing over at the District Attorney for help. Finally the prosecutor objected to one of Clint White's questions.

"The objection is sustained."

Clint was standing next to the jury box. He stopped and dropped his head and rubbed his chin and then looked up at the judge, and in a booming, disbelieving voice said, "The objection is sustained?"

The old, white-haired, white judge recoiled in his chair and for a moment turned whiter, seemed to be out of breath, lost his voice and then said weakly, "Yes, Mr. White."

I revered the man. Almost every time I saw him in the courthouse, I tried to find some excuse, some reason to talk to him, however briefly. He knew that; I could see it in his eyes. He was usually patient with me but at times short with me too. The longer I was in the office, the more I wanted to try a case against him. But when the time came, a month before I left the office, I was scared to death. The experience was like being locked in a small cave with a huge, angry black bear.

The case was as petty as most of the cases I prosecuted in the Oakland Municipal Court. The vice squad had raided an ongoing dice game. The participants fled in every direction, but eight were caught and brought to trial. Clint represented all of them. In those days whenever he tried a case in that municipal court, the word would spread throughout West Oakland and blacks would flock to the courthouse to watch their hero. It was by far the best show in town and the admission was free. But it was much more than a show. It was their chance to watch one of their own do what every one of them wished they could do.

So the courtroom was always packed when Clint was trying a case, and our case was no exception. As we selected the jury, the all-white jury pool shrank and shrank, and there were correspondingly fewer and fewer white faces in the courtroom. When the 12 jurors were finally seated, they and the judge, his clerk, his court reporter and bailiff were the only whites in that courtroom. Everyone else, except me, was black. Legal scholars and judges like to point out that the Constitution says that every man is entitled to a jury trial by his peers. But on that day, if those 12 jurors from the Piedmont District and the Oakland Hills were the eight defendants' peers, then I was Paul Newman. As I looked around the courtroom, despite all my sorry goals, I was not a proud prosecutor.

The case was open and shut. The police had caught the defendants red-handed. What was there to try? Yet as I sat there and watched and was subjected to Clint's power and magic, I became more and more worried that I would become the laughing-stock of the office, the pathetic loser of the most open and shut case that had ever been tried. The officers told the truth. But by the time Clint was finished with them on cross-examination, they were thoroughly shaken. "Do you mean to tell me, officer..." in that booming, outraged voice again and again. He rattled and ridiculed me, not explicitly but in his tone, with that clear, indignant voice. But he saved his best for last, something I had never seen before, have never seen since, and will never forget.

In a criminal case, after all the evidence has been presented, the prosecution argues his case to the jury, followed by defense counsel's argument, and then the prosecution has the final say in rebuttal and the jury deliberates. I pointed out pedantically to the jury that I had proven all the elements of the gambling charges beyond a reasonable doubt, and asked for a conviction on all counts and sat down.

The judge turned and looked at Clint. "Mr. White."

Clint sat for several moments, hand over his mouth, rubbing it, thinking. Then he rose. That big, black hulk of a man stood and faced that white jury, but instead of addressing them from counsel table or moving in front of them in the jury box, he walked slowly, ponderously around the table, past the jury box and into the witness stand just a few feet from the jury. He sat in the witness chair, bowed his head and rubbed his forehead for several moments, thinking. Tension rose. The courtroom was tight with silence. When he looked up, he still didn't speak. Instead he faced each one of the jurors, one by one, eye to eye. Only then did he begin, in that clear, clean voice, "You know, I grew up watching my mother work in a white man's kitchen and I'm here to tell you..." The jurors buckled. The spectators whooped and cried. The judge pounded with his gavel and said loudly, "There'll be silence and order in this courtroom or the courtroom will be cleared!" The spectators hushed, became restrained, but there was glee and joy on their faces. Once again Clint White was doing what they had never done and would never be able to do.

"Proceed, Mr. White."

"And I'm here to tell you what it's like watching your mother work in a white man's kitchen!..." On and on he went in that booming voice using the facts of the case and the police actions, not to argue a defense, but rather to point out, and hammer home, the injustice of our entire legal apparatus. I thought he would never stop. I felt like I had shrunken to the size of my toenail. A few times I looked over at the jurors. They were withered and beaten. Somehow, despite all my fears, they convicted the eight defendants.

Two days before I left the District Attorney's Office, I saw Clint in a courthouse hallway. I went up to him and said, "Clint, I'm leaving. I'm quitting. I'm going to San Jose to be a defense attorney."

He looked at me with those strong, black eyes and said, "Ruiz, I'm glad. I'm glad you finally realized that it's about time that you quit playing around and got out of here and went down there and helped your people."

Clint White went on to become a Superior Court Judge and later a California Appellate Court Justice. He should have been the first black California Supreme Court Justice.

Chapter 5

When I passed the California Bar examination in 1965, the largest number of Mexicans living in any U.S. city was concentrated in Los Angeles. The second largest group of Mexicans in California lived in San Jose. I had been to Los Angeles once and had been put off by its size. On the other hand, I had lived and worked in San Jose and liked it. In 1965, the number of Mexican-American lawyers north of Los Angeles to the Oregon border was small. There were two in San Jose, one in Fresno, one in San Francisco and one in Oakland.

I had always thought that my way into the white world would be as a lawyer. Once I was a lawyer that path all but disappeared, because it soon became crystal clear that there were then no Mexicans in the white legal world. I had had some contact with the Mexican-American lawyer in Fresno. He was a sole practitioner with a small office and had only Mexicans for clients. Now I was seeing that the same was true in Oakland, San Francisco and San Jose. Clearly in 1965, Mexicans need not apply at white law firms. The Christian Brothers had gotten me the job in the Alameda County District Attorney's Office. On my first day in the office, my supervisor introduced me to one of the two Mexican-American Oakland police officers. "George, I want you to meet Ronald Ruiz. We hired him just for you."

As able and gifted a lawyer as Clint White was, I never saw him represent a white client, nor did I expect him to. White people didn't hire black lawyers. Nor did I expect that white people would hire Mexican lawyers. Except for those cases in which the court appointed me to represent an indigent, white defendant, it would be many years before I had a white client. In a way, Clint had made that irrelevant. "Ruiz, it's about time you stopped playing around here and went down and helped your people."

The day I left Oakland, I drove out to St. Mary's and Brother Robert. This time he was pleased. As we walked about the campus, he smiled and said to a passing Brother, "He's going down to San Jose to work as a Public Defender, defending his people.'

In 1966, I opened a law office in San Jose as a sole practitioner. Except for the city employees I had sold insurance to, I knew no one in San Jose. But given the large number of Mexicans living there, and the fact that the two Mexican-American lawyers practicing law there had very little trial experience (a third Mexican-American lawyer had joined the Public Defender's Office), I believed that I could quickly and easily develop a client base that would provide me with a good living. I was half right. I wanted to be a criminal defense lawyer and every day the court calendars in San Jose were replete with the Spanish surnames of Mexicans, not unlike most cities where the bulk of the criminal defendants are made up of racial minorities. From the start, I could have had as many cases as I wanted. But Mexican defendants had little money. I was offered tool sets and old cars for fees. Early on, I tried a murder case to a jury for $700 and paid more than that out of my own pocket for psychiatric expert testimony.

Fortunately, I had enough business sense to introduce myself to the local judges. In those first days, I stalked the halls of the Municipal and Superior Courts without a client to my name. I made it a priority to sit in courts where defendants were being brought for their first proceedings, and visited those judges in their chambers whenever I could. I made it clear that I was a Mexican-American, spoke Spanish, had been a Deputy District Attorney and had trial experience. The judges were receptive. Their courtrooms were saturated with brown-skinned defendants. A Public Defenders Office had just opened in Santa Clara County but there were still many cases that had to be assigned to private lawyers. Those court appointments provided food, clothing and shelter for my family during my first 18 months practicing law in San Jose. I will always be especially grateful to Superior Court Judge Joseph Kelly for the court appointments that he consistently gave me in those lean months.

One defendant in one of my first court-appointed cases would continue to make his way back into my thoughts over the following years unlike any of the others. Hector Padilla was 19 when I became his lawyer. He and six other young men were charged with two murders arising out of a high school graduation party they crashed in East San Jose. Hector and his friends had dropped out of school and their parents' society years before. They identified only with themselves and established their own set of values. They did not call themselves a gang and did not give themselves ominous monikers as youngsters that followed would, but they were one and the same. Hector was convicted of second degree murder and sentenced to 15 years to life in the state prison.

A few years later while he was serving his sentence at San Quentin, his parents gave him a pair of tennis shoes for Christmas. He was wearing those shoes in the prison yard one day when another young Mexican inmate from Los Angeles stopped him and demanded that Hector give him those shoes. The assaulter was a member of the Mexican Mafia, the then reigning prison gang in California, and he expected quick compliance. Hector refused and a struggle ensued. Hector left his assailant wounded on the prison yard and walked away, still wearing his tennis shoes. That incident spurred the creation of a rival prison gang: the *Nuestra Familia*.

On the streets, San Jose became the headquarters for the *Nuestra Familia*, just as Los Angeles was the headquarters for the Mexican Mafia. Over the years, some of the defendants I represented had some connection with the *Nuestra Familia*, or had been subjected to its brutal, senseless violence, as well as that of the Mexican Mafia. In 1992, I was court-appointed to represent Vicente "Chente" Arroyo, the then head of the *Nuestra Familia* and one of the most remarkable men I have known. Mr. Arroyo, along with other gang members, was charged with multiple murders in perhaps the largest death penalty case in U.S. history. I worked on that case for four years and for much of those four years, I worked only on that case. What I heard, saw, read and learned during that time, often made me wish that Hector's parents had never given him those tennis shoes or that Hector had simply turned them over on demand.

Some 25 years lapsed from the day that Hector was sentenced and the next time I saw him in the mid1990's. I was looking at a court calendar posted on the courtroom door just before court began. I saw Hector's name on the calendar and turned to see if he was one of the many waiting in the hallway for the doors to open. I recognized him, but only after a while. He was still of the same height and stature, and though he was then somewhere in his mid-forties, he looked ten to fifteen years older. His face was deeply lined and seemed forever sad, and his eyes were blood-red. I went up to him and said, "Hello Hector, do you remember me?" He looked at me with those sorrowful eyes for a full minute. He was under the influence of something. Then he slowly, solemnly nodded and moved past me. Poor bastard, I thought, and thought too that I understood why he had come to court in that condition, to face a new felony charge that might well put him back in prison for the rest of his life.

During my first nine years practicing law in San Jose, I worked day and night and weekends, desperately needing to prove, no longer that I wasn't a

Mexican because that would never be, but rather that I was at least equal to, if not superior, to whites. Five mornings a week, I was out of bed at 5:00 or 5:30 and having breakfast at Pete's Diner a few blocks from my office by 6:30. By 7:00, I was at my desk which gave me some two hours to prepare for the day before court began. After morning court, I returned to my office and worked through the noon hour, skipping lunch because I had already learned that eating at noon was not only a waste of time but more importantly, it made me sleepy and ineffective during early afternoon court sessions. At 1:30, I went back to court, usually returning to my office between 4:00 and 4:30. Then I would make and return phone calls, see clients or potential clients and/or their families, and anyone else who had made an appointment. Three nights a week, I was home by 7:30 for dinner. My wife and kids had long since eaten. Thursday nights I worked the jail because no matter how late I stayed, there was only one court day left that week. Those nights, I was seldom home before 11:00.

Working the jail, or hustling it as I used to call it, was a must. I was building a client base. During those first years of my practice, I spent more time with defendants in that jail than any other private attorney in town. Inmates came to believe that I cared about their cases. They never had much money, but if they were desperate enough and convinced enough that I would ably represent them, at times their families and friends gathered enough money to retain me. And in those early years, there were many weeks that I would return to the jail on Saturdays and Monday nights as well.

Within three years, that frantic pace was beginning to take its toll on me, one I couldn't ignore. I would wake on Saturday and Sunday mornings to a tension in me that made my skin tingle and throb. I was irritable and quick to anger. Life for those around me was not pleasant. All day long Saturday and part of Sunday, I tried to rid myself of that tension but couldn't. I was afraid to drink or smoke. But what I feared most was that if the tension remained, I wouldn't be able to work on Monday or the remainder of the coming week. Somehow though, on Monday morning, my relentless need to prove myself always prevailed and I was once again the lawyer I needed to be throughout the week.

On one such Sunday in early March, I took my family on a drive from our rented home in San Jose to the coastal town of Santa Cruz, thirty miles away. To get there, one had to cross the coastal range known as the Santa Cruz Mountains. They are not really mountains but rather big, beautiful, wooded hills that peak at 3,200 feet. As we reached the summit, a light, rare snow was falling and traffic had come to a halt. We sat there for maybe an hour, and the silence and peace of those hills captivated and calmed me. A few years before, I had been introduced to the untouched beauty of the Kings Canyon back country in the Sierra Nevada Mountains. It was a beauty that enthralled me in a way that I have never forgotten. That Sunday afternoon, I once again felt the peace, calm and beauty of Kings Canyon. It led me to begin searching for a home in that coastal range.

Months later, I was driving on a back road of that sparsely populated coastal range with Stefan, my oldest son, who had just turned six, when I saw an old abandoned house on a hillside. I asked the closest neighbors if the house was for sale. They told me it wasn't but that an old man who lived down the road wanted to sell his house and five acres. I found the wood-framed, dull-red house they had described and introduced myself to the owner, Harry Wolf. He was a grizzled but pleasant old man in his late 60's who had great difficulty walking. He said that he had lived there for more than 40 years; that he had built the house and roads around it and had sold off some of the original acres. He said that he loved the place; the look on his face said it all. But now he was too old and frail to live there and maintain its upkeep. He didn't want to sell, but he had no choice. It was for sale, although there was not a single sign anywhere saying so.

The five acres had a large clearing on the front side of the house. Giant, awesome redwood trees stood on one side and behind it, thickening even more as the property deepened. The parcel had a creek that ran through the center of it. The sound of the running stream was magical. Harry had cut paths and laid bridges all over the land that allowed him to drive an old, World War II army jeep over every part of it, and then onto an old logging road that went up a steep grade through towering redwoods to a pasture on the summit. He took us for a ride in that jeep and even before we left the five acres I was spellbound. But then we drove up to the solitary, uninhabited summit. From there I could see the Monterey Bay and the blue Pacific seven or eight miles away as the crow flies. I was ecstatic and then depressed. I didn't have the money to buy his wondrous place. We drove back down to the house in silence and I thanked him for his time and said I was sorry but I just couldn't afford his place.

"I only want $40,000 for it," he said sadly, almost pleading.

"I don't have $40,000, Mr. Wolf. As I told you, I have a small law practice and a family of five. I'm able to make ends meet now, but not much more than that."

"How much of a down payment can you give me?"

"I'm sorry, sir, but I'd be embarrassed to tell you how much I can give you down. You might as well know that."

"Look son, I love this place. It's meant more to me than most anything in my life. I saw the way you looked at it, and I can see the way you'll love it too. I know you'll care for it, the way it should be cared for. That means a lot to me. That's why I want you to have it. That's why I need to have someone like you to have it. Give me $2000 down and I'll carry a note for the rest of it. You can pay me $400 a month until it's paid off."

All I could do was nod. That old red house and those five acres were to be my home for more than 20 years. Although I added three bedrooms as my family grew, to me, the house would always be those original front five rooms. And it would always be Harry Wolf's house, too.

That house and those five acres, the Branciforte property, were my salvation, I would not have survived my craziness but for them.

A year or so after we moved onto the property, I stopped commuting to San Jose on Saturdays. Instead I stayed in my office on Friday nights for as long as I needed. Then on Saturday mornings, I went out to the garage and worked on cases until 9:00. I stopped then because I knew the kids would be coming, looking for me, and because the tension in my body was telling me that I had to stop. I could feel and sometimes see the blood throbbing in my arms and hands. It was time to stop. It was time to relax. It was time to get ready for Monday, for another week of hell, for another week of proving myself. By then, I had learned that the only way I could relax, come to any kind of peace with myself, was to work on those five acres.

When we moved onto that parcel, the only utility we had was electricity. Our water came out of the mountain on the right side of the property into a cistern next to the creek. From there, a small electric pump drove it up the hill and over to the house, a hundred yards or so away. No electricity, no water. After a major storm, we could go days without water, lights or the use of the electric stove in the kitchen. Until I learned enough to set up a generator in the garage. The uninsulated house with single pane windows was heated by a fireplace and a wood-burning stove. Eventually as the house grew, we ended up with four wood-burning stoves. It took a lot of wood to keep the house heated six months out of the year during the cold, rainy season in those mountains. Initially, I decided to fell my own trees and cut and split the wood. But after a near disaster, I conceded that it was safer and cheaper in the long run to buy wood, which still meant making kindling, splitting, stacking, and hauling the wood to the house as needed. It was work that I needed to do every bit as much as it needed to be done.

Those enormous, beautiful, redwood trees needed and drank gallons of water each day and I had a forest of them. The weather and the mountains provided them with that water, some winters we had more than 50 inches of rain. The house sat in a gorge and once the rains started in October, the trees and the fading sun kept the air cold and wet. The rain kept me busy. The downpours and the ensuing avalanches of water shooting down the mountain on the right side of the property threatened to flood the garage and wash away my driveways if I failed to dig and maintain culverts. The rising creek had to be kept clear so that the foot bridges wouldn't be swept away. In April we planted an acre of garden in front of the house and, in time, a pasture alongside it that ran up the hill and had to be irrigated and mowed. There was plenty to do outdoors from April to September, and come October, I would begin getting ready for winter again.

Now my weekends were filled with manual labor. By mid-afternoon on Saturdays, the worries of the office and my clients and their cases and my ever-present need to prove myself began to subside. By Saturday evening, I was exhausted but the throbbings, the little jerkings and twitchings in my body had stopped and I dared have some wine. I slept soundly Saturday nights and as late as I could on Sunday mornings. When I woke, I felt like a new man. The wonderful world that was awaiting me outside was mine. But even before I was dressed, I was dreading the change, the challenges, needs, that would come with the next morning. I would go outdoors as quickly as I could to lose myself again, not just in physical labor but in the beauty of my surroundings. There were times just after a heavy rain that I would stand at the bottom of the driveway as brown water rushed noisily down culverts I had dug, and look out over the quiet of my meadow and the meadows beyond to Loma Prieta. The sky would still be heavy and dark and the air had an unparalleled stillness and freshness, but I knew that the rain had passed. In those moments, the barks and limbs of the bare, deciduous trees that lined the meadows would be black and strong against that grey sky and another year's growth of wild, rich, green grass.

Sometimes in the third or fourth week of August, I could feel the change of the seasons in the air and I would look at the garden, at the brown earth that had already given most of what it would give and sense it's relief: it was done for another year. I had developed a love for that land and I was beginning to understand and appreciate what countless men before me must have felt for their land.

On some Sunday afternoons, I would stop whatever I was doing and go to the back part of the property where the creek was strong and the trees were many and walk among those giants. What then went up a hundred feet and more were second-growth redwoods. The first growth had been logged at the turn of the century and their stumps were at least three times larger than the new tree trunks. Those stumps were usually head high and on a Sunday afternoons I would often climb up on them, and lie on my back and look up with wonder at the young branches a hundred feet above me, watching the wind gently weave through their leaves. Nothing seemed more beautiful, more simple, more priceless. Sometimes I would sit against a stump and try to imagine what those trees must have seen and endured years and years before I was born, or look at the young trees and try to imagine what they would silently see in the centuries to come, knowing that all the drama and trauma I was seeing, thinking and feeling week after week would mean nothing to them as they lived on.

There were times on the weekends when we had a medical emergency and I had to jump into the car with my wife and sick child and drive over to the hospital in Santa Clara, unwashed, uncombed, unshaven, wearing dirty boots and jeans, with a T-shirt or sweat shirt. Once there, I would wait in the parking lot, slouching down in the car while my wife took the child into the hospital, afraid that someone might see or recognize me in my grimy clothes. Whenever I drove over the mountain to Santa Clara as a lawyer, I was as clean as clean could be and carefully dressed in a suit and tie. As I slouched in the car outside the hospital on those weekends, it occurred to me that perhaps there would never come a time when I would not feel ashamed of being me.

One Sunday afternoon, a white colleague who had been curious about my living in the Santa Cruz Mountains showed up uninvited at our red cabin with his wife and kids. It had to be March because the air and ground were still wet, muddy and cold. The kids had been running in and out of the house all weekend tracking mud everywhere, and I had let the fires go once I started working outside, so that the house was filthy and cold. I was dirty and so were the kids. My wife was the most presentable, but that was no comparison to my colleague's wife in her city, Sunday best. Standing outside in the mud-squashed driveway, the looks and words of the adults were awkward and nervous. Their three children stood quietly next to their parents, wide-eyed. They were invited in. The wife was horrified. She hadn't said a word and was looking down at the mud-streaked floor. The young lawyer tried several times to strike up light conversation but nothing worked other than to make their presence more excruciating. Their kids tentatively followed ours, and once they began to interact, ten bodies in those five small rooms were just too many. The young lawyer tried to excuse their uninvited arrival, edging toward reasons for an early departure, which only added to the awkwardness. They left after a few minutes, but I never forgot their visit, or my own dismay.

Every year I paid my obligatory California State Bar dues but did not participate in any of the State Bar or County Bar functions. I stayed away from local lawyer social functions and after attending a few legal seminars, I stopped going until they became mandatory. Aside from feeling that I didn't belong, didn't fit in, there was another reason. Wherever there was a gathering of criminal defense attorneys, whether socially or at seminars, the war stories soon surfaced and then dominated. Success was everywhere. Brilliance, talent, cunning, genius, astounding strategies filled the air. In truth, we were defense attorneys and were getting our butts kicked soundly and regularly, tasting defeat every day. I was very much aware that whatever success I had in representing my clients, which wasn't much but probably as much as most, was not because of my skill as a great orator or my charisma or superior intellect, but rather from my fear-driven work borne from a sad need to prove myself.

Most of the not guilty jury verdicts that I received came in my early years of practice. As the years passed, they were fewer and further between. The mood of the state and of the country in criminal cases had shifted far to the right. When I began practicing law, the California Penal Code stated that one of its objectives was rehabilitation. Not long after, that provision was stricken by the state legislature and the stated purpose became punishment, solely and simply. Year after year, mandatory sentences for offenders became longer and harsher, so long and so harsh that California prisons were bursting at the seams.

There were two cases in the first nine years of my practice that made a great impression on me. Ray Cuellar was a man in his early thirties, married, and the father of three young daughters. He worked as a body and fender man in an auto shop when I first met him. He was facing a heavy prison sentence, and as we were preparing for his trial, Ray would come to my office in the early evenings after his work day, his eyes blood-red and moist. But he would be very relaxed.

"You look like you're floating."

"Yeah, but I'm O.K. I smoked some after I finished at the shop. Been putting in as many hours as I can in case things don't go too good with the case. I have to leave as much bread as I can for the wife and the kids. I can't stop thinking about this case and the weed is the only thing that can mellow me out."

It was 1968 and Ray Cuellar had picked up two counts of sales of marijuana in Merced California. He had gone there one weekend to visit an old friend, a *compadre* who had baptized one of his kids, but unbeknownst to Ray, his *compadre* had been arrested on a marijuana charge some weeks earlier and had accepted the police's offer of leniency if he would turn over some of his suppliers. The night Ray arrived at his *compadre's* home, he gave his friend two baggies of marijuana in exchange for thirty dollars, and was promptly arrested. Sales of marijuana at that time carried a mandatory five-years-to-life sentence in state prison. It was a serious crime then and indeed a very serious crime in tiny Merced, California. Ray's jury trial was in Merced, beginning early one morning and the jury returning its verdict near midnight: guilty on both counts. Ray was sentenced to state prison for five years to life.

It would be some years before the marijuana laws changed drastically, but change was already fermenting at the time of Ray Cuellar's conviction. The sons and daughters of the white electorate, of white judges and white legislators had taken to using marijuana. Before then, black and brown people had been the principle users of marijuana and those draconian sentences were aimed at stopping them, at safeguarding white society. Once those white kids began facing those harsh sentences, and life in California jails and prisons themselves, change came about as quickly as the legislature could make it happen. Today, a sale of thirty dollars of marijuana might bring a suspended sentence of 30 days in the county jail, if charges were even filed to begin with.

There were many unique and strange things that occurred during my handling of the People vs. Rachel Salinas case. In 1973, Rachel Salinas, a young, beautiful, intelligent woman, was accused of murdering her handsome young husband. The young couple had moved to San Jose shortly after their marriage in the Central Valley. They seemed like an ideal young couple, working at good jobs, living in a nice neighborhood with everything pointing to a fine future. Then one day Rachel shot her husband at point blank range on the back porch of their duplex apartment.

The case was unusual from the beginning. I was retained by Rachel's family, or so I thought. There were stories that my fee had in fact been paid by the family's parish priest in the Central Valley. I didn't pay much attention to those rumblings until I learned that Rachel had worked for the priest before her marriage. In what capacity? The insidious stories got worse: delivering monies from him to Rome. It sounded preposterous. When I asked Rachel, she said that she had worked for the priest doing odd jobs around the parish. Yes, she had been to Europe and Rome a few times, but on vacation. Yes, those trips were paid for by the priest but it was ridiculous for anyone to think that she was delivering money to the Vatican. I thought so too, then. But later on began to wonder.

Even before I was retained, as the family was initially meeting with me, I knew that the case had already been assigned to Ulysses Beasley in the District Attorney's Office and there was definitely a part of me that was not looking forward to trying that case against him. Ulysses Beasley was the first black prosecutor in the Santa Clara County District Attorney's Office, and he was a good one, as good in the courtroom as anyone they had. Beasley, or "Bease" as I called him, grew up five blocks from me in West Fresno about the same time I did. I hadn't known him then because he was a few years older than me and had attended local public schools while I had gone to private Catholic schools. His early years had to have been tougher than mine, and yet he had not only survived, but had prevailed. He graduated from Fresno State and for many years worked as an investigator for the California Alcohol Beverage Control Agency while going to night law school and passing the Bar exam. He had been an athlete in his younger days: a boxer and a football player. Despite an enormous stomach, he still had something of an athletic build.

We met in the San Jose criminal courts. Our legal careers began about the same time and we were friends even though it was generally held that prosecutors and defense attorneys shouldn't be friends. Often in private moments in and around the courthouse, we would laugh, talk and joke about Fresno, about the shortcomings of white prosecutors and white defense attorneys and about our experiences with white juries. Our friendship was sealed early on one day when Beasley said, "You know one of my best friends down there in Fresno was Rudy Savala. You know Rudy Savala?"

"Rudy Savala?"

"Yeah, Rudy Savala, short, dark, little Mexican guy."

"Rudy Savala from Pinedale?"

"Yeah, that's him."

"Rudy's my cousin."

"No. Really?"

"You're talking about Rudy Savala who used to live out there in Pinedale with all his good-looking sisters? His folks had a little store?"

"Yeah, that's him."

"He's my cousin, Bease."

"Man. I always knew there was some reason I had to like you," with that big toothy grin.

For years, Beasley seemed to visit Fresno about once a month, and upon his return he was sure to talk about his visit. Often, Rudy's name came up. I seldom visited Fresno and though Rudy was my cousin, I had never had much contact with him.

Beasley was gregarious and on the surface, warm and friendly. He loved to talk to people, all people. He liked to entertain them, make them laugh. He was a master of the aw-shucks, corn-pone that kept white folks smiling, laughing and loving him. He was the antithesis of Clint White. As proud and arrogant and intimidating as Clint could seem, Beasley could appear to be sweet, gentle, and warm, not too bright and not at all threatening. But Beasley was no fool. When it came to knowing, gauging people, he had few peers. And when it came to white people, white jurors in particular, he knew and understood them better than Clint and far better than me. Well hidden beneath that stumbling, country-bumpkin, toothy smile was a toughness, a fierceness and a brilliance too, that had brought him from his hard beginnings to where he was then. He was the best trial lawyer in the District Attorney's Office and maybe the best they had ever had. His string of guilty jury verdicts was unassailable, and that in a county that had but a handful of blacks living there.

The Amos and Andy Show began as a radio program in the 1920's. It was created by two white actors familiar with minstrel traditions and achieved great popularity among white Americans into the 1950's. The show depicted African-Americans in a sitcom version where their bungling attempts, laced with word-play humor, at business, social climbing and everyday challenges were doomed to comical failure. As early as the 1930's, blacks protested the lower-class characterizations and the crude, repetitious and moronic dialogue. But the show's popularity continued to increase and in 1943, it became a weekly half-hour comedy program. The show was adapted to television in 1951. But the NAACP's protests and boycott of the sponsors' products brought a cancellation of the video version in 1953.

One of the show's characters was Calhoun, a grossly bespectacled, buffoon black lawyer whose bizarre attempts to master the English language and legal concepts had white audiences howling. I often thought that Beasley must have studied the Amos and Andy Show. Because there was Beasley, time after time in front of a white jury, mispronouncing words in his heavy vernacular, correcting himself with that toothy self-conscious smile, deliberately twisting legal jargons and concepts so badly that he would have to stop and explain them in an apologetic poor-man's English, all the while smiling in an aw-shucks manner. The white jurors loved him, loved this humble, sweet man who knew his place and couldn't or wouldn't possibly deceive them. And they were quick to return guilty verdict after guilty verdict for him.

When the Salinas family first approached me, I had never tried a case against Beasley although I was well aware of his record and his trial tactics. The more the family appeared ready to retain me, the more I was tempted not to take the case, to tell them I was too busy, had too many other commitments. That same fear had already taunted me in other cases and would become stronger as my cases became more serious. But that fear I always overcame with another fear, a fear that I wouldn't respect myself if I turned and ran. Better a humiliating defeat in court than to run.

My style was very different. Soft spoken by nature and very uncomfortable to this day when speaking in public, especially without the use of a microphone, I was not a gifted, talented, natural trial lawyer. A judge once described me to my sister, "When he starts in trial, there are times when you can barely hear him. But when he gets going, watch out. He explodes." A woman juror in opulent Palo Alto came up to me after her jury had deadlocked in a driving with a suspended license case. She was angry. "Mr. Ruiz, I want you to know that I didn't appreciate you shouting at me for 20 minutes during your closing argument."

No matter how emotional or excited I might have become in a trial or how much I shouted or exploded, none of that was ever planned or contrived. Almost every time I walked into a courtroom to begin a jury trial, I was scared and exhausted. I had worked so hard and worried so much in preparing for that trial that invariably the night before I couldn't sleep. No matter how many cases I had tried before, no matter how much success I had before, as I walked into that courtroom on opening day, none of what had gone on before was proof enough. Once again, I couldn't bear to let the world see how truly inadequate I was.

As formidable as Beasley would have been to any defense attorney then, he was that much more formidable to me. Because no matter who the white prosecutor against me was in any given case, I always had one pillar of self-support to help me along: the belief that no white lawyer had ever been through what I had been through, had worked as hard, persevered as long, or used more wits and cunning to survive. But now, here came black Beasley, from the same West Fresno, with probably even fewer opportunities than I had had, who had probably worked harder, and who likely needed to be tougher, smarter and persevere more than I had had to. I wanted to run from that case but I couldn't. Running would never be an answer. I took Rachel Salinas' case.

I used to think that in the more serious cases, at some point during the trial, the defendant didn't matter anymore, that he or she was beside the point, that the case had really become a contest between the two opposing lawyers and their egos. I'm sure that Beasley and I reached that point early on in the case of The People of the State of California vs. Rachel Salinas. After that point, as difficult as it may have been for either of us to believe, there was a Rachel Salinas and she was sitting there at the same counsel tables with us, facing a murder charge.

Rachel Salinas was remarkable in her own right. At 26, she was pretty, petite, demure, with large brown eyes, a delicate mouth, a soft olive complexion and a shy, self-effacing look, she would have captured the heart and brought out the protective instincts of many a man. Though she had only been to high school, she had traveled to Europe and Rome three or four times. She loved

Rome and Italy and spoke of her travels with an intelligence and articulateness that surprised me. As far as I knew, there were no other Mexican-American girls from poor families in central California with only a high school diploma vacationing in Europe and Rome in the late 1960's and early 1970's. She was bright and grasped legal concepts quickly and easily, weighing them evenly and with a good sense of how they would affect her. She had no prior criminal record, but had remained in jail awaiting trial for some six months. Life in the jail had to be new and obviously harsh for her, but she dealt with it stoically and with dignity.

I visited Rachel in the jail once and sometimes twice a week as she awaited trial. She cried often. Hers were not loud, showy or even hysterical tears. Rather they were silent, intermittent tears that dropped unheeded from the sides of her eyes. There was sadness and remorse in those tears. Bail in homicide cases, if set, was always very high, and I assumed that she wouldn't be able to post it. That made getting an early trial date a priority. It wasn't until after the case had been tried, that I began to think that even if she, with the help of her family and the priest, had been able to post bail, she probably would have chosen to remain in custody anyway.

It took the Salinas family about two weeks to raise the funds to retain me. In the meantime, I met with different members of the family. What they told me was that Rachel's husband had been very jealous and had beaten her many times over their two year marriage, and was about to beat her again when she shot him in self defense.

The police report read differently. There had been no signs of struggle in the duplex on the day of the shooting. There were no marks or bruises or anything on Rachel's body that would indicate a beating that day or for at least several weeks prior. Likewise, there were no marks on the husband's body to indicate that he had been in a physical altercation that day. The ballistic expert said that the husband had been shot several times in the chest from a distance of six to ten feet. There were no prior reports of domestic violence between the couple in any police files. The neighbors had heard no prior quarrels, nothing except gun shots on that day. The husband's family told the police that Rachel was very ambitious, a social climber who was disappointed with her husband and the marriage and wanted to leave him. If their son was jealous it was because Rachel was very flirtatious, craving the attention of other men. They had never known their son or brother to be violent or physically abusive to anyone.

The gun in question was his. He always kept it in the house in his dresser, but unloaded because he was concerned about any accident. The report did say that when the police officers arrived at the scene, Rachel was hysterical and kept crying, "He beat me for the last time!" The gun was lying next to her husband's body.

More often than not when I saw Rachel in the visiting room, she seemed to be grieving and remorseful. Often she seemed lifeless. Sometimes her skin was grey, her eyes were never more than half-opened, and many of her words were whispers and her movements were slow and few. I did not have the impression that any of this was posed or put on. Yet despite what her appearance might be on a given day, she always had a poise and dignity about her that I found remarkable.

The first time I saw her, she told me that her husband had been very jealous and had beaten her often during their marriage. If he saw another man look at her, he would fly into a rage. She had become more and more afraid of him and had tried to leave him, but unsuccessfully. On the day of the shooting, he had come home after she had and for no reason, flew into a rage and was about to beat her again. She ran, and as she did, she picked up the gun which was lying on a shelf in the hallway. He ran after her. When she reached the back porch, she turned the wrong way and, seeing no way of escape, shot him. I didn't stop her, interrupt her or try to contradict her then. There would be plenty of opportunities later to discuss the police report with her.

Rachel's story remained the same before, during and after the trial. She had clear answers to all my questions. Why had there been no sign of a struggle in the house on that day? She said that there hadn't been a struggle because there had been so many struggles and beatings in the past that she ran, knowing what was coming. Why no marks or bruises on her to show signs of present or past beatings? She had never bruised easily, her parents could verify that. And her husband was careful to hit her where the bruises had less tendency to show. Why no police reports of prior domestic violence? She was too embarrassed and ashamed to let others know what she was being subjected to by her husband. Why had the neighbors not heard any of the previous altercations? The duplex was very well insulated. Where did her husband keep the gun? Usually in his dresser drawer, but on that day when she came home from work she had noticed it lying on the shelf in the hallway. Did she think it was loaded or unloaded? She didn't know. She didn't think. She didn't have time to think. He was going to beat her again. Besides, before that day, she had never used a gun, although she had seen them used, but was afraid of them, and wanted nothing to do with them. Was she flirtatious? When I asked, she gave me a quick, contemptuous grimace, turned her face and shook her head. But there were a few times over those six months, when she gave me looks that made me wonder.

As the trial neared, it gained quite a bit of attention from other Deputy District Attorneys, Public Defenders and defense counsel. It wasn't uncommon for one of them to approach me with something like, "I hear you and Beasley are going to go at it in a murder case soon. That ought to be something to see." Yes, for our white colleagues I imagined it would be quite a spectacle. The big-bellied nigger who himself got away with murder in the courtroom with his deliberate folksy stumblings that allowed him to put before an amused and adoring jury what was otherwise inadmissible, and the wild, screaming Mexican who lost control and had little respect for, or idea of the proper decorum expected from any civilized lawyer in court.

Something was happening in the previously all-white segment of the criminal justice system in Santa Clara County. A black man and a Mexican with their unorthodox styles had risen in the ranks and I suspected that at least some of our adversaries and colleagues were rankled by our success. Now, with so many of them expressing an interest in our upcoming trial, I of course thought that they were gleefully waiting to see which one of us would fall and how badly we would butcher each other. One of us had to lose and I was convinced that it would be me. How ironic and fitting, I thought, to have battled through one white barrier after another, just to be put back down to where I belonged by a black man.

I prepared for this trial as I had prepared for no other because I knew how well prepared Beasley would be. I knew very well how hard that lackadaisical, bungling, good-natured appearing black man worked. I outlined the transcript of the preliminary examination in great detail, and had reviewed that outline so many times that I could point to the page and line of a witness' prior testimony in seconds. I had all but memorized the police report, the autopsy report and the ballistic report. I went to the evidence room and examined the physical evidence several times. I visited the duplex and that back porch three times. And I began preparing my witnesses for their testimony weeks in advance. I spent hours with Rachel going over her direct and cross examination. I had watched Beasley in trial enough times so that I could emphasize again and again to her where and how I thought he would come at her. But as hard as I worked, no one could have convinced me that Beasley wasn't working harder.

There was never any doubt that Rachel had shot and killed her husband. That was a given. But in order to gain a conviction of second degree murder which the prosecution sought and which carried a 15-year-to-life prison sentence, Beasley would have to convince the jury beyond a reasonable doubt that Rachel had intended to kill her husband, and that she had not shot him because she thought he was about to beat her. If the jury thought the latter, they could find the shooting to be an involuntary manslaughter with a sentence of 12 months in the county jail.

Only two people had witnessed the shooting, and one was dead. The direct evidence, what Rachel saw, heard and believed, was in her favor. The circumstantial or indirect evidence wasn't. There was no evidence of any struggle or altercation before the shooting. There was no record of any prior beatings other than what Rachel might have told her family and that would be contradicted by the testimony of the husband's family and friends. Her husband had not been armed with a weapon of any kind and was shot at a distance of six to ten feet from her. Then there was the matter of the gun. His family said that it was always kept in his dresser, unloaded. How then did it happen to be in the hallway fully loaded?

My hope was that Rachel would present herself credibly not only when she testified, but throughout the trial. Present herself so well that the jury would believe her, like her, be sympathetic and yes, pity her. My fear was Beasley himself. As the trial approached, time and again I imagined him doing his little corn pone dance in front of the jury, saw his aw-shucks bumblings and toothy, twinkle-eyed corrections, slipping everything imaginable into both, warming their hearts, assuring them without a word that they could trust him, that he would never lie to them, that he could not and would not ever seek a second degree murder conviction unless it was truly warranted. Try as I might, I couldn't think of a way to stop him.

In my mind, in those last days leading up to the trial, Beasley seemed to have every advantage except one. Homicide cases usually took two or more weeks to try and were physically exhausting. Beasley loved to eat and he was badly overweight. His legs, arms, shoulders and neck were stark reminders of what his once lithe, athletic body had been. But his belly had far outgrown the rest of him. I had started jogging some years before, insurance against the stroke or heart attack that I feared might come from the strain I was putting myself through week after week. Being in much better physical condition than Beasley, I fancied that the longer the trial went on, the more rapidly he would tire, the more easily he could be agitated to a point where the jury could see who Beasley really was.

Three days before the trial, I added as much weight as I could to my regular running gear. I wore heavy work boots, work pants, two sweat shirts and a heavy winter jacket. On the morning of the trial, not having slept much that night, I ran in the dark with that added weight, but instead of running along the road, I ran up and up into the pathless mountain above my house. It was a miracle I didn't injure myself. I ran as hard as I could for as long as I could, pushing myself to hurting, but always thinking of one thing: Beasley.

The jury we selected was comprised of six white women and six white men. I thought it was as good a mix as Rachel could have. Women tended to be more compassionate with defendants. On the other hand, they could be much harder on another woman than men. I was hoping that Rachel could bring out the protective, sympathetic strain in those six men.

Today I'm convinced that the case was decided that first day as we selected the jury, before any evidence was presented. I was so consumed with fear that Beasley was about to win the jury over in the selection process, that I began objecting to much of what he said and did from the very beginning, something I had never done before and would never do again. "Objection, Your Honor. The purpose of voir dire is to select a fair and impartial jury, not to curry favor with them!" "Objection, Your Honor. Mr. Beasley's prolonged and repeated excuses and explanations for his bumblings, even though he does it with that big smile, is not proper voir dire!" "Objection, Your Honor. Mr. Beasley is lecturing the jury on the law in his off-the-cuff apologies!" "Objection, Your Honor. Mr. Beasley's shuffling and gyrations, his grins and grimaces as he stands before the jury are improper and unneeded!" I went on and on. I was irritating Beasley, but I was also irritating the judge who was not someone you wanted to irritate. But I couldn't help myself. Many of our colleagues were in the audience and I could sense their exasperation over my incessant, petulant, silly objections. The judge had sustained some of my objections but not nearly as many as he had denied and now he was looking at me with a stern, angry look every time I stood up to object.

I erupted. I don't remember exactly what I said but it went something like, "I object! I'm sick and tired of sitting here watching Mr. Beasley's Amos and Andy Show theatrics in his determined attempt to ingratiate himself with this jury. I know him well and I know that this is all just a big act..."

The judge was pounding the bench with his gavel. "That's enough, Mr. Ruiz! That's enough! Sit down and be quiet!"

I sat down, silent and shaking. The judge cleared the courtroom. Then, with only Beasley and myself and the court personnel present, he said, "Mr. Ruiz, I find you in contempt of court. And I order you to pay a fine of $300 by six o'clock this evening or otherwise surrender yourself to the jail and remain there until the fine is paid. Now, I'm going to admonish you once and only once. So listen carefully. If there is another repetition of your conduct in court this morning, I can assure you that you will very much regret it. Do I make myself clear?"

"Yes, Your Honor."

To me then, three hundred dollars was a lot of money, but I paid the fine well before six o'clock.

Whatever embarrassment or shame I felt soon wore off when I recognized the change in Beasley when we returned to finish selecting the jury. He was quiet, but angry. The aw-shucks, bumbling business was gone. There was an edge to him that got meaner and meaner as the trial went on. I was quiet, controlled, but angry too for the duration of the trial. But the $300 fine had paid off. I don't think the jury cared much for the angry, mean black lawyer or the wild, angry, crude, Mexican lawyer that were there with them for another two weeks. But their attention was solidly focused where I had hoped it would be: on Rachel Salinas.

I have coached many defendants and witnesses in how to present themselves before a jury. Most of the time, it has been a waste of time and effort. They have usually been just who they are when they have testified, only more nervous and frightened. But from her first minutes on the witness stand, I knew that my efforts to coach Rachel hadn't gone to waste. She handled herself better than any defendant I ever represented. She was genuine, nothing concocted. She came to court every day in a simple cotton dress and flats. She was well-scrubbed, neatly combed and wore no make-up. She couldn't have been prettier. She sat next to me with her chin slightly downcast looking at no one and nothing. When I whispered a question or comment to her, she would nod once or twice or shrug; seldom did she shake her head. She cried throughout the trial. But there was no drama in those tears, no theatrics, no hysteria. The tears fell slowly and silently. By mid-afternoon there were large splotches on her dress and the redness around her eyes couldn't go unnoticed. As the trial moved forward, I saw that the jurors were more carefully eyeing her. She was winning them over. I let her be, said nothing to her of what I thought I was seeing for fear that I would upset everything.

When I questioned her on direct examination, there was rapt silence and attention in the courtroom. All eyes were on her. Her answers were clear, concise and soft-spoken. There was no sniffling, no wiping of her eyes or nose, no pausing or momentary gasping. The tears fell slowly, involuntarily, almost drip by drip on either side of her face. She testified that she had arrived home from work and was changing her clothes in the bedroom when her husband came home. Within moments, he accused her of flirting with other men, of wanting to go out with them. She didn't answer. To answer, she thought, would only add fuel to the fire, as it had in the past. He came at her. He was going to beat her again. She ran out of the bedroom, slamming the door behind her. She ran down the hallway and as she did, she heard him come out of the bedroom in pursuit. She saw the gun on the shelf and picked it up without thinking. She ran through the kitchen and into the back porch, and then realized that she had run in the wrong direction because there was no further escape. He came out of the kitchen in a rage and started towards her. She pointed the gun at him, more to stop him than anything. She didn't know if the gun was loaded. She had never handled it before. He kept coming. She pressed the trigger, the gun went off, several times and her husband fell to the floor. When she stopped, when she finished, the silence boomed, hollowing the courtroom. You could feel emotions stretching from one wall to the other. After a long silence, the judge recessed the trial until the following morning, when Beasley would cross-examine Rachel.

From the courthouse, after her testimony, I drove to the duplex. The landlady had let me examine the vacant apartment before and I was hoping to get one last look at the scene, to more thoroughly prepare Rachel for the cross-examination that was coming in the morning.

I rang and knocked but there was no answer. The landlady wasn't there. I decided to wait. I went around the back and sat on the porch steps just a few feet from where the shooting had occurred. The sun was at a slant, shining down on the driveway before me. I saw a glint in the gravel. I went to the other side of the driveway where the reflection was. Lying two inches apart were two unspent bullets. My first reaction was to leave them, not pick them up. But I did, and I saw what I must have been afraid I would see. They were the same caliber, the same type of bullets that were fired from the gun that had killed Rachel's husband. I kept telling myself that those bullets meant nothing, proved nothing. But my mind wouldn't stop. If the gun was always kept in the husband's dresser unloaded, something Rachel had never denied, then how did the gun get to a shelf in the hallway fully loaded? When was it loaded? How was it loaded? Why would the husband have dropped bullets in the driveway? Why would he have loaded the gun in the driveway and then left it on the shelf? No, the bullets proved nothing. But if it was Rachel who had loaded the gun, Rachel, who had never handled it before, wasn't it more likely that she, rather than he, would have dropped two bullets in the driveway? And who would have been more likely to load the gun outside the duplex? Less likely to have loaded the gun inside the duplex?

My world was falling apart. My impulse was to throw the bullets as far as I could from that driveway. But there were houses and duplexes all around me. Someone might see me. Someone might have already seen me. I wrapped my fingers as tightly as I could around the bullets and walked as quickly as I could to my car. I drove onto Highway 17 headed for Lake Vasona but reminded myself that it was a city park and there were always people walking around there. Lake Lexington was beyond it in the Santa Cruz Mountains. No one would see me there. But I hadn't gone another mile before I knew that I had to show the bullets to Rachel, confront her. I was tormented by the thought that she had loaded the gun outside in the driveway and then gone into the duplex and shot her husband. I kept telling myself that it was quite a stretch. There was really no way to know how those bullets had gotten in the driveway. No way to know how long they had been lying there. The husband could have just as easily have dropped those bullets there one day as he got out of his car after buying bullets. Anyone could have dropped those bullets there long ago. But no, I had to show the bullets to Rachel. I had to ask her.

I turned the car around and went to the women's jail. Rachel came to the visiting room. She was quiet and sad and wouldn't look at me. Did she know what I had found? We sat there somberly. I didn't know how to begin. Finally I said, "Rachel." She looked at me with eyes that said, Please let me be. "Have you ever seen these before?"

She looked long and hard at the bullets but without a word or a nod or a glance at me.

"I found them in your driveway near the back porch. Have you ever seen them before?"

She started to cry, the same silent, stoic tears.

"Did you ever have these in the driveway?"

She shook her head slightly as tears fell, without a word or a look at me.

"Rachel, I have to know. You have to tell me. You have to answer me."

We sat there for some twenty minutes, I repeating the question in different ways. All she did was shake her head ever so slightly and cry. She never looked at me.

It was dark when I left the women's jail. I drove my car a little ways and then stopped next to a wooded, grassy, empty plot of land and threw the bullets into the darkness.

The next morning, I expected the worst. When the deputies brought her into the courtroom, it seemed a certainty. She looked terrible. She had already been crying and her face was drawn. We were in the second week of the trial and it had taken its toll. Or was it the bullets? The jurors watched her every movement. The deputies seated her in the witness stand even before the judge took the bench. She sat erect for several minutes with her eyes downcast, alone in her world, as the jurors and Beasley watched. Then the judge came out. "Good morning," looking around the courtroom and then, "Mr. Beasley." Beasley stood and I thought, Here it comes.

But Rachel stood her ground. Her answers were short, concise and she didn't waver or contradict herself. The tears came early: silent, stoic. He had beaten her many times in the past. She hadn't reported it because she was ashamed. She always did what she could to hide the bruises and cuts. Beasley wasn't shaking her. He got angry, mean and loud. She was scared, she repeated. She ran down the hall. She saw the gun. She took it, not meaning to shoot him, just wanting to stop him. But he wouldn't stop and before she knew it, she was shooting. The louder Beasley got, the more the jury was repulsed.

After a day and a half of deliberations, the jury returned a verdict of guilty of involuntary manslaughter. Rachel hugged me and cried hard. When I looked around, Beasley was gone. Two weeks later the judge sentenced Rachel to a year in the county jail, but with the time she had already served and credit for good time, she would serve a little less than three additional months.

Not long before she was to be released, I went out to the jail to visit Rachel, to say goodbye before she returned to the Central Valley. She was pretty, but still sad and mournful. She thanked me for my work but there wasn't much else to say. As I was leaving she said, "I think I should tell you something."

I stopped and waited.

"One of the jurors has been coming to visit me."

"One of the jurors from your trial?"

"Yes."

"Why?"

"I don't know. But he's come every weekend since the trial ended."

"What for?"

"He says he loves me. That he fell in love with me during the trial. He says that he wants to be with me when I get out of here. That he can make me happy. He leaves money for me on the books."

I was stunned. "Which juror? Which one?"

"You know, the one in the front row on..."

"No, no. That's O, K. I don't want to know." I had had enough of Rachel Salinas and her trial, and I didn't want any more. I didn't want to go back to court again, now on the issue of improper juror conduct. I left.

Two weeks later, I received a call from a deputy at the women's jail. "Mr. Ruiz, Rachel Salinas' family is here and they're asking that you come down here and we think it would be a good thing if you did."

"Why?"

"Well, today's Rachel's release date and her family's driven up here to take her home. But she's refusing to leave."

"What?"

"Yes sir, she won't leave and the family thinks you might be able to persuade her to leave."

I drove out to the jail. One of the guards took me to her cell. She was sitting on her bunk, crying.

"What's wrong, Rachel?"

"I'm not going."

"What do you mean you're not going? This is your release date. You're free to go. Your people are out there waiting for you. Come on, let's go."

"I'm not going. I don't want to go. I want to stay here."

"You can't stay here. You've done your time."

"I want to stay."

This went on for some time. Finally, I went out and talked to the deputies and the family. I wanted her out of the jail, out of my life. I wanted no more of Rachel Salinas and her case. The last thing I wanted was to be back in court with her and the judge asking her why she didn't want to leave the jail. It was decided that three of us, one of her male relatives, a male deputy and I, would return to her cell and carry her out of the jail. And that's what we did. The deputy lifted her from behind, her relative and I each grabbed a leg and carried her out of the jail, in her jail clothes as she screamed and wrenched and cried until we put her in the back of the family's car and they drove off. I never heard from Rachel Salinas again.

It was several months before Beasley and I spoke again. I was avoiding him, dreading the next time I had to try a case against him. I had been lucky in Rachel's case. Everything had fallen in place for me. I knew only too well that wouldn't be the case the next time. I also knew that Beasley had a long memory and that he would be merciless the second time around. Then one day as I was going into a courtroom as he was coming out, we were literally face to face. "Hi, Bease." "Hi, Ron." His was as clumsy as mine. But we talked, very stiffly at first, but we talked. We had been through so much of the same, had wanted so much of the same, that we talked. Gradually over the months that followed, we became close again, privately laughing, talking, joking and comparing courtroom and Fresno notes and updates on my long-lost cousin, Rudy Savala. But we never mentioned Rachel's case and somewhere in me there was always that dread for the next time.

A couple of years went by and we had yet to try another case against each other, when Beasley invited me to have lunch with him at Original Joe's. Beasley loved to eat and he loved the good food and generous portions at Original Joe's. As we sat and ate, Beasley told me about health problems that were forcing him to leave jury trials. He was being reassigned to ministerial calendars and tasks in the District Attorney's Office. It saddened me but I felt some personal relief, too.

Beasley handled those routine and monotonous calendars and tasks for many years. He was still very much the good-natured black man who enjoyed making everyone laugh and like him with that bungling, aw-shucks, toothy smile. In time, I began thinking that some of the bungling was no longer an act.

As I watched him in those later years, I couldn't help but remember what a very good trial lawyer he had been. There were times when young white lawyers came out of a courtroom where Beasley was handling the calendars, laughing about his incompetency. Each time I wanted to spit on them.

I wasn't practicing law in San Jose when Beasley died and I didn't hear about his death until sometime later. There may have been others who have shared so many of the same life experiences that Beasley and I shared, but I have only known Beasley.

Chapter 6

In 1973, during the seventh year of my law practice in San Jose, I decided that unless I was in a jury trial, I would find time to write a novel between the morning and afternoon court sessions and on weekends. Leaving Villa Montalvo, I had vowed never to write again. Since returning to law school, I had read nothing except law books, written nothing except legal motions and briefs. Yet the desire, the need to write kept gnawing at me, increasing each year as I became more settled as a lawyer. By mid-1973, I had begun writing again, notes mainly, usually of some disappointment or sadness. Gradually the notes increased in frequency and length but seldom more than two paragraphs. There was never enough time. The notes were an outlet. I confided in no one, and the more frequent the notes, the stronger became my need to vent. But why use writing as a vehicle after having failed at it so miserably for almost three years? My love of music and the respect and admiration I had for self-expression had kept the fire burning.

For three summers, beginning when I was 10 until I was 13, I spent a few weeks visiting with my cousins in San Francisco. I worshiped my cousin Rudy who was three years older than me. He was a good athlete, handsome (the girls were always chasing him) and as cool as he could be. Every afternoon and for hours on Saturdays, Rudy and his friends listened to Jumpin' George and his Sepia Serenade Comin' Across the Bay From KDIA in Oakland. It was black music, rhythm and blues. The beat was there and the blues were there. Muddy Waters, Louis Jordan, Howlin' Wolf, Jimmy Witherspoon, Jimmy Rogers, Memphis Slim. How I loved that music. Maybe in the beginning it was because Rudy and his friends loved it, but by that last summer, it had nothing to do with them. I loved it myself. Its roots were the same as the music I had listened to outside those black bars in Fresno on Sunday afternoons, but far up the scale.

In 1956, when Elvis Presley became the heart throb of young white America, I was dismayed. The songs he sang were black songs and, to me, poor imitations. Worse, the creators of those songs had never, and would never, see a fraction of the money or fame that Elvis, or the white musicians that followed, garnered from their creations.

Another kind of music awaited me in 1956. I was a junior in college and had no appreciation or liking for classical music. Some of the students listened to and even studied by it. That was beyond my comprehension. Some, as well as some of the Brothers, went to San Francisco to listen to the symphony during the season. I had no interest. But I took a liking to the music of Dave Brubeck and his Quartet. His music was popular with college students then. Several of his albums had been recorded live at concerts he had given on college campuses. He was one of the first jazz musicians to grace the cover of Time magazine. And he lived in the Oakland hills on the other side of St. Mary's. The sounds from his piano and Paul Desmond's alto sax fascinated me.

Also in 1956, I met Ernie Palomino. Ernie was a few years older than me, pencil-thin at five foot seven. Almost everything about him was long, thin, delicate and fine: hands, fingers, arms, neck, legs, chest. His face was narrow, jawless, slanting down to a small, pointed chin with a thin-lipped mouth that was often pursed. His nose was pointed and fine. But his brown eyes bulged grotesquely out of that delicate face, emphasized even more by the coke-bottle glasses that he wore. When he spoke, his voice was squeaky, high-pitched. Speaking, articulating did not come easy for Ernie, though he spoke all the time. He had difficulty finishing thoughts and sometimes sentences. You could see his mind struggling, searching for words that would explain or give meaning to what he had just said. When the words did come they were sometimes too big or too new for him. But then, he liked telling how, in his first week of high school, he had found it so unbearable that he actually rolled out of the classroom window onto the lawn below and left the school grounds never to return. He had a laugh, a cackle that could come at any time, whenever he or anyone else was speaking and he thought, not infrequently, that what was being said was absurd.

I met Ernie in my parents' living room during one of my college breaks. I walked in on one of his visits and I could see that Mom, while polite, was tolerating him, but Dad was animated. He and Dad were speaking in Spanish about the art work Dad had done in a ceramic factory in Mexico City before coming to the United States. When Ernie left, I asked, "Who's he?"

"He's a very good painter," Dad said. "He's becoming famous here in Fresno."

Mom left the room and returned with a handful of newspaper clippings. "He's getting a lot of publicity," she said.

I scanned the clippings. There were several large black and white photographs of his paintings and articles praising his work. The Fresno Bee had described him several times as "Fresno's own, young, promising artist."

"What's he doing here?" I asked.

"Oh, he just likes to come here and visit with us," Mom said.

"Why?"

"Maybe because he doesn't have any family or anyone, and he feels right at home here with us."

Later, my sister Eleanor said to me, "He's got a crush on Marian. So he comes here all the time trying to see her. But Marian won't have anything to do with him, and if she knows he's coming, she leaves. If he comes when she's home, she hides in our bedroom and won't come out 'til he leaves."

The newspaper articles had caught my attention and my envy too. I had never before read any article in the Fresno Bee praising a Mexican-American. I read them again. They described a self-taught young artist, a high school dropout, who supported himself with odd jobs once he left high school and began drawing because he "liked to draw." He drew and drew until by chance, one of his drawings was seen by a woman who had an interest in the arts. The woman tracked down Ernie and once she saw his multitude of drawings, not only encouraged him to paint but gave him the funds to do so. Now his paintings were being recognized as the work of a remarkable young artist, not only in Fresno but as far away as the Bay Area.

The next time Ernie came to our house when I was there on semester break, I waited until he had visited with my folks and then I met him outside. I told him I had heard and read about his work and wanted to talk to him about it, wanted to learn how and why he did it. He liked that and surprised me by saying that he knew I was going to college and had never met a Mexican who was going to college, and would like to talk to me too. We became friends and each time I came home from St. Mary's, I spent more time with Ernie than anyone else.

Fresno was then planning to expand its downtown. To do so, it had condemned several old houses adjacent to downtown. Those houses stood alone and vacant, without water or utilities, except that Ernie lived in one of them. And he made no secret of it. The house he chose, and there were several blocks of them, couldn't have been more public. It sat alongside a street that was heavily traveled. Any passerby, especially at night, could see that someone was living in that abandoned house. That didn't seem to matter to Ernie. Perhaps because by then he had become "a proud son of Fresno," which I thought was why he had never been evicted.

It was a small house, completely stripped. The vent hole and smoke and grease stains on one wall said that had been the kitchen. Two rooms with a closet and window in each were the bedrooms. The bathroom had a rusted iron tub and a hole in the floor. Ernie lived in the biggest room which opened onto the front porch, whose floor was leaning heavily downward. In that front room, he had brought in an old couch and a table and two chairs. On the table were a kerosene lamp and some candles. On the floor in a corner of the room was a mat with some blankets.

I spent many nights talking to Ernie in that old house, and Ernie loved to talk. He had opinions and ideas about everything, especially now that so many people were interested in him, people who were constantly exposing him to things that were new to him. Many of his opinions and ideas were half-baked and poorly informed, not to say that mine were much better. He had a habit, at times, of stopping in mid-sentence or mid-thought and laughing, cackling at the ridiculousness of what he was saying or at his inability to finish his thoughts. Then after laughing, he would stop, turn to some other subject or ask me what I thought.

One subject Ernie never cackled over, though he railed against it often, was Americans' pursuit of material things. "They think a big, new car, flashy clothes, expensive jewelry, a bigger TV set, is going to make them happy. They sacrifice, put themselves in debt for it. For what? They're still miserable after they've got it. How long is it gonna take them to understand that none of those things have anything to do with happiness?" Initially I wondered if that contempt was really envy. He had nothing. But years later, when he had money, his life style hadn't changed.

Time and again he assailed me. "Ronnie, I can't believe it! I don't understand you! You talk the talk and walk the walk, and yet you say you want to be a lawyer? Can't you see where you're headed? What do you want, a lot of money? Wanna be a big shot? Lord it over the rest of us poor Mexicans?" I used to think: That's because you know that you could never be a lawyer, that you'll never be anything but a starving artist. But my answer would simply be, "That's what I wanna be." He would persist until he saw that he was pushing it, that he had gone too far. Then he would stop, drop it. My friendship meant something to him.

Ernie's beginnings could not have been more difficult. His father was a cripple and his mother was a shut-in who never left the one room bungalow they lived in. She was terrified of going outside and kept the door and windows locked and the shades drawn. They lived on whatever his father could earn on odd, menial jobs. When his father died just before Ernie started high school, he was on his own. He survived on odd-jobs as well. Though he was self-taught, his drawings were stark, graphic, detailed depictions of the hardships he had known.

His early paintings, the ones I knew, were startling. They also dealt with the same horror-filled experiences of his youth, but they were much more powerful than the drawings. The canvases were many times larger and the colors intensified the starkness and the pain. Ernie said that he admired the work of the Mexican painter, Jose Clemente Orozco, and years later when I saw Orozco's magnificent murals on the walls and ceilings of the Guadalajara orphanage, vibrant reds, yellows, whites and blacks and a man being hurled into the flames of Hell, I thought of Ernie. One of Ernie's paintings I'll always remember. It was on a six foot by four foot canvas. The dominant colors were red, yellow and brown. The thick brush strokes and the subjects' hair and clothing gave a sense of the wind blowing. A forlorn brown woman was standing behind a fence from which there was no escape. She was holding the hand of a brown toddler who was also peering out into hopelessness through that fence. Behind them stood the small ramshackle structure that was their home.

A year after I met Ernie, I stood with him on the lower floor of the De Young Museum in San Francisco. On the floor above us was an exhibit of the Edward G. Robinson Collection that was on national tour. On the lower floor, we stood watching people view Ernie's paintings and drawings. There were many "oows" and "ahhs" as people entered the room, many startled and dismayed expressions. The viewers moved cautiously, reverentially up to and around his work. Some shook their heads and whispered among themselves. We watched for more than an hour. Ernie said not a word. He simply watched, his small mouth pursed, but in a good way, matching his gleaming eyes.

After viewing his exhibit at the De Young Museum, Ernie and I paid a visit to San Francisco's North Beach later that night. The Beat Generation was in its heyday and if San Francisco was its capital, North Beach was its home. The place was teeming with wanna-be artists, writers and poets. Bearded, beret-wearing, pipe-smoking men, many carrying portable typewriters, were everywhere. I had been to North Beach once before and that had been enough for me, but Ernie hadn't been and wanted to go. We ended up at Miss Smith's Tea Room on Grant Street. That night, Allen Ginsberg and Gregory Corso happened to be there. Ginsberg's book of poems "Howl" had received national praise and attention. But I wasn't buying any of the North Beach scene. Sometime during the evening Ginsberg gave an impromptu talk. Many gathered around him. Ernie and I were in the front row, a couple of feet from him. While Ginsberg was speaking, I must have made some snide remark because he stopped, looked at me and asked, "What is the sound of a single hand?" I shrugged and he slapped me across the face. "That's it!" he said. That was the end of our night in North Beach.

The respect and admiration I had for Ernie, I had for no other peer. His dedication, hard work, courage and discipline made a lasting impression on me. However, as accomplished an artist as he was, he was also a talented musician, a drummer.

In those days, the black musicians in Fresno were divided into two groups. One group was cashing in on the new-found craze for rock and roll. The other group was intent on emulating the black jazz greats on the east coast. Ernie was a drummer for both, was accepted and comfortable with both. Hayward Lee was a young, husky sax player with a quartet that he called something like Hayward Lee and the Blasters. Ernie was the only non-black in the group. The young whites in Fresno were crazy about Hayward Lee. Every weekend, he would fill a Fresno ballroom. Ernie used to say, "You otta see those white kids mobbin' that place, dancin' and shoutin' to Hayward's music. What's so fucked up about it is that Hayward's got a white chick for a girlfriend and he won't let her come into the place because people might think that she's his woman. So that girl sits in Hayward's car parked two blocks away waiting for him from the time we start at nine until one in the morning."

The cool blacks used to snipe at Ernie, "You gonna play with that turkey again? Ernie, you know damn good and well that Hayward don't play music, man. Hayward honks. That ain't music man, that's honkin' and you know it. How can you sit there and backup all that honkin for four hours?" Ernie's answer was short and simple. "Hey man, I need the bread. I need to eat." For some time, Ernie's sole source of income was Hayward Lee. Snipe as they would,

Ernie was the cool ones' drummer, always the only non-black in the group. He jammed with them late at night and on Sunday afternoons, sometimes in little clubs and sometimes in their homes. There was never much money in it, but they were beyond that. Elvis had brought black music to white America and white musicians were reaching out, trying to recruit black musicians to play with them. Ernie said that the black musicians had an unwritten code: "Man, don't go play with Whitey. You're just gonna make that fool sound good. Let him sound the way he's always sounded. Like shit. Don't help him."

If you ever saw Ernie play, you wouldn't see much of him. His slight, pencil-thin frame was mostly hidden by the drum sets. You could see his twig-like arms and tiny fists moving up and down and around with an amazing pace and grace. From time to time you would get a glimpse of him, of his coke-bottle glasses and his beak-like nose moving from side to side. But you could always hear his sounds driving, filling every note for the other musicians.

Early on I told Ernie that I too liked jazz, that I liked Dave Brubeck.

Ernie was merciless. "You like Brubeck? Man, that ain't jazz!"

"What is it then?"

"I don't know but it ain't jazz. He plays some kind of semi-classical stuff on that piano. And Desmond plays nothing but sweet, syrupy shit on his sax. Sweet music for all those white rocking chair people ain't jazz. That's Tommy Dorsey and those guys."

I was hurt and humiliated. But Ernie was relentless. "You wanna hear jazz? Then listen to Max Roach or Art Blakey. Those cats play jazz."

Ernie always began with Roach and Blakey, because they were drummers. But a long list followed: Bud Powell, Thelonius Monk, Horace Silver, Charley Mingus, Lester Young, John Coltrane and Miles Davis. I listened to those great jazz musicians. At first, because I wanted to be hip and because I wanted to be Ernie's friend. But I grew to love that music and listened to it long after Ernie and I parted ways. Fifty years later, I still listen to and enjoy their music, always dazzled by the fact that those black geniuses had no formal musical schooling and probably not much formal education either.

I've watched many groups play jazz. I've seen some of the East Coast greats play. Unfortunately, there is one performance that stands out in my mind above the rest. It was while I was living in San Francisco after leaving Villa Montalvo. I went to a Sunday afternoon show at the Jazz Workshop featuring Charley Mingus and his Quintet. Mingus was then considered the premier jazz bass player. He was a big, light-skinned man who towered over his instrument. His Quintet was made up of two saxophones, a trombone, the drums and his bass. All of the group was black except for the white trombone player.

On stage there was no doubt who the leader of the group was. Mingus' command and control was on everything. I was thrilled to be there, to see and hear this great musician's group play, thrilled through the first set. At the intermission, the group left the little stage. Twenty minutes later, they returned, first three and then Mingus. For whatever reason, the trombone player was not on the stage. Mingus looked around, clearly annoyed. The he began to shout, scream. There were about 50 people in the club and the first shouts took us aback. "Hey Frankie, where in the fuck are you! Get your silly white ass out here before I go back there and kick it out here!"

No Frankie.

"Did you hear me, you sorry white motherfucker! I said get your stupid white ass out here!" He was screaming.

The curtain behind the stage ruffled, then parted, and there stood Frankie, head bowed and frozen.

"Move, I said! Before I come over there and move you! You can't play worth a shit! And now you pull this! I'm telling you for the last time! MOVE! Or I'm gonna come over there and move that flabby white ass of yours!"

Frankie moved, slowly, not just beaten but shattered, over the few feet to his trombone.

"Now put that fucking thing in that pasty white mouth of yours and you better not fuck up this set the way you did the last or I'll beat the holy fuck out of you right here in front of everybody!"

Frankie put the trombone to his lips and for a long, long moment there was silence until Mingus said, "One, two, three."

The music began but I wasn't listening. I couldn't listen. I was staring at Frankie. When the piece ended, I left. I was already familiar with the saying that the worst tyrant is the ex-slave. I had just witnessed living proof of that. How quick the oppressed are all too often ready to inflict the same cruelty that brutalized them on others.

During my two-plus years of wandering about as an aspiring novelist, I saw Ernie whenever I could. Then, just after returning to law school in San Francisco, I saw him for what turned out to be the last time for many years. I was no longer a practicing Catholic and Ernie had dropped out of the Church long before me. My contempt for the Church was great but Ernie's was greater. My wife and our parents were Catholics and it was important for them that my first child be baptized a Catholic. I relented. But the Baptismal ceremony required godparents. My wife had asked her sister to be the godmother. Who was to be the godfather? Ernie was the only friend I had, so I called him.

"Are you out of your fucking mind? Have you gone completely crazy? You're gonna baptize your kid and you have the fucking balls to ask me to be the godfather! What do you think I am? Who do you think you are?"

"Ernie, I have to baptize her and you're the only guy I know to ask. You're my friend. Do me this one favor, please Ernie."

We went round and round until finally I heard that cackle and he said, "O.K." But no sooner had Ernie agreed than I began to worry. Ernie would speak his mind in that squeaky voice on any topic, whenever he chose, no matter what the occasion or who was present. I could already see and hear him ranting and raving at the Baptism about those bastard priests who sucked every penny out of dirt-poor Mexicans to build their gold-encrusted churches, how those savage priests had made slaves out of the Mayas and destroyed their wonderful temples to raise their own ugly churches over them to prove who the true God was, how they had ravaged the Mayas' culture, burning their books and codices. Maybe I shouldn't have asked him after all. And what would he look like at the Baptismal? Most of the time he looked weird, wearing used clothes from Goodwill and The Salvation Army. Maybe the priest, seeing him, wouldn't let him be the godfather. Then again, maybe Ernie would change his mind and not come.

But Ernie did come to San Francisco to be the godfather. His clothes were as presentable as I had ever seen: pressed slacks, a clean, starched dress shirt and polished shoes. But how was I to control his mouth? That morning we had several private conversations.

"Ernie, when we get to the church, please don't start bad-mouthing the Church."

"Bad-mouthing?"

"Yeah, you know how you always like to go off on how the Church and the priests have been ripping off poor Mexicans since the time Cortez hit Mexico."

"Ah, man."

"No, none of that. And the priest is gonna ask you if you're a Catholic and what are you gonna say?"

"No, I'm not."

"Shit Ernie, if you say that, the kid won't get baptized and everybody's gonna be pissed-off as hell at me."

"But I ain't no fucking Catholic."

"Listen to me. Listen to me. You know what they say: Once a Catholic always a Catholic. So once you're baptized, and you were, you've told me that, you'll always be a Catholic, in name only, even if you don't practice anymore."

"I'm no fucking Catholic."

"But you are. In name you are because you were baptized. Only in name you are. It's like your name's Ernie. You'll always be Ernie. So if the priest asks you if you're a Catholic, all you have to say is 'yes.' That's all."

"Shit man, you asked me to do you a favor and I said O.K., but you never brought up any of this crap."

"Please Ernie, do it for me."

The priest didn't ask and Ernie didn't tell. In fact, Ernie said nothing at the Baptism except "yes" each time the priest asked him if he was willing to carry out his Catholic responsibilities in case of the parents' deaths. Of course, I was standing next to him nodding yes and pressing gently but firmly against him in response to each of those questions. The baby was baptized. But it would be many years before I saw Ernie again.

Once I resumed my law studies and then began practicing law, my visits to Fresno were few and far between. When I did go, it was with my family and usually for special occasions. We would leave the Santa Cruz Mountains on Saturday morning and return as soon as we could on Sunday. The visits were always taken up with family and there was never any time to visit Ernie. But Mom and Dad kept me posted. Mom saved every article about Ernie in The Fresno Bee and was always eager to show them to me. To my surprise, Ernie had become a Professor of Art at Fresno State University. How anyone who had rolled out of a high school window in his freshman year and never gone back was a university professor was beyond me.

It was eight or nine years after the Baptism, when on a visit to Fresno, Mom told me that Ernie had visited them and left his address, saying that if I ever came to Fresno he would like to see me. I drove over to his home in a blue collar neighborhood in East Fresno. It turned out that he had purchased two modest houses there, one for his wife and kids and one for his studio. I met him in his studio. It was a small, old house, sparsely furnished and without a hint of affluence. His clothes were still shabby. He was rounder around the waist, which was exaggerated on his pencil-thin frame. Although he could always slip into a pensive mood, that afternoon the pensiveness never left him. He was married and had several children and that responsibility was weighing heavily upon him. His professorship was the first steady job he had ever had, and in some ways it sounded like just that: a job. The schedules were too rigid, his associates were difficult and not on the same page as him, and the students could be troublesome. I was feeling similar pressures, and after we exchanged grumblings, there was nothing more to say. It felt so odd. There had been a time when we could spend hours talking on any given subject. Now there was nothing more to say. I felt as if we were worlds apart. I left within the hour, telling him where I lived and if he was ever in the area to stop by.

Perhaps a year later, he came unannounced with three of his kids on a weekend afternoon to visit me in my home in the Santa Cruz Mountains. His kids immediately began running around with mine, and I walked him around the five acres, extolling its virtues. He wasn't interested. Worse, he cackled several times, the same cackle he had often used to express what he thought was an absurdity. This visit was more awkward than our last. Not long after the tour, he left.

The next and last time that I saw Ernie Palomino was in 1994. It was at a reading in Fresno for my then recently published first novel, *Happy Birthday Jesus,* the dark, grim story of Jesus Olivas. The reading was well attended, and it was a while before I noticed Ernie sitting in the crowd with a woman. It surprised me. After the reading, people came up for signings and comments. Ernie was at the tail-end of that group. When he approached me, he, the creator of the darkest, starkest paintings I had ever seen, shook my hand and said, "Ronnie, when are you ever going to write something nice?" Then he grinned and left.

Once I returned to law school there was little time for anything else. When I started my law practice there was even less time. People were paying me money to help them, too often money they could ill-afford to pay, because they believed in me. I could see it in their eyes, hear it in their voices: the hopes, the expectations, the pleas. The hated, dry, dull, law books were for the most part gone. They had been replaced with people and their very real stories of hardship. Replaced too, by judges and prosecutors, courts and courtrooms, and by the ministerial duties of running an office and making money. My family was there too and, as always, poorly attended to by me. That left so little time for anything else.

Yet at times at night, after everyone had gone to bed, I would pull out some of my old jazz albums and play one cut softly, sitting back and letting myself go to another place, another time, back when I had time and none of the constant pressures I was feeling then. Horace Silver playing "Senor Blues." So many different strains: West Indies, Cuban, New York funk, blues and counterpoint. Another place, another world and Horace was taking me there. Thelonius Monk on "Round About Midnight." He never ceased to amaze me. How could this unschooled man make so many discordant sounds pleasing? Dave Brubeck and "Take Five." Sweet it might be but no, Ernie, Tommy Dorsey could never play that. Brubeck up and down, repeating counterpoint after counterpoint while Desmond's lyrical sax taunted me. One album, one cut per night, and then I could go to bed having experienced another world, another being for a few moments.

My car radio also allowed me a few moments of escape. A few of the FM stations in the Bay Area were playing music that I liked. On my trips to outlying county courthouses, I could find 20 to 30 minutes of good listening. The Paul Butterfield Blues Band, Jimi Hendrix, and the revival of Muddy Waters. Welcome intrusions from the pressures I had just left in one courthouse and those awaiting me in the next. Even some of the country western music fascinated me: Roy Orbeson, Johnny Cash, Merle Haggard. Simple, straight ballads about the lives they were living, hearing, feeling and seeing. How I longed to write about those things.

Then came Bob Dylan, exploding onto the American music and cultural scene as no one had before. By 1964, he was everywhere. He spoke to my mind and twisted my emotions as no musician ever had before. *Blowin' In The Wind. A Hard Rains Gonna Fall. The Visions of Johanna.* On and on he went. After eight years of living in a literary wasteland, I had only to turn on my car radio or play one cut from one of his albums at night to hear as fine a poet and musician as I had ever heard. A poet? Yes, indeed. I bought all of Bob Dylan's albums as soon as they were released. I listened to them every chance I had. Many of his lines ran through my mind day after day. More than any other artist, Bob Dylan kept the desire, the need to write, burning within me.

But write about what? Write about what I was seeing and living every day as a criminal defense attorney representing a racial minority and the poor. Day after day, I was seeing Mexicans in jail garb being taken from a holding cell and being brought into a courtroom on new felony criminal charges, 30 or 40 of them every afternoon in a single courtroom. Ninety to 95 percent of those brought into that courtroom were Mexicans. In Oakland, the percentage of blacks in that situation was even higher. In rural, mountain counties where there were no Mexicans or blacks, it was the poor whites that constituted that majority. Yet those percentages never seemed to strike a chord with anyone. I used to say in those early days to anyone who would listen, and I don't mean were interested, that it cost the state more money to send one of those Mexicans to prison than it would to send him to Harvard. That still holds true.

Every year I dreaded going to court after the New Year. Because each year the state legislature, in its infinite wisdom, was adding new felonies to the Penal Code, increasing the length of sentences for existing felonies, and adding to the number of mandatory prison sentences. But the mindless electorate's solution to the crime problem was to lock up those filthy animals forever, and the politicians in the state legislature who were in the business of being reelected could never let themselves be viewed as being "soft on crime." The prisons grew and grew until they became the largest yearly item on the state budget. Did this "tough on crime" solution solve anything? Today, California's recidivism rate for parolees, now well-trained after their long sentences, stands at 70%. The highest in the nation.

As I write this, California is bankrupt. Six thousand five hundred prisoners have been granted early releases this year and there will be many more next year. Others who would have routinely been sent to prison for years are now being sent to county jails and a year's sentence instead. The state budget has to be slashed and, needless to say, the prison system's budget. Still, the politicians are reluctant to slash their draconian sentences that have flooded the state prisons with inmates, afraid to be viewed as "soft on crime."

Let me make myself clear. Violent offenders should be locked up in prisons and kept locked up for as long it takes to protect society. But what I was seeing was that the bulk of felony arrests (crimes that warrant a state prison sentence) were for the sale, possession for sale or possession of drugs, as well as for numerous drug-related crimes, such as burglaries, robberies and other forms of theft that had at their root the need to support a drug habit. Each year,

I was seeing more men and women being convicted of those crimes and going to prison for longer and longer periods of time.

What were the prisons like? If you weren't a hardened criminal when you entered prison, the chances were very good that you would be one when you left. Prisons are a school for crime. By the 1960's, gangs permeated California's prisons. The gangs were formed along ethnic lines: brown, black, and white gangs. The gangs were frequently at war with one another. Upon entering a prison, many an inmate felt compelled to join a gang as a means of surviving, of protecting himself against rapes, beatings and stabbings. Once you were a member of a gang, you did as the gang ordered, or else. What the gang ordered was often more ruthless and violent than anything to be found outside the prison walls. As the inmate population grew, the gangs grew. The California prisons cracked down hard. Their repression was brutal. Some of the punishments exacted for what were perceived to be violations of prison rules and regulations were extreme. Certain parts of the prisons were designated to house and mete out special punishment for those offenders.

One prison in particular was extremely harsh in its punishments. That prison was located outside Soledad, California, some 70 miles south of San Jose. The inmates' cries of inhumane treatment there grew louder and louder, leading to a United States congressional investigation headed by Senator Robert Kennedy. The prison reacted by filing new criminal charges in state court, on offenses that had normally been dealt with in the prison, new charges that would significantly increase the length of the sentences of "inside offenders." Indigent inmates now found themselves once again in the state criminal courts.

For sometime before I met her, Faye Stender had been single-handedly advocating for the rights of prison inmates. She was a bright, 40-year-old lawyer who passionately believed that prison inmates should be treated as human beings despite their criminal histories. All of her work was done *pro bono*, and she also paid for her own expenses as she went from prison to prison. Her husband's successful law practice allowed her to do what few lawyers thought was important. When the Soledad Prison began filing criminal charges in Monterey County, Faye Stender began looking for lawyers to represent the inmates. When she called me, I told her that my calendar wouldn't permit it, that I simply didn't have the time to travel to Salinas to try what were sure to be jury trials. She wasn't easily put off. She came to my office. I was annoyed, but that didn't last long. In a matter of minutes, this tall, willowy, white woman had put me to shame. She was quick to point out that almost all of the defendants were Mexican-Americans, almost as if I had a special obligation. Which I tried to hide, but which she uncovered in a matter of minutes, not so much by what she said, but rather by what she had been doing. For years I had loathed what I saw happening to Mexican-Americans in the criminal justice system. Now a white woman was doing something about it, and she was sitting across from me asking me to join her. I couldn't say no.

She assigned me the case of the People vs. Ralph Chacon. At the age of 19, Ralph Chacon had been convicted in Bakersfield of stealing a case of beer at knifepoint from a convenience store. Eighteen years later, he was still in prison, now in the infamous "O" wing at Soledad where there had recently been a riot. For several hours, the inmates had gained control of that unit and had held guards hostage. They were ultimately subdued and order was restored. As a result, Chacon and other inmates were indicted in a Salinas court on new felony charges that would add many years to their existing sentences.

Soledad Prison is situated on the east side of Highway 101 in the agriculturally rich Salinas Valley, some 20 miles south of the city of Salinas. Behind it are acres of rich farmland. Across the highway are the dark San Lucia Mountains, the western border of the Los Padres National Forest, and beyond that, the Pacific Ocean. Once inside the prison at that time, you entered a long, dark, wide, cement hallway that seemed to go on and on, at times I thought for a mile. On either side of that hall were rows of two-story wings, a half block deep and set a half block apart. The wings were designated by the letters of the alphabet. More than halfway down that gargantuan hall on the east side was the specially designed "O" wing where Chacon was housed and where I met with him on several occasions. Chacon's cell was known as a maximum security cell. It was an 8'x10' windowless cell with no light fixtures and only a slit in its steel door which could be slid open from the outside to pass a food tray or to allow a guard to look inside. There was nothing in the cell except a hole in the center of the floor where the inmate could urinate or defecate. The inmate wore no clothing in that cell and he could only stand, sit or lie on the floor.

I visited Chacon on Sunday afternoons. When he was brought out of his maximum security cell, he was issued white coveralls and then brought to a small interview room where I was waiting. He entered the room rubbing his eyes. It would take him a while for his eyes to adjust to the light.

Before my first meeting with Chacon, I knew nothing about him other than what was in the prison offense report. It said little more than that he had been one of several inmates who had been involved in a smoke and gas-filled riot in an attempt to take over "O" wing. When a guard told me that they would be bringing Chacon down to see me, I was not prepared for what I was about to see. He entered the room, went to the chair across the table from me, pulled it out and to one side and sat down. My first impression was that he was 5'6" or 5'7", thin, with black hair and a pale complexion. Ralph had moved the chair at an angle from the table so that he was facing the door, not me. I waited for him to turn and face me, but he didn't.

"Ralph, my name is Ron Ruiz and I'm going to be your attorney."

No response, not even a blink. His eyes remained fixed on the door.

"You're Ralph Chacon, aren't you?"

Again, nothing.

I was annoyed. I had driven all this way on a Sunday, wasted a Sunday, for this? I waited, calmed myself, reminded myself what this poor bastard was facing. "Ralph, the charges you're facing in the Salinas court are serious. If you're convicted, you could spend the rest of your life in here. Come on, turn around. Let's talk."

Nothing. Was he game-playing me? I had had hundreds of interviews with in-custody inmates by then, and had been subjected to a variety of attempts to manipulate me. I decide to wait him out, not speak again until he did. I watched him. I waited. He was a strange one. Not once had his gaze left the door. I focused on his eyes. No movement. I watched for a blink. None. Then it struck me that his complexion was not really pale but grey, ash-like, with blotches of light yellow. I hadn't seen that color before on any Mexican, or anyone for that matter.

After what I thought must have been fifteen minutes, I decided to leave. I'd driven all this way for this? I didn't need him. He needed me. If I left now that would teach him. It wouldn't take him long to realize that he would be walking into that Salinas courtroom alone. I got up to leave but stopped. I couldn't leave, not then. Because I didn't really know how long I'd been there. Had it really been fifteen minutes or ten or less? I had been careful to wear a suit and tie to look like a lawyer as it was my first visit to that prison. When I entered the prison, I had signed in as an attorney from San Jose. Then the guards asked me for my Bar card and my driver's license. They examined them both carefully.

They conferred among themselves and then asked for a business card. They asked why my business card bore a San Jose address and my driver's license had a Santa Cruz address. I said that I commuted every day.

"And you drove over here from Santa Cruz on a Sunday to see one of these guys?"

"Yes."

To me, at that point, they didn't believe that I was a lawyer. I was probably the first Mexican lawyer they had ever seen. Two of them went into a side office and one stayed with me at the front counter. The two were gone for several minutes. When they returned, one of them said, "O.K., you can go in." Once inside "O" wing, the guards there had disbelieving looks too, but now with smirks. As I stood then looking down at the still mute Ralph Chacon, I thought, Leave now after five minutes and it will confirm all their suspicions. Then they might stop me and question me as to why I really came down here. I sat down. This time I would time my stay: fifteen minutes. If Chacon didn't speak to me by then, I would leave. I waited 20 minutes and left. Not once had he spoken to me or stopped staring at the door, even after I had tried again. "Ralph, we have to talk. What they have you charged with is very serious."

For several days, I was angry and baffled. My ego was bruised. I wanted to call Faye Stender and bitch, make her feel defensive. But I couldn't. She had flattered me with the good things she said she had heard about me from other lawyers. She had told me she was assigning me one of the more difficult cases because she knew I could handle it and do a good job. How could I now call her and tell her that Chacon wouldn't even talk to me? It was then that Bobby Soto's name came up, brought up by another lawyer in the case who said he had interviewed him. He said that while Soto was also housed in "O" wing, he had not been named as one of the defendants in the riot case. He had found Soto to be bright, straightforward and credible. He thought Soto was worth talking to, if only to get another version of what had happened and what went on in "O" wing. Depending on the guards' testimony at the trial, he thought Soto might be a good rebuttal witness. That gave me a new direction. I went to Soledad again on the following Sunday, intent on talking to Soto first, asking him about the riot and "O" wing and what he knew or thought of Chacon.

Bobby Soto was indeed bright and articulate. But he was much more than that. He was a sturdy, handsome, fiercely independent, young Mexican in his mid-twenties who had yet to be broken by the guards or the other inmates. He had gone to prison three years before on a robbery charge, and had continuing difficulties with the guards, which finally led to his being housed in "O" wing. He thought the guards were mental and physical midgets, and he let them know that. He had refused to join any gang, which made him a prison-wide target and he seemed to pride himself in that.

"All I can tell you is that I was in my cell when it happened and I had no part in it. I don't know who was involved in it and I don't want to know."

"Was Ralph Chacon involved?"

"I don't know, but it's hard for me to believe that he was."

"Why?"

"The guy's a space cadet. He's out of it. That's why."

"What do you mean?"

"You've been with him, haven't you?...The guy's in his own world. He's always staring out into space. He never talks to nobody."

"How do you know that?"

"I've been out of my cell with him a few times. Believe it or not, they pull us out from time to time just to search those fucking holes we live in. I don't know what they think they're going to find. Sometimes, they just pull us out. Then there's times like when one of us will be out for a medical and the other guy's got an interview. I've been out there with the dude a few times alone and a few times with some of the other guys too. He's just not there. His body's there, but his mind is someplace else. Some guys laugh at him. Some shake their heads. I kinda feel sorry for him. But why would anybody want him in a fucking riot? He'd just get in the way."

"Can't the guards see this?"

"The guards see what they want to see. They don't believe anything we say or do and we don't believe anything they say or do. They probably think he's gaming them."

"Why did they file charges on him?"

"Except for a few guys, I don't think they really know who did what. See, they probably think Chacon's hooked up with one of the gangs. And if they think you're hooked up, then they're gonna hang you with the gang. They know I'm no gang banger. They've put me in so many holes for fighting with those punks that there's no way they could slap charges on me for being a gang banger."

"Is Chacon in a gang?"

"Hell, I don't know. But it doesn't matter if he is or isn't. If these fools think he is, then he is."

"How do you get along with Chacon?"

"Man, how am I gonna get along with a dude that won't even talk to me or look at me?"

When Soto left and while I waited for the guards to bring Chacon, I had no idea how I would deal with him. When he entered this time, I watched him with different eyes. He's not gaming me, I thought. I said nothing. There was nothing I could say. I was too engrossed in watching that grey, sallow, expressionless face, those fixed eyes. The offense report said that he was 37. He looked more like 47. A case of beer worth 20 dollars, at knife point, 18 years ago, and now this. This for a case of beer! Americans could parade around the world pointing their fingers at human rights violations, my answer was Ralph Chacon. Had he lost his humanity when he stole a case of beer from a convenience store in Bakersfield 18 years ago?

When I finally spoke, I said, "Ralph, I'm your lawyer. I want to help you. But I can't help you unless you talk to me. Talk to me, Ralph."

No answer. Not even a blink.

I stood and moved my chair, placing it directly in front of him. His eyes didn't shift, didn't move. I sat down. Those eyes were meeting mine. Looking at me without seeing me. I reached out and touched his hand. It was as cold and stiff as my sister's was on the day she died. "Ralph please, you have to talk to me. I can't do anything for you if you won't talk to me."

Nothing. I sat there for what I thought was a long time. Finally, I stood and put two of my business cards in his hand and left.

It was two weeks before I saw Ralph Chacon again. In the meantime, my thinking was that I probably had no alternative but to file a motion with the Salinas court asking for a hearing to determine Chacon's competency to stand trial based on his inability to assist me as his attorney in conducting a defense, as provided under Penal Code section 1367. What that meant was that the criminal proceedings would be suspended and Ralph Chacon would be sent to the prison at Vacaville for evaluation until the doctors there determined that he was able to stand trial. In the event that he was not able to stand trial, he could be held in Vacaville for the maximum term of the offenses. I had to explain all of this to Ralph before I could file the motion.

A few days before I returned to Soledad, I received a letter in the mail which had all the markings of a letter from a prison inmate. Neatly printed on the envelope were my name and office address with a return to Ralph Chacon, his prison number and his Soledad address. I looked at the envelope several times. How could he have written to me? I opened it, anxious now, and found nothing but a pencil drawing of the face of a kitten. The face took up the entire single page. There was nothing else on it, not a single letter or line. The kitten's eyes were large and the face amazingly life-like. I recognized the paper as that issued to inmates for writing. I sat there for several minutes trying to make some sense of the drawing and the letter itself. I took it with me when I returned to Soledad.

I asked to see Soto first. He came, rubbing his eyes. "Give me a minute, man." What a difference. Soto was fit, strong, alert and articulate. Ralph was sullen, thin, lost and mute.

"How do you do it, Bobby?"

"Do what, man?"

"Survive in here, maintain the way you do? Stay strong?"

"I have to, man. It's my will against theirs. They're trying to break me. If I let them, I'll turn out like Chacon. He's not the only guy that they've cracked, there's a hell of a lot more like him. Guys be screaming out their minds. Hanging themselves the first chance they get. That's what this place is all about, breaking us. If you don't conform, if you don't fit into their mold, then they put you in these holes until you do, or break, or somehow show them that it's not gonna happen to you."

"But how do you do it? Alone in that darkness, day after day, with nothing, not even clothes. Nothing except a shit hole."

"It's like I'm fighting for the rest of my life. If I give in, if I break, I'll become like Chacon. Then life ain't worth living. That's what I keep telling myself in that hole, what I can't let myself forget in that hole. It's about surviving. I've got to stay strong now or life won't be worth living."

"How long have you been in here?"

"Going on four months."

"How much longer will they keep you here?"

"I don't know. But I'm not giving them any excuses to keep me longer."

I showed him the drawing. "Ralph sent me this."

"Hmph."

"You think he drew it?'

"I don't know. I don't know if he can draw or not. But whoever did it, did a pretty good job."

"How could he draw that in the hole?"

"He could. About once a week they drop some of that paper and a stub of a pencil through the slit. They do that because they know that they can't cut us off from our lawyers. Then they leave the slit open long enough to let some light in."

"Who wrote this?" showing him the envelope.

"Probably the guards. When you finish writing, you slip the paper back out and they do the envelope."

"But you have to tell them who it's going to, don't you?"

"Yeah, unless they know who you're writing to. From what I hear, Chacon's been in the joint a long, long time. I doubt he's got anybody left to write to except maybe you. And if you gave him one of your cards, he could have given them one of those."

When Ralph came in, I positioned my chair so that his stare was fixed on me. I told him about the motion and what it meant. There was no response. His stare remained the same. I waited, thinking. Then I took the letter out of my coat pocket and showed him the drawing. His eyes did shift to the kitten, fixed on the kitten and the corner of his lips rose slightly, as if to smile, and for the first time he looked at me and saw me, and I thought nodded. But that was all.

At the upcoming hearing I would need psychiatric testimony to prove that Ralph couldn't assist me in conducting his defense. But where was the money to come from to pay for a psychiatrist? The only forensic psychiatrists I knew who would be willing to travel to Soledad and examine Ralph, review my file and then testify in Salinas had their offices in Palo Alto and San Francisco. I calculated that with their travel time, if I was lucky, I was looking at a minimum fee of $5,000. My time and work on Ralph's case was *pro bono*. I could absorb that. But $5,000 was a lot of money to me in 1973.

While worrying about the fee, someone told me that a Mexican psychiatrist had opened an office in Berkeley. The idea appealed to me. Ralph would be difficult to examine no matter who the psychiatrist was. But a Mexican psychiatrist might be more understanding, more compassionate, and set a more reasonable fee. I drove to Berkeley. Dr. Carlos Perez's office was a small room with a desk, three chairs and a couch. His reception room was a bare, narrow aisle with a bell on a shelf that I rang to announce my arrival. I entered his office and shook his hand. There he stood, brown like me. No question, he was a Mexican. I felt so comfortable, uninhibited that I said, "Wow! A Mexican psychiatrist!" His answer I've never forgotten. "*Si, y ya estamos usando calcetines.*" ("Yes, and now we're even wearing socks.") I told him about Ralph and the case.

When I finished he asked, "Who's paying your fee?"

I hesitated and said, "I'm doing it *pro bono*, but I'm not asking you, nor am I expecting you to do the same. I'm willing to pay a reasonable fee."

"And I'm willing to take the case."

"What will your fee be?"

"Let's not worry about my fee. I'll tell you as we go along."

"I have to worry about it. I have to pay it."

"Let me put it this way, Mr. Ruiz. Whatever I decide my fee should be, it will be a reasonable one. You'll just have to trust me."

"O.K.," was all I could manage, but I was very much hoping that "reasonable" would be somewhere well below $5000.

"Agreed?"

"Yes." But what was "reasonable"? I was afraid to ask.

A week later, I received another letter from Ralph. This time it was a pencil drawing of two kittens on the same lined-ruled prison sheet as the first, and nothing more. Does he even know how to write, I asked myself for the first time? I knew nothing about cats or kittens but these kittens were more striking that the first. Their large eyes had so much hope and sadness. Or was that my imagination? One thing for certain: they upset me.

Two weeks after I had met with Dr. Perez, he phoned me. "I've seen Mr. Chacon twice. The first time he was just as you described. Total muscle rigidity and no reaction to anything I said or did. The second time I saw him he seemed normal. Slow and not very bright. Making eye contact. Answering my questions, albeit at times with great difficulty. He seemed to have normal body movements. Then, a little more than half-way through the examination he became rigid again. Wouldn't answer me, look at me or move. I'm convinced that he's suffering from schizophrenia with catatonic features, specifically catatonic stupor. I'll have no problem testifying to that in court. However, just to be sure, I'm going to see him a third time. I will have to testify that during part of my second examination, he did have normal reactions and movements and did answer my questions. So I think it's best to see him a third time."

I was at first elated and then worried. Worried about the normal reactions which I had not, and would never see, and what the third examination might reveal. Worried too about the disappearing "reasonable fee." As it turned out, Ralph was in the same catatonic state in the third examination as he had been in the first.

"There's no doubt in my mind," Dr. Perez said after his third visit, "that Mr. Chacon suffers from a severe mental disorder. To put it simply, he's a very sick man. What caused it, neither I nor anyone will probably ever know."

Before the hearing, I received another letter from Ralph. I stared at the envelope for a while, fingered it, but didn't open it. I knew what it was and I didn't want to see any more of his kittens. I put the unopened envelope in the top drawer of my desk. Two days later, I opened the envelope. When I saw this kitten's pleading eyes, I stuffed the drawing back into the envelope and dropped it into the bottom drawer of my desk.

After the hearing date was set, I learned that we had been assigned to what by all accounts was the toughest, orneriest, crankiest judge on the Salinas bench. His draconian sentences for criminal defendants were legend. By then as a criminal defense attorney, I pretty much expected those assignments. What did it matter? I reasoned in an initial state of self-pity. If the judge found Ralph able to stand trial, I had no defense and he would quickly be convicted and sentenced to the maximum term. If he found him unable to stand trial, he would go to Vacaville probably for the maximum term. But my conscience intervened. It did matter. If we went to trial, Ralph would be convicted of crimes he had not committed. Better to take his chances at Vacaville where at least he wouldn't be saddled with more felony convictions.

On the first day, we began the hearing late in the morning. The courtroom was empty except for the Judge, the District Attorney, Ralph and me, the court clerk, the court reporter, the bailiff and two armed prison guards. The old courtroom was big and poorly lit, which I thought helped Ralph. He was in that rigid stupor state and the courtroom dimness seemed to add to the grimness of his situation. Dr. Perez was on the witness stand the entire day. He was excellent, never wavering from a firmly held opinion that Ralph was suffering from schizophrenia with catatonic features. The District Attorney challenged him with the brevity of his contacts with Ralph: three interviews over three weeks, totaling a little more than five hours.

"Are you telling this court, Doctor, that based on those three brief interviews with Mr. Chacon, it's your professional opinion that he is suffering from schizophrenia with catatonic features?"

"Yes, it is."

"How can you be so certain, Doctor?"

"I'm absolutely certain."

"Based on what?"

"On my studies, my training, and my experience."

"Wouldn't you say, Doctor, that the guards who saw him every day for the past seven months, who conversed with him, took him in and out of his cell, provided him with food and drink daily, and sometimes with writing materials, would be better positioned to give us a more accurate opinion as to his mental condition?"

"Not necessarily."

"Why do you say that, Doctor?"

On and on it went. The District Attorney's position was that Ralph was feigning, that the guards who saw him on a daily basis would establish that, and that defense counsel's paid expert witness was doing exactly what he was expected to do: earn his fee. The next morning the District Attorney called the custodian of the prison medical records to testify that Ralph Chacon had never been treated for, nor complained of, any mental illness, despite the fact that he had been seen by several prison doctors over the course of 18 years. Then came the parade of "O" wing prison guards.

Early in the afternoon of the second day, as the next to the last guard was testifying, the old judge sat up in his chair and said, "Stop, Mr. District Attorney! I've heard all I want to hear. I've watched this defendant sitting in my courtroom for two days now and I'd have to be an idiot not to recognize that this man is catatonic. I order these criminal proceedings suspended and that Mr. Chacon be sent to the prison at Vacaville for evaluation and to remain there until that facility finds that he is able to assist his attorney in the conduct of his defense. That will be all." Then the old man left without another word.

When Dr. Perez left Salinas after his testimony, he said in answer to my question. "Call me when it's over and we'll talk about the fee." Which I did as soon as I returned to my office. I told him what the judge had decided. Then he said, "In good conscience, I can't charge you a dime more than what you've been paid in this case. The next time we meet, buy me a few tequilas." I would have gladly done so, but we never met again.

Over the next year and a half, I received three letters postmarked "Vacaville" with three more drawings of kittens from Ralph Chacon. As always, there was not a word or another line printed. But I did not receive any notification from Vacaville telling me that Ralph was able to stand trial and was being remanded to Salinas for further court proceedings. From mid-1975 to the fall of 1980, I closed my law office, gave up my law practice and worked for the California Agricultural Labor Relations Board in Sacramento and around the state. From time to time I checked for mail at my old office. During those years I received a few more kitten drawings from Ralph, still at Vacaville, but nothing more. Then sometime in 1979, I received a letter from a woman unknown to me with an address and an envelope post-marked Oceanside, California. The letter was brief and poorly written. It said that she had been visiting Ralph in Vacaville for the past several months, that he was about to be released from Vacaville, and that she planned to have Ralph live with her and maybe someday they would marry.

It was two months after Ralph's hearing in Salinas that I decided to set aside time each day to write a novel. I had a lot to write about.

Chapter 7

In California cases involving major felony crimes, the defendants are generally represented by the Public Defender. The reason being that they cannot afford to pay for the services of a private attorney. However, when the Public Defender declares a conflict of interest, then the court must appoint private counsel to represent one of those defendants. In cases where only one defendant is charged, that conflict of interest could arise where, for example, the Public Defender has represented the victim of the crime in the past, or has represented one or more of the potential witnesses that the prosecution will call in its case against the defendant. In cases where there are two or more defendants, the Public Defender will automatically declare a conflict of interest, keeping one defendant, while the court appoints separate attorneys for the remaining defendants, because under California law each defendant is entitled to separate counsel. As a result, I was appointed by the court to represent defendants in several major felony criminal cases.

Three major criminal cases in which I was court-appointed are very memorable to me for different reasons. The first one is the case entitled The People of the State of California vs. Richard Rodriguez and Leroy Mims.

The pendulum in the Santa Clara County criminal justice system began to swing to the right in the mid1970's. In those days, two Superior Court departments were used exclusively for criminal cases. They were known as the Superior Court Criminal Division. Next to the courthouse was the county jail which was connected to the two courts by an underground tunnel. Every defendant charged with a felony was arraigned, that is, had the charges read against him, entered his plea, and had his case set for trial in one of the two courts. If a jury trial was estimated to take two or more weeks, it was routinely transferred to one of the 14 Superior Court departments located downtown in the Civil Division, as were other cases when the two criminal departments became log-jammed.

When I first began appearing in the Superior Court Criminal division in 1966, the two judges assigned there were Judge Joseph Kelly and Judge

John Racanelli. Both were good, moderate judges and I enjoyed being in their courtrooms. Every Friday morning, the Master Sentencing Calendar began at 9:00a.m. and often ran until 12:30, sometimes beyond. There were usually 40 to 50 cases set for sentencing as a result of plea bargains entered into between the District Attorney and defendants. The Probation Department always submitted a report with a recommended sentence to the Judge. In court, the Judge allowed the District Attorney and Defense Counsel to speak on behalf of his or her client. I generally had three or four cases on that calendar each week and had spent several hours preparing to refute the probation report. I was long-winded, but each of the Judges heard me out, and I often felt that I had gotten a lighter sentence for my client.

In 1973, Judge Bruce Allen was assigned to the Criminal Division, filling a third department. Judge Allen was a tough, hard-nosed judge whose sentences were harsh and long: a hanging judge. However, at that time a California statute allowed an attorney to challenge, or excuse, one judge per case on the grounds that the defendant or his attorney did not believe, under oath, that he could receive a fair trial before that judge. We defense attorneys immediately began challenging Judge Allen, which pretty much rendered him useless for criminal cases. But the judges were not to be played with. The following year, Judge Kelly was assigned downtown and here came Judge James Wilson, who was even tougher and more conservative than Judge Allen. Not only was Judge Wilson assigned to us, but he was also made the Presiding Judge of the Criminal Division, which meant that he had complete control of every case in the Criminal Division.

In just a matter of days, defense attorneys were faced with a completely new and different regime. If we were assigned to Judge Allen for trial and challenged him, then we were sent back to Judge Wilson who would just keep the case in his department for trial. If Judge Wilson initially assigned a case to himself and we challenged him, then we would be assigned to Judge Allen. In either case, though it was never verbally articulated, we soon learned that we and our clients were going to pay a price for having exercised a challenge. The second judge made that clear in his rulings, in the consideration or lack thereof that he gave us, and at times even in the gravity of the sentences that our clients received. It wasn't long before the wholesale challenging of judges ceased.

Judge Wilson's Friday morning Master Sentencing Calendar bore no resemblance to that of his predecessors. To begin with, it never went past 12:00, and at times ended well before 11:30. Unlike former judges, his sentences never fell below that recommended by the Probation Department. On the contrary, they all too often exceeded that recommendation. At sentencing, the statute afforded an attorney an opportunity to speak on behalf of his client; but the statute made no mention of how long one could speak. Judge Wilson was well aware of that. "That's enough, counsel. You've made your point.... Is there anything else, counsel?.... I'm well aware of that, counsel.... I've heard enough, counsel, and I'm prepared to proceed.... There are some 47 cases on this morning's calendar and the court doesn't appreciate unnecessary delays.... Is the defendant ready for sentencing?"

All the hours I had spent the night before, poring over Probation reports searching for ways to refute them, structuring notes for my in-court presentation, all that work did nothing more than irritate Judge Wilson. The more I pressed, the more irritated he became, until at times I felt that as a result of my persistence, he had given my client an even harsher sentence than he had originally intended. I started paring down my attempts at eloquence to what I felt was the heart of the matter, what I believed I had to say but being careful to say it as quickly and concisely as I could. Even then, I still irritated Judge Wilson. To him, I was another hopeless, naive, bleeding-heart liberal who would never understand or appreciate how the law had to deal with these depraved degenerates for the good of society.

As much as I disliked being in their courtrooms and as much as I struggled whenever I was there, I nevertheless respected both men. Judge Allen lived in the Santa Cruz Mountains. I'm sure he worked whatever land he had up there because he drove a battered pickup truck to the courthouse, often with a well-worn chain saw in its bed. He dressed very simply and carried a brown bag lunch to his chambers in the morning. The courts usually recessed for lunch from noon to 1:30 and many judges managed to stretch that into a two-hour lunch by adding minutes on either side of the equation. Not Bruce Allen. He ate his brown bag lunch in his chambers as he worked on case files and read the latest cases decided by the higher courts. His pickup was always one of the first in the judges' parking lot and among the last to leave. Nor did he ever "dodge" assignments or "milk" cases once they were assigned to him, that is deliberately slowing down the pace of the trial by taking unnecessary or long recesses or beginning a trial each day at a late hour or ending at an early hour so that he could avoid further assignments. I never doubted, no matter how much I might have disagreed with him, that in his mind he was doing what he honestly believed was the best thing to do in any given case.

Judge Wilson was cut from the same cloth as Judge Allen, but he was a much more imposing figure. Some of that had to do with his physical appearance. He was a big, broad-shouldered man with a square jaw and sharp, chiseled, facial features, and a look that could stare through you. As intense a man as any I've ever known, I'm sure he was convinced that the criminal justice system's greatest ill in Santa Clara County and the nation was the leniency of the courts in dealing with criminal defendants. And he was deeply committed to correcting that ill. He worked incredibly hard. I can recall going into his chambers late in the afternoons, very late, for case review sessions with the District Attorney. Stacks of case files would be piled high on his desk. His look, even at that hour, was grim and determined. What I will never forget was something I saw time and again on those late afternoons. James Wilson was a solidly built man, yet as he sat behind his desk in his shirt sleeves in his air conditioned chambers, the sides of his shirt under the arm pits were heavily stained with sweat.

There were other more moderate judges in whose courtrooms I was much more comfortable. Some of those judges I liked personally and also respected. But there were other judges in that group for whom I didn't have the same level of respect that I had for Judge Wilson or Judge Allen, even though their sentences may have been less severe for my clients and their treatment of me much more tolerant.

One spring morning in 1974 shortly before 7:00a.m., a man stepped out of his home in the Rose Garden, one of San Jose's finest neighborhoods, and started toward his car in the driveway. He was on his way to work. He had taken only a few steps when, from across the street, two men got out of a parked car and, for the next minute, fired a barrage of bullets before leaving him slumped and dead in his driveway with 40 bullet wounds in his body. Within an hour, a lone Sheriff's deputy stopped a car southbound on highway 101 outside of Morgan Hill for a traffic violation, some 20 miles from the scene of the shooting. The two occupants appeared hostile, suspicious and black, and the deputy radioed for assistance. When he approached the vehicle, the driver and passenger put up no resistance but were uncooperative. Other officers arrived and the occupants' evasiveness and hostility led to a search of the vehicle that produced an arsenal of guns and ammunition. A radio check verified that some of the guns and ammunition matched the description of those that had been used at the shooting at the Rose Garden neighborhood. The two men were arrested and taken into custody.

Prior to that day, I had twice been invited to meetings at a home in the Rose Garden by a leftist group, The National Lawyers Guild. The house was a beautiful, two-story home with a fine yard and garden. It was as nice a home as I had been in. I've never been comfortable in organizations and groups, and after those two meetings I decided not to join the organization. But the owner of the home, Joan Hammer, a tall, stately, beautiful, white-haired woman, had gone out of her way to make me feel comfortable. I liked her very much. Her daughter, Betsy Hammer, was another matter. Pretty, bright, vivacious, this 19-year-old woman was already a burning leftist. And I had difficulty understanding what that beaming young woman, who could have graced television and magazine ads as an All-American girl, was doing with these disgruntled leftists.

The morning of the shooting, the courthouse was filled with talk of the Rose Garden slaying. But little was known then. The next morning, however, the newspaper devoted front page coverage to the shooting. It said that the victim was a black man who had recently been paroled from San Quentin Prison and who had been living in a Rose Garden home. The suspects were not talking to the police but had been identified as Richard Rodriguez and Leroy Mims, both from Los Angeles. They had apparently traveled to San Jose to execute the man now identified as James Carr.

In most murder cases, the media coverage diminishes or disappears after three or four days. Living in Santa Cruz County, I didn't subscribe to the San Jose newspaper and found little time or opportunity to read it. After the first few days, I didn't give the killing much thought, thinking it was an open-and-shut case that would be plea-bargained out by the Public Defender for something less than the maximum sentence.

Three weeks later, I received a call in my office.

"Mr. Rue-ez?"

"Yes."

"This is Judge Wilson."

"Yes, sir."

"I've just appointed you to represent Leroy Mims. He's one of the two individuals involved in that Rose Garden shooting a couple of weeks ago. He

appeared in my court this morning and I put the matter over to Thursday afternoon at 1:30 in my court for identification of counsel and arraignment and plea.
I expect you to be in my court then."

"Yes, sir."

"Good."

I sat there baffled. Judge Wilson had just appointed me to a high profile
murder case. Why? I annoyed the man. He seemed to have little use for me. At
best, he tolerated me, and then with effort. Why would he toss such a case, any
case, my way and expend County funds on me?

Then the barbarousness of the case set in: forty bullets blasted into an innocent man's body. The weight, the gravity of the assignment followed as well
as the realization that in a little more than 48 hours, I had to appear in court
with whoever this man was who had killed another human being in the most
brutally imaginable way, and act as his attorney. Fear flooded through me. Was
I capable of handling this case? Did I need this grief? Should I call Judge Wilson
back and tell him that I couldn't take this case? Tell him that my caseload would
not permit it? Pride and fear, the fear of cowardice, prevented me from making
that call. And something else, something that now appears foolish, but something that plagued me the entire time that I practiced criminal law: the belief
that if I held myself out to be a criminal defense attorney, then I couldn't refuse
to represent any defendant, no matter how heinous the charge might be.

Then, knowing that I was to be Leroy Mims' attorney, there was no time
to waste. I dropped everything and drove over to the District Attorney's Office.
They knew I had been appointed and had a packet of discovery ready for me:
police reports, lab results, photos and autopsy reports. After receiving them, I
sat in my car in the County parking lot reading them as quickly as I could.

More surprises. The scene of the shooting was the driveway of the same
house I had visited in the Rose Garden. The victim, James Carr, was married
to Betsy Hammer, and upon his release from prison moved into her home. Carr
had been a model parolee, working in construction and also attending classes
at the University of California at Santa Cruz. But he had been a cellmate of
George Jackson while at San Quentin and the police were theorizing that the
killing may have had some connection with a black prison gang. George Jackson was one of three black inmates in the California prison system known as
the Soledad Brothers, the leaders of a black militant group inside prison. After
his death, George Jackson became a martyr and hero to black militants both

inside and outside the prison system. The prison authorities' statement of the facts surrounding Jackson's death was questionable at best. They claimed that he managed to smuggle a hand gun into the prison in his Afro-haircut after a visit with his attorney, and said that he was shot to death by prison guards as he was attempting to escape by scaling a towering prison wall.

The District Attorney's Crime Lab had examined the bullets recovered from James Carr's body as well as some found at the scene of the shooting. The bullets found in the suspects' car appeared to be of the same type and make. The lab expert had fired some of those bullets from the guns found in the vehicle and, after a comparison, concluded that the bullets that killed James Carr were fired from those same guns.

It was an open and shut case. There was nothing to defend. Better to plea-bargain it away as quickly as possible, and get the lightest sentence I could get for Leroy Mims. I would never take this case to a jury trial, never dare to. What an excruciating experience it would be to stand before a jury and try to defend this man and his acts. Is that why Wilson appointed me? To watch me squirm as I tried to wiggle my way out of a nightmare? I stared out my windshield across the parking lot into space. There was a rap on my side window that startled me. I turned.

"Hey! What the hell are you doing in there, Ron?"

It was another defense attorney and I was embarrassed. Papers, reports, photos were strewn on the passenger seat next to me. A packet of papers was on my lap. "Huh?'

"Don't you have an office? Looks like you're spacing out in there. You're taking this stuff way too seriously. We've got a spare room in our office that you can use as an office." He was smiling.

"No. No," shaking my head. But I didn't roll down the window. I didn't need any more of him. "I'm just waiting for someone, that's all. I got tired of waiting and started flipping through this file."

"Pretty big file."

"Yeah," I said, looking away, window still up, determined not to say another word, to make him leave even if it were awkwardly. He did leave. And I scrambled to put all the materials in some sort of order, not only because I didn't want a repeat of what had just happened but also because I realized that it was past noon and I had appointments sitting in my office waiting to see me.

Then as I started the engine, I knew exactly why Judge Wilson had appointed me. And I could hear his words, "My court...my court...my court." He had assigned this God-awful case to himself, to his court and had appointed me to try it there. It made sense. As much as I annoyed him, I imagined the outrage he must have felt towards Mims and Rodriguez for the atrocity they had committed in one of San Jose's finest neighborhoods. It was an open and shut case. He would give them the maximum of maximum sentences. There would be no plea bargaining. He would force me to try this thing in front of a jury. I was well aware of the number of times he had rejected the District Attorney and defense counsel's plea bargain for a lesser sentence as "unacceptable to the court." In other words, not harsh enough, thereby forcing a jury trial. Not to mention the number of times he had exceeded the Probation Department's recommended sentences. No, he was going to make me try this open-and-shut atrocity to a jury. He had to be thinking, Mr. Rue-ez, let's just see how much you really love these animals, let's just see how much compassion you really have for them.

Almost without exception, all of my court-appointed clients were in custody and I had made it a practice to visit with them in the jail at least once before our first appearance in court. They generally had some questions, concerns or complaints that I could at least attempt to address before we appeared together in court for the first time. It made that first court appearance so much more palatable for the client and me. There was nothing worse than having the judge call a new, in-custody, client's case and to see him for the first time standing among the 14 other defendants in the jury box, knowing he's probably facing a long prison sentence, and approaching him for the first time. Then, positioning myself as close to him as possible and saying in a high whisper so as not to disturb the judge, "Hi, I'm Ron Ruiz and I'm going to be your lawyer in this case."

Because of my already filled calendar, the earliest I could see Leroy Mims was the next day at noon, which still was some 24 hours before we were due in court. I took the elevator up to the third deck and the maximum security unit in the old jail where he was housed. The deputy there knew me.

"What can I do for you, counselor?"

"I want to see Leroy Mims. He's in max."

He studied me for a moment. "You're *his* lawyer?"

"Yeah."

"O.K. counselor. But it's going to take three of us to pull him. Those are my orders. And I'm the only deputy up here now. I'll have to get two more bodies up here to pull him. So it's going to be a while."

"I'll wait."

"O.K. then, have a seat in one of the interview rooms."

I was seated in one of the two 8x8 square foot interview rooms for at least fifteen minutes before I saw two more guards approach the watch station and remove leg irons, waist chains and cuffs from a drawer. Then the three started toward the hall that led to the maximum security unit. The three were big enough to cuff a horse. Five minutes later, I could hear the leg irons clinking against the concrete floor, growing louder and louder. Here he comes, I thought, bracing myself.

The first thing I saw when the door opened was the red-streaked whites of two eyes in a black face filled with anger and hate. And they were directed at me. His nostrils were wide-open, inflamed, as if he were snorting. He was a big man but at that moment, he seemed twice his actual size. The deputies moved him to a white plastic chair across the small white plastic table from me and sat him down. Then they stood at the door for a moment looking at me, waiting for me to speak, giving me a chance to say that I wanted him unchained or at least uncuffed. That always made a chained client feel better. But I couldn't say it. I didn't want him unchained or uncuffed. They started to leave and then the last one stopped, turned and looked at me again. I said nothing. I wanted those leg irons and waist chains and cuffs kept exactly where they were. They closed the door and left.

As soon as they did, I could see and feel the rage leaving him. His shoulders slumped and the white, maximum security jump suit that had been stretched tight against his black frame loosened. He lowered his look, his eyelids now half-closed. He let out a long, strong exhalation of breath, and then breathed softly and easily as he slumped. When he looked at me again, I saw a broad, thick, yet fine, handsome, black face whose eyes were no longer red-streaked.

"Who are you?"

"I'm your lawyer, Mr. Mims."

"Please don't call me 'Mister.' My name is Leroy Mims. I've never been a 'Mister' to anybody except sell-out niggers."

"Shall I call you Leroy?"

"Call me anything you want, but not 'Mister'.... You say you're my lawyer? I didn't ask for no lawyer. I can't pay for no lawyer. Are you a Public Defender?"

His voice was calm, thoughtful, his look questioning but not hostile. "I'm not a Public Defender. The court appointed me to be your lawyer. The Public Defender is representing your co-defendant, Richard Rodriguez. The law doesn't allow the Public Defender to represent both defendants in these kinds of cases."

"I didn't ask for no lawyer."

"You don't have to. The court automatically assumes that you're not able to pay for an attorney in a serious case like this, so it appoints one for you."

"Who pays you?"

"The court."

"The judge pays you?"

"Not exactly. The County pays me."

"The County pays the District Attorney too, right?"

"Yeah."

"And the County pays the Public Defender too, right?"

"Yeah."

"And the County pays the cops that arrested us and the goons that just dragged me over here to see you, and all those goons that were standing in the courtroom the other day when they brought me and Richard into court the first time. They were just standing everywhere with their loaded .38's, just hoping that Richard and me would make one false move. The County pays them too, right?"

"Yeah."

"And the County pays that judge over there too?"

"Not exactly. The state does."

"But it's all coming out of the same pocket, the government pocket, right?"

"Yeah."

"So you're all eating out of the same dish?"

"I guess you could say that."

"Don't you think I'd be better off with my own paid lawyer than with one of you guys? You're all eating out of that same dish, so it seems like you're all gonna be more careful not to step on each others' toes, or push too hard against somebody lined up there eating with you. Seems to me like a paid lawyer ain't gonna have the same problem."

"I don't agree with you."

"You really don't think I'd be better off having a lawyer I paid for myself rather than having one of you guys?"

"Not necessarily."

"Well, I don't know why I'm going off on that. 'Cause I sure as hell don't have any money to hire me a lawyer anyway.... What'd you say your name was?"

"Ron Ruiz."

"How do you spell that?"

"R-U-I-Z."

"Puerto Rican?"

"No, Mexican." Some blacks hated Mexicans as much as they hated whites. But I saw none of that. He just nodded to himself.

"Well, you know I think I'm actually better off not having a lawyer. I didn't ask for one, but that asshole judge over there gave me one anyway."

"What do you mean?"

"Well, they're gonna convict us anyway you look at it. But they're going to have a hell of a time doing it, and it's gonna take a hell of a lot more time in that courtroom, cost them a shitload more money, if I'm my own attorney. 'Cause I can raise a hell of a lot more shit in that asshole's courtroom than any of you lawyers can even think of doing. And no matter what I do, how outrageous I act, what are they gonna do to me? Give me more time? They're gonna give me all they can give me anyway. But I can have a hell of a lot more fun in there, just raising hell by myself, playing the part of the fool and driving that tight-ass judge crazy, than I ever could with you representing me. Couldn't I?"

I didn't answer. But I did know that judges dreaded defendants who insisted on representing themselves because that inevitably led to complete chaos in the courtroom and especially during the trial.

"So what do I have to do to get you off the case?"

"I'm not on it yet."

"Yeah, but that hard-ass over there said that he'd have a lawyer there for me tomorrow, and that must be you."

"All you have to do is say that you want to represent yourself, that you don't want a lawyer. That's all."

"Then that's what I'll do then. Thanks for coming up and don't take it personal."

"I'm not." I closed my file, rose and stepped to the door.

"Do me a favor."

I stopped and turned.

"Tell those white goons out there that they don't have to prove how tough they are every time they pull me or take me back to the cell."

I nodded. Once I closed the door behind me, I saw that the three guards were still at the deck station. One of them said, "Finished, counselor?" I nodded and started for the elevator thinking, Finished? Yes. Indeed.

Among other things, I had worried that at the trial I would have to cross-examine Betsy Hammer and her mother, Joan. They were eye witnesses. This had to be a horrible ordeal for them. I had been in their home and they had been gracious and kind to me. Unfortunately, I didn't know them well enough to recuse myself from the case. As I left the jail that afternoon, I realized that I didn't have to worry or even think about anything else connected with Leroy Mims' case.

As I entered Judge Wilson's courtroom the next afternoon, one of the Public Defenders came up to me and said, "I've got Rodriguez and I understand that you have Mims."

"Well, not yet."

"I thought I'd let you know that Rodriguez is going to enter a not guilty plea today, ask for a jury trial and not waive time. What about Mims?"

"Uh. I don't know."

"You haven't talked to him?"

"I have, but I don't know what he's going to do."

"I suppose it really doesn't matter what Mims does, if Rodriguez doesn't waive time, Wilson'll set both of them for trial in seven weeks or so."

I nodded.

Except for the eight in-custody defendants seated in the jury box, lawyers, the court personnel and eight armed deputies positioned around the courtroom, there were only a handful of spectators, mostly media people, present. It was a light afternoon calendar of seemingly little importance except for the fact that Richard Rodriguez and Leroy Mims' names appeared at the foot of it. Had those two names not been there, the eight armed deputies wouldn't have been there and neither would the media. Neither Rodriguez nor Mims were in the courtroom yet.

At exactly 1:30, always as if on cue, Judge James Wilson stepped onto the dais from a side door and his bailiff rapped his gavel and said loudly, "All rise!" which I often thought was unnecessary because Judge Wilson was such an imposing figure in that black robe and with those dark intense eyes, that everyone would have automatically stood. He was all business from the moment he stepped onto that dais until the moment he left it. There was never any time wasted on pleasantries, smiles, greetings or farewells. That afternoon as soon as he was seated, he looked over at the jury box, then at the Public Defender and myself and said, "Deputies, bring out Mr. Rodriguez and Mr. Mims."

As if rehearsed, four deputies met in front of the jury box and then moved in two rows forward and then up the three steps to the iron door of the holding cell. Deftly, the heavy door was unlocked, swung open and after a few words, Richard Rodriguez and Leroy Mims stepped out onto the landing, towering over everyone in the courtroom except for the deputies who were standing beside them. I had read that Rodriguez was Puerto Rican and was surprised to see how light-skinned he was. He was not a small man, five foot ten, 160 pounds, but next to Mims who was at least six foot one, broad, muscular, powerfully built, he seemed small. They were dressed in white jump suits. Mims' blackness in those white coveralls made him even more striking. They stood on that landing unlike any two defendants charged with murder I had ever seen stand in court before, not nervous, frightened, obsequious, repentant nor respectful, but rather bold, proud, defiant even as they looked straight ahead at everyone and everything.

I saw Judge Wilson watching them, saw him hold his breath, hold himself and his outrage. Then he turned to the Public Defender and me and with a slight movement of his head signaled that we were to go up to the landing and stand beside our clients. I followed the Public Defender, thinking what a fool I was about to be made out to be in front of everyone. I imagined how everyone would be reading the next day about Mims' rejection of me as his attorney, as not being able or worthy enough to represent him. I stood beside him. He seemed twice my size. Judge Wilson began his mantra. "Let the record show that the defendants, Richard Rodriguez and Leroy Mims, are present in court represented by their attorneys, the Public Defender and Mr. Rue-ez. Gentlemen?"

I looked down expecting Mims to begin reciting his rejection of me. But he said nothing.

Instead the Public Defender entered a plea of not guilty for Rodriguez, requested a jury trial and said they would not waive time, thereby requiring that the trial begin within 60 days. Now I was certain that Mims would begin his grand denouncement, but again he remained silent and Judge Wilson was staring at me. "What about your client, Mr. Rue-ez?"

I looked at Mims and he said to me, loud enough to be heard throughout the courtroom, "I ain't pleading guilty to nothing, and I ain't waiving no time, and I want a jury trial."

That took me by surprise and I paused.

"Mr. Rue-ez?" Judge Wilson was glaring at me, almost as if I were responsible for Mims' impudence.

"Mr. Mims pleads not guilty, requests a jury trial and will not waive time, Your Honor."

"Very well. Set the matter for trial in my department 48 days from today's date. That will be all."

Quickly, the deputies moved Rodriguez and Mims back into the holding cell. As the Public Defender started down the steps, I looked over at Judge Wilson. He was scowling and I left the courtroom as quickly as I could.

Outside, I was dumbfounded, so much so that rather than remain in the courthouse, I walked across the street to the parking lot and sat in my car before my next scheduled court appearance. Up to that point in time, Leroy Mims had to be one of the strongest personalities I had represented. And he had told me in no uncertain terms that he was going to represent himself, that he did not want me to be, nor did he need me to be, his lawyer. Yet he had spoken not a word of this in court. That silence had nothing to do with timidity. I could still hear his gruff, loud words as we stood on that landing. I could still see the way he and Rodriguez had stood when they were first brought out of the holding cell. Proud, defiant, challenging anyone and everyone even though they were charged with one of the most heinous murders that I was to ever encounter.

Not once during our first meeting the day before in the jail, had he ever denied killing James Carr. Not only had there been no denial, there hadn't been one iota of remorse. He never once mentioned James Carr. Did he even know James Carr? What had James Carr done to him to warrant 40 bullets, to warrant such a vicious killing? The police had theorized that it had been an execution, and sitting in my car then, I found myself thinking that too.

Under California law, a defendant charged with a felony had a right to a jury trial within 60 days of the day that he first appeared in the Superior Court for arraignment on that charge. If the defendant did not waive that right and was not brought to trial within 60 days, those charges had to be dismissed. Since the vast majority of defendants charged with murder waived time, most murder cases came to trial a year or more after the date of the homicide. Because Mims and Rodriguez had not waived time, I was now faced with trying that horrid case before Judge Wilson and a jury in seven weeks. There was no time to waste

I spent every spare moment I had reviewing Mims' case file. The first thing that struck me was that while the witnesses' descriptions of Rodriguez as one of the gunmen were almost letter-perfect, the same could not be said for their description of Mims as the second gunman. The shooting had occurred around 6:45a.m.on a weekday morning. The visibility had been good. The great number of shots had attracted the attention of many in the neighborhood. There were several eye-witness descriptions of the two men, including those of Betsy Carr and Joan Hammer. The consensus was that one of the gunmen was white or Latino and the other was a black man. The description they had given the police immediately after the shooting of the white or Latino man fit Rodriguez, but varied, often notably, when it came to the black man. There were similar variations when the witnesses viewed lineups and photos of the lineups.

In the vehicle, the police also found a notebook and receipts detailing daily expenditures, as well as a text on guerrilla warfare tactics written by Mao Tse Dung. The book had apparently been stolen from the UCLA library in Westwood, was well worn, and was the only book in the suspects' possession. It seemed as if every cent the two men had spent on their trip to San Jose had been itemized: rent, gasoline, toiletries, pharmaceuticals and food, including cash register receipts from McDonald's, Burger King and Jack in the Box. The notebook also established that Mims and Rodriguez had been in San Jose for some twelve days before the shooting, that they had been tracking James Carr for many days, that they were making daily calls to Los Angeles from pay phones, and sometimes changing their plans because of those calls. Not a single cent was spent, or at least not listed, for alcohol, cigarettes or entertainment.

I visited the studio apartment they had rented in San Jose for those twelve days. It was located in a long, narrow, cheaply constructed, two-story apartment building near San Jose State University on a lot where there had once probably stood a stately, old home. A sign on the front of the building said: STUDIO APT. FOR RENT. I asked to see one of those apartments on the pretense that a younger brother of mine would soon be enrolling in the university and would be needing a place to live. A woman first showed me a studio apartment on the ground floor and then I asked to see one on the second floor. Once there, I asked to see the studio I knew Mims and Rodriguez had rented, which was still vacant. It was one room with a bathroom and a counter against one wall that had two electric burners and a mini refrigerator. There was nothing more except the plastic Venetian blind that covered the sole window.

"None of your studios are furnished?"

"No."

"So my brother would have to bring his own bed, bedding, dishes, utensils, everything?"

"That's right."

I looked again. None of it made any sense. The cheap, cracked tile floor ran unimpeded to the wall; from there the wall ran up to the ceiling unobstructed. Only a small light fixture in the center of the ceiling broke up the space.

"My brother said that some of his friends just rented one of your studios, and I think it might have been this one. They recommended your place to him."

"I don't think the ones who rented this place last were your brother's friends. I think they were black people."

"Black?"

"I don't know much about them. But like I said, I think they were black. They weren't here too long. They just came and left. We didn't even know they were gone."

"How could you not know that one of your renters had left? They'd have to move all of their things out, wouldn't they?"

"You would think so. But they just left. Didn't tell us and didn't leave a single thing behind. It was days before we knew they were gone."

As I drove back to my office, I tried to make some sense of what I now knew. Every item that had been found in their vehicle had been on a two page sheriff's report. There was no mention of bedding, sleeping bags or even blankets; no towels, soap or toothbrushes. They must have slept on the floor fully dressed. How else? How did they dry themselves when they bathed, if they bathed? No mention of cups or glasses or any kitchen utensils? How did they drink? From the faucet? And what had they done during the hours and days that James Carr worked in construction? Sit in that bare room and read Mao's work on guerrilla tactics? Why such a bizarre, Spartan existence before executing someone? I had to talk to Leroy Mims.

I went up to the jail about 6:30 that evening. The jail would be quiet then. Shift changes would have taken place, the inmates would have been fed, and the different array of visitors from the outside world would be gone by then. It would be a good time to have a serious talk with Mims. Another deck officer advised me that there would be a delay until they had enough guards on the floor to take Mims out of his cell. I waited in the interview room. This time when the guards and Mims approached, I could hear a struggle going on. I looked and saw Mims in leg irons, waist chains and cuffs writhing and twisting between three guards as they pushed, pulled and jerked him toward the interview room. I could hear him cursing. The interview room door flew open and the guards picked Mims up and carried him two steps into the room and sat him down hard on the chair across from me. Mims' eyes were wide with anger, but he stopped writhing. All four men were breathing heavily and I thought I could hear, almost feel, Mims snorting. Then the guards stepped away from him and stood at the door and one of them said, "You want the chains off, counselor?" I shook my head several times hoping that Mims wouldn't see but he did.

After the guards left, it was a full two minutes before Mims looked at me and said, "What's the matter? You afraid of me? You think I'm gonna hurt you or something once these fucking chains are off me?"

"Well..." I didn't know what to say. "You were mighty pissed off when they brought you in here. What was I supposed to think?"

"What you were supposed to think is that this ain't got nothing to do with you. That's what you're supposed to think. It's between me and them white pigs. Every time those stupid, ignorant animals come to pull me out, they talk to me the way you talk to a mule. To them, I'm nothing but another dumb, fucking nigger. But I got news for them. I'm not. So they're not gonna talk to me like that and have me do what they say. That's when they have to try to show me who's boss, like the fucking, ignorant assholes they are. I could kick the shit out of any one of them. But there's three of them. So they're gonna do what they want to do. But that doesn't mean I have to go along with it, even if they fucking chain me up. That's what that's all about, but it ain't got nothing to do with you."

He stopped and we were silent for a while, with me worrying that the next time I came I would have to ask the guards to take the chains off.

"So what did you come up here for?"

"Well, I'm your lawyer. Right?"

"Yeah."

"I didn't hear you tell the judge that you didn't want me to be your lawyer."

"True. I never said anything like that."

"So as your lawyer, I think we need to talk."

"About what?"

"About the case."

"What about the case?"

"You want me to defend you, don't you?"

"Defend what?"

I stopped. I didn't know what to say, where to begin. "Well...for one thing, none of the witnesses have really been able to identify you and..."

"Wait a minute! Wait a minute! You go into that cesspool that you call a court and do what you have to do, but don't come in here and try to get more information out of me."

"But...I just thought..."

"I don't give a damn what you thought. I don't know you and you don't know me. And I sure as hell don't know you well enough to trust you. Any time we talk about 'the case', as you call it, there's bound to be stuff that's gonna come out that one way or another is going to go past you."

I didn't know what to answer.

"Now look, I'm not putting you in the same category with all them white pigs out there. At least not yet. I just don't want to talk about 'the case.' Ain't nothing personal. I'm just not gonna do it. Understand? So you just go on and do what you have to do and we'll both be O.K."

"But if you don't want to talk about the case, then what is there to talk about? Why should I even come and see you?"

"You don't have to and I won't take no offense if you don't. Besides, it's just me and my road dog, Rodriguez, back there where they got us. We're right next to each other and we can talk all day and all night to each other if we want to. Of course we know the cells are bugged. So we talk about everything that doesn't matter and about some things that those silly white morons wouldn't understand even if we drew them pictures. So we're having a good time back there. Better enjoy it while we can. Because in a few weeks we'll be headed somewhere where we might never see each other again. But that's O.K. too. We know why we're here and we know what's coming."

The death penalty was not in effect in California at that time. As I left the jail, I was convinced that Leroy Mims knew, had accepted, did not fear and in some ways might have felt justified with what was to come: a life sentence in prison.

But I was in a quandary. I had nothing to prepare for a jury trial that was going to take place as surely as I was breathing. There was no defense to prepare because my client did not want a defense presented. I decided then and there to stop working on the case, not spend another minute on it. That resolve lasted as long as the beginning of that evening. Because the fact remained that *I* was involved. If I didn't continue working on the case, if I didn't know it as well as it could be known, then the District Attorney would make me out to be a bigger fool than I was destined to be before Judge Wilson, the jury, the spectators and the media. Even if Mims' defense no longer mattered, *I* did. So I continued working on the case and as I did, the witnesses' inability to identify Mims taunted me.

I saw Mims eight days later. When I heard the clanging of the leg irons, I turned but saw no sign of a struggle or resistance. Maybe they had reached some kind of an accord. Maybe Mims would talk to me about the case now. No. His first words were, "Hope you didn't come up here to talk about the case, little brother."

Those words dashed my hopes and yet warmed me: "little brother." I paused for a moment before I said, "As much as I'd like to talk about it, I know you won't. But I try to see all my clients at least once a week when they're in custody. It just makes everything a lot easier for both of us."

"I do have something to tell you. You know when they pull us out for showers and exercise up there on the roof, me and Rodriguez get a chance to mix with some of the brothers. And the word is that you're alright, that you don't fuck over any of us. But that don't mean I'm gonna talk about this case. You probably had to work hard to become a lawyer. Probably wasn't handed to you. But don't kid yourself for a minute. Lawyer or no lawyer, you're still a pawn in the white man's system. They let a few of us get up there so they can brag to the world about how great they are. But if you or any one of us thinks that we're ever gonna call the shots in the white man's world then you're really fucked up."

The visit didn't last long because after a few "How you been?" and "How's everything?" I asked, "Where you from?"

"There you go again, little brother. Except for what I've heard about you from some of the other dudes in here, I might have to think that you were trying to set me up. Now you ought to damn well know that these little rooms are bugged."

"They can't do that. It's a felony if they do that."

"Come on now, you can do better than that. So who's gonna report them to the cops? The guys that installed them or the guys that are listening? Shit! And who are they going to report it to? Their captain who ordered them to do it? Wake up, little brother. Don't get all drugged out on the white man's system. That's exactly why I can't be giving you no personal information. They're dying to find out whatever they can about us."

On that visit the guards didn't ask if I wanted the chains removed and neither did Mims nor I mention it. But a week later, again on a visit in which there was no apparent conflict between Mims and the guards, one of the guards asked, "You want the chains off, counselor?" I could feel Mims watching me from across the table. I looked at Mims. He was watching me.

"Yes, take them off."

"You sure?" I nodded. Off came the chains and cuffs and then the deputies were gone too. Sitting three feet away from me, across a skimpy plastic table, was this six-foot- one-inch, 200 pound-plus, giant of a man who had committed one of the most brutal murders I had ever heard of.

He broke the silence. "Nervous, little brother?"

I didn't answer.

"There's no need to be. I'm not going to do nothing. But I wanna thank you for what you just did. I appreciate it. And now I know that what the other brothers say about you is true."

I was still without words.

"Well don't worry, we're not going to talk about the case or about me, but I would like to stay a while and talk to you.... I know what we can talk about.

We can talk about you. You got nothing to hide from these assholes who are bugging us here, do you?"

I shook my head.

"Where you from, little brother?"

"Fresno."

"Never been there but I've heard it's a pretty reactionary place."

"I left there when I was 17 and I've never gone back, and I don't miss it. So I guess that means I never cared for it very much."

"You married?"

"Yeah."

"Any kids?"

"Yeah, four."

"How long you been a lawyer?"

"Eight years."

"You like it?"

"Yeah."

"What do you think of the justice system in America?'

"It's not perfect. But I can't think of any other that is."

"Have you studied up on other systems?"

"No."

"Little brother, you better start broadening your world."

The following week Mims had the worst of his altercations with the guards as they were bringing him to the interview room. He was struggling and cursing so much that they carried him, one on each thigh, some fifteen feet to the interview room where they sat him in that plastic chair with enough force to break it, although it only crumpled a bit. He was furious when they left, snorting and gritting his teeth. But the only thing he said for however long we sat there was, "Look, I don't wanna talk. I just wanna sit here for a while and calm down and not let them take me back in the condition I was in when they brought me. Because when I get that way, I know I've blown it. But sometimes I just can't take their shit, their humiliation. I'm a man, you know, and I wanna be treated like a man.... Give me a few minutes and then you can go out there like we're finished talking."

I visited with Mims the evening before the trial was to begin. I told him how the trial was to proceed. First, the jury selection with questioning by the judge and the lawyers. Once the jury was selected, the District Attorney would give an opening statement outlining what he intended to prove. Since we had no defense, I would waive an opening statement. Then the prosecution would call witnesses to prove their case and the defense lawyers could cross-examine them. The defense could call witnesses on its own behalf. Did he have any witnesses that he wanted me to call? No. Did he intend to testify? No. Did Rodriguez intend to testify? No. The attorneys would then argue their case to the jury, after which the jury would deliberate and decide their guilt or innocence. Had he understood everything that I had said? Yes. Did he have any questions, comments or thoughts? No.

My last words to him were, "I'll see you in the morning."

His were, "Yeah, you will."

At exactly 9:00a.m., Judge James Wilson stepped onto the dais from the door that led to his chambers and took his seat above us at the bench, the name given to a judge's large desk on the dais. Alert, tense, sharp-eyed and ready, he surveyed the courtroom. Present were his clerk, the court reporter, the bailiff, the District Attorney, the Public Defender and myself. Except for the defendants, that was the core of any trial. But on that day, there were an additional four armed deputies in the courtroom, one on each side of the doorway and one on each of the side walls near the railing that separates the Bar and the jurors from the spectators. Finding everyone in their places, Judge Wilson said, "Deputies, bring out the defendants." In the wall behind the Judge were two doors. The one to his left was the wood-paneled door to his chambers; the one on his right was an iron door behind which was a holding cell and steps that led to the underground tunnel to the jail. The four deputies formed a half-circle around the iron door. One of them unlocked it and Mims and Rodriguez emerged. It took me a split second to recognize them because now they were dressed in street clothes that had been provided by Friends Outside, a support group which accepted used clothing donations, cleaned and mended them, and provided the large majority of in-custody defendants with trial clothes. Mims and Rodriguez now wore clean, neatly pressed khakis and long-sleeved, white shirts. But above their donated court shoes, they still wore leg irons.

Then Judge Wilson said, "Mr. Rodriguez and Mister Mims, please take your seats next to your attorneys at the counsel table." His voice, the tone, the level, the firmness, left no doubt who was controlling that courtroom. The deputies stepped aside and the defendants did as the Judge said, leg irons clanging on the courtroom floor. When they were seated, Judge Wilson said, "Mr. Rodriguez, Mr. Mims. I want you to look down at the floor next to your leg irons.... See that metal ring there? That ring is attached to a metal bar that has been cemented into the floor. The leg irons you are now wearing can easily be attached to that ring. Once that is done, you will not be able to get up out of the chair you are now sitting in. I'm going to have your leg irons removed for now. But if at any time during the trial, if either or both of you become disruptive in any way, I will immediately have you shackled to those floor rings. Do I make myself clear?"

Mims and Rodriguez stared back at Judge Wilson but neither did nor said anything other than continue to stare.

"Do I make myself clear?"

Again, only the stares.

Judge Wilson glared back. As he glared, I thought that the only thing preventing him from having the defendants shackled then and there was his worry that at this early stage of the trial, with nothing more than their stone-walling and jurors not even present, he might cause a reversal from a court of appeals of a conviction that he was sure to get. In the silence that followed, the courtroom became as tense as he was. For seconds, neither side would budge.

Finally Judge Wilson said, "I think I've made myself very clear. Test me if you want, gentlemen. Deputies, remove the defendants' leg irons."

Once the leg irons were removed, he turned and said, "Mr. Bailiff, please go and summon a jury panel. I told the jury commissioner that I wanted a panel of 70. Make sure there are 70 in that panel."

"Yes, Your Honor."

During the 30 years I practiced criminal law, there was an instruction of the law that the judge was required to give every jury before they deliberated which, almost without exception, arose at the time a jury was being selected. It was an instruction that I abhorred. It said: "A defendant in a criminal case is presumed innocent of the charge against him until the prosecution, based on all the evidence, proves to the jury beyond a reasonable doubt and to a moral certainty the truth of the charge." As I sat in court waiting for the prospective jurors to be brought in for the case of People vs. Richard Rodriguez and Leroy Mims, I felt that there could be nothing in the realm of human experience that could be further from the truth. Over the years, I had been in courthouse hallways where prospective jurors were waiting to be called into a courtroom to begin the jury selection process, and had heard remarks that demonstrated just how ludicrous that instruction of the law was. One I have never forgotten. On that day, I found myself in the middle of a group of 40 or 50 people shuffling their way through a courthouse hallway. From their comments, I understood that they had been told to return after lunch so that the jury selection could continue. Two well-dressed men in suits and ties were in front of me. It seemed apparent to me that they were not accustomed to dealing with the seedy-looking people -the defendants, their families and friends- that daily visit the criminal courthouses. One of the men said to the other, "What are you doing down here, Harry?" "Oh, I'm down here to do my civic duty and convict one of the sons-of-bitches. And you?" "Me too."

I turned in my chair and watched the prospective jurors, as I always did, when they entered. Sometimes it disarmed them to see me watching them, but usually they were more concerned with finding a good place to sit and looking at the courtroom surroundings and didn't notice me. They were all white. Santa Clara County had few blacks then and there were rarely any blacks in the jury pool. Occasionally there would be a Mexican-American, and at times an Asian or two. But on that day, they were all white. They had been summoned for jury duty at the Criminal Division of the Superior Court and many of the people they had seen in and around the building that morning may have confirmed that they were to be jurors in a criminal case. A few met my eyes while they were still standing but they quickly looked away. Once seated, they looked around the courtroom again. For sure they saw the stern-faced Judge sitting above us, the four armed deputies, and at our counsel table, two men in suits flanking one man they probably presumed to be a Mexican and a black man, both dressed in khakis and white shirts. They must have surmised by then that the Latino and the black man were charged with criminal offenses. Did they then presume them innocent? Not from the looks of discomfort I saw on their faces.

The bailiff rapped his gavel and I turned to face Judge Wilson. "Ladies and gentlemen," he began, "the case you have been called upon to sit as jurors is a criminal case. Madam Clerk, will you please read the information."

A small woman seated below him rose holding a single sheet of paper before her and read, "The People of the State of California vs. Richard Rodriguez and Leroy Mims. The District Attorney of Santa Clara County hereby accuses Richard Rodriguez and Leroy Mims of a violation of section 187 of the Penal

Code, murder, in that on the seventh day of May, 1974, they did willfully and unlawfully shoot and kill James Carr in the City of San Jose...."

The gasps, cries and stirrings were unmistakable. The reaction was immediate and loud. The horrible homicide had occurred some two months before and had received extensive media coverage. Did anyone in that room at that moment presume Leroy Mims and Richard Rodriguez innocent?

The clerk then drew 12 names at random from a box on her desk and those 12 persons were seated in the jury box. Judge Wilson questioned them first. He began by thanking the prospective jurors for coming and reminding them of the valuable civic contribution they were making to the criminal justice system in their community. Then he asked if there was anything at all about this particular case that would prevent any of them from being fair and impartial in deciding it? There was no response. Had they heard, read or known anything about the case that would impair their ability to be fair and impartial? Again no response. He said that the case would take one to two weeks to try. Would that present a problem for anyone? Several hands went up. Those people spoke primarily about conflicts with their work schedules, but Judge Wilson found that none warranted an excuse from jury service. Then he turned the questioning over to the attorneys.

The law permitted questions relating to the jurors' abilities to be fair and impartial in deciding the case and nothing more. Any attempt to educate or influence the prospective jurors at that stage of the proceedings was not to be tolerated, and that was especially true in that court. But Judge Wilson's questioning had been nothing more than a hurried generalization. In his view, Mims and Rodriguez were blatantly guilty and were wasting taxpayer money and his time by demanding a jury trial. The sooner they were found guilty, the better for everyone. While Mims and Rodriguez might well have been making a mockery of the process, so too, in my mind, was Judge Wilson. Nor can I remember a trial in my more than 30 years of practicing criminal law when the highfaluting pretense that defendants were presumed to be innocent by a jury of "their peers" grated on me more.

I chose to question the prospective jurors individually and when it was my turn to do so, I stood and moved away from the counsel table and went to the jury box just a few feet away from the man sitting in juror seat number one.

"Sir, are you aware of a shooting and killing that occurred in the Rose Garden here in San Jose in the early morning hours of May some two months ago?"

"Yes."

"And you understand that if you're chosen to sit on this jury, you will be deciding the guilt or innocence of my client, Leroy Mims, on that day?"

"I do."

"Did you read about this case in the newspapers?"

"Yes."

"How many times?"

"Well, of course I read about it when it first happened. It was all over the front page. And I read about it for several days after that until it kind of died down."

"And did you see any news accounts of it on television"

"Oh, yes. When it first happened, it got quite a bit of play."

"Did you discuss the case with anyone? Family members, friends, people at work?"

"Everybody was talking about it at work and at home too."

"In those newspapers accounts and what you saw on television, do you remember reading that two suspects were apprehended by the police a short time after the shooting?"

"Yes."

"And you probably read or heard that they had been put in jail here in San Jose, correct?"

"Yes."

"Was there anything then or since then that you might have heard, read or seen that would lead you to believe that the police had arrested the wrong men?"

"No."

I walked back to the counsel table and stood behind Mims. I put my hands on his shoulders and said, "Sir, I'd like you to look over here at my client, Mr. Mims."

He blinked several times as he looked and it took a few moments for his eyes to settle, but he did give Mims a wary look.

"As you look at Mr. Mims now, sir, can you say, after all you've read, heard and talked about that you presume Leroy Mims innocent at this moment?'

"Well...not really."

I looked up at Judge Wilson and said, "At this time, Your Honor, the defendant Mims moves to excuse juror number one for cause."

It was my understanding that any prospective juror who said at the beginning of a criminal jury trial that he did not then presume the defendant innocent had to be excused for cause.

"Not so fast, Mr. Rue-ez, not so fast. I have some questions for the prospective juror," as he gave me that look of annoyance that I knew so well. "Sir, you understand that while the law does state that a defendant in a criminal case is presumed to be innocent until his guilt is proven beyond a reasonable doubt and to a moral certainty by the District Attorney, all that really means is that not until you've heard *all* the evidence in a case can you actually decide that a defendant is guilty. In other words, can you keep an open mind until you've heard all the evidence in this case? Can you?"

"I think so."

"The defendant's motion is denied. Proceed, Mr. Rue-ez"

But I persisted, and a few jurors later when I asked, "Can you tell me, Ma'am, that after all you've heard, read, seen and talked about this case, that you still have an open mind and can presume him innocent until you've heard all the evidence in this case?"

"No," she said, "I know too much about this case already. I've served on juries before and I've never seen armed guards in the courtroom like there are here now. No, to be honest, I think he's guilty and I really don't think that there's going to be anything said in this case that's going to change my mind. I can't imagine that he'd be sitting here like this with all these armed guards if he was innocent."

Judge Wilson couldn't shake her and there was a quiet hush as she left the courtroom. I saw no reason to look up at Judge Wilson then.

A few jurors later, another juror said that he did not presume Mims innocent and didn't believe he could change his mind. Judge Wilson was scowling. But that turned out to be a pyrrhic victory. Because from then on all the prospective jurors who did not wish to be inconvenienced with two weeks away from their normal lives, and there were plenty of them, merely said that they could not presume Mims innocent and stuck to it. On the other hand, individuals who wanted to stay and be seated as jurors did so, for the most part, because they wanted to see justice done, be part of justice, to wit: convict Mims and

Rodriguez. Still, the selection of the jury took two days instead of the one that Judge Wilson thought necessary. That was something of a satisfaction for me.

The District Attorney spent the first day of testimony calling witnesses who lived near the scene of the shooting, who had seen and heard some of the dreadful spectacle. All said they were drawn to their windows by the first shots. Some saw two men shooting at a fallen man, some saw two men running to their car, and some saw only a car driving off with two men in it. All were able to identify the vehicle from photographs shown to them in court. Those who saw the two men were positive that one of the men was Richard Rodriguez. With only one exception, they could only say that the second man was black, but were not as certain that he was Mims.

The two principle prosecution witnesses were Joan Hammer, in whose home the victim had been living and her daughter, Betsy Carr, the wife of the victim. My cross-examinations of the two women were difficult. Joan Hammer, tall, elegant, white-haired, beautiful, looked at me with disbelief throughout the entire time I questioned her. Her eyes said, How can you do this, Ron? How can you stand there with these men that you know killed Jimmy and defend them? Worse, How can you continue to question me as if I'm lying, as if I have some reason to lie, when you know as well as I do that I'm not lying? Don't you understand, can't you appreciate what they've done to us and what you're doing to us now? But the words she spoke were soft, thoughtful, straight-forward, just as they had been in her home when I was there. Yes, she had seen them firing at Jimmy's fallen, still quivering body. Rodriguez was definitely one of the gunmen. The other man was black. That was the most she could say.

Betsy Hammer, widow and young mother, came to court looking like the high school girl she had been only two years before at a private Palo Alto alternative school. She cried during the District Attorney's questioning and was still very much red-eyed and tear-streaked when I began questioning her. But she didn't cry during my cross-examination of her. The rage and hate she felt for me were all consuming. There was no space for tears. Her eyes were bitter and biting. They never left me. They challenged me, cursed me, damned me at every second. I was no different than the two animals sitting at the counsel table. I was one with them. No, I was worse than them because I knew better, because I had been welcomed in their home and knew who she and her mother were, and was now betraying them. And for filthy money, no less. Yes, she saw them shooting Jimmy. And it was him, him, him, pointing at Leroy Mims who was absolutely one of them.

The last witness of the afternoon was a portly, middle-aged man who within a few hours of the shooting had given the police a detailed description of both men. He was a close neighbor of the Hammers who had as good a vantage point as any. He testified that he was certain that Rodriguez was the light-skinned gunman and thought that Mims strongly resembled the black man. On cross-examination I asked if he had been interviewed by the police after the shooting. Yes. Did he spend much time with the police? Quite a bit of time. Why? Probably because his window was so close to the shooting and because he was able to give a full account of what he saw and a detailed description of the two gunmen. Was the shooting fresh in his mind when he spoke to the police? Yes. Fresher than it is now? Of course. Was there any doubt in his mind then that the description he was giving the police was accurate? None whatsoever.

In the police report, he described the black man as 5'9" or 5'10", 170 to 175 pounds, average build, with "medium dark" skin. I showed the witness a copy of the police report and asked him if that was the description he had given them? Yes. Did it accurately describe the man he had seen? Yes. I had him read the description aloud.

Leroy Mims had been sitting at the counsel table the entire time the witness had been in the courtroom. I was standing about ten feet away from the witness and a foot from the center of the jury box. I turned and asked Mims to stand and come to where I was, so that the witness could get a better look at him. When Mims stood, there were murmurs in the courtroom. As he neared me, I motioned for him to stand next to me. He did and that put him inches from a juror in the front row, and she immediately let out a loud cry and tilted her seat as far back as she could from Mims.

Judge Wilson was furious. "Mr. Rue-ez, remove yourself and your client away from the jury box!"

Presumption of innocence?

We moved and then I asked the witness, "How tall would you say Mr. Mims is?"

"Five foot nine or ten."

"Or six foot one or six foot two?"

"He could be six foot."

"Or more?"

"Maybe an inch more."

"How much would you say he weighs?"

"180, 190 pounds."

"How about 220 pounds?"

"Well…"

"Look at him. At least two hundred pounds?"

"Maybe."

"How would you describe his build?"

"Well, he's big but you could still say he's of average build. Not all big built men are necessarily well built."

"Could you say he's well-built?"

"You could say that?'

"No, what I'm asking is whether *you* could say that?"

"Yes, some people could say that."

"You described him as 'medium dark.' What did you mean by that?"

"Well, he's a black man. So he's dark."

"Aren't there many shades of dark?"

"Yes, that's why I said 'medium dark."

"Looking at him now, could you say he's very dark?"

"I imagine some people could say that."

"Could *you* say that?"

"Well, yes, somewhere between medium dark and very dark."

I left the courthouse buoyant, floating: maybe there was something to try in this case after all. I sat through several waiting appointments in my office, doing my best to listen, but still reveling in the doubt I thought, hoped, I had placed in the jurors' minds. I got home after everyone had gone to bed still buoyed by my last cross-examination. I was awake and excited by 5:30 and left the house before 6:15, eager to start another day of trial. I had breakfast in San Jose and once at the office, I reviewed yesterday's mail, drafted answers, wrote checks, and left notes for my secretary regarding phone calls and appointments that had to be made. For the first time since the trial began, I left my office not dreading what the day would bring. Things were looking up. Now there seemed to be glimmers of hope everywhere.

The bailiff was waiting for me in the hallway when I arrived outside Judge Wilson's courtroom around 8:45. "The Judge wants to see the attorneys in chambers before we start. The D.A.'s already in the courtroom. Just as soon as the Public Defender gets here, I'll take the three of you back to see the Judge."

I had no idea why Judge Wilson wanted to see us, but as we waited for the Public Defender, I fantasized for a moment that Judge Wilson was going to demand that the District Attorney dismiss the charges against Mims. But only for a moment because there was no way I could ever visualize him speaking those words. When the Public Defender arrived, the bailiff took us back to the Judge's chamber. Judge Wilson waited until we were seated before he began. "Mr. Rue-ez, we have a problem."

I looked at him, puzzled.

"Your client is refusing to dress in civilian clothes."

"What?"

"Since 7:30 this morning, Mr. Mims has refused to put on the clothes that Friends Outside have left for him. I've had the guards bring him down to the holding cell in his coveralls and shower slippers. The guards have also brought down his court clothes. It's four minutes to nine and I don't want to keep the jury waiting. I want you to go into that holding cell and have him put on his court clothes. You have five minutes. I'm not going to keep the jury waiting. If he refuses, you can tell him for me that I'm going to have the guards bring him into the courtroom dressed as he is and shackle him to the floor. Now go talk to him and let's not keep the jury waiting."

The bailiff had kept the jurors in the hallway. Only the deputies and some guards were in the courtroom. I was let into the holding cell. Mims was sitting there alone, dressed in his white coveralls and shower slippers. He was staring at the floor and did not raise his eyes when I entered.

"What's going on, Leroy? What happened? Why won't you get dressed for the trial?"

He wouldn't answer or look at me.

"Leroy, you gotta get dressed."

Still no answer.

"Leroy, if you don't get dressed the Judge is going to have those deputies take you into the courtroom dressed like this, put you in your chair, and chain and shackle you to the floor. If that happens, the jury'll convict you in two minutes."

He looked at me. His eyes were red, angry and sad. "Let that motherfucker do whatever he wants to do. And let that cocksucking jury convict me in one minute. I don't give a good fuck what any of them do. This whole thing is one big charade. Can't you see that? Didn't you see that woman juror in the front row jump and holler when I got close to her yesterday? And you think she's not going to convict me? Didn't you see that sorry motherfucker yesterday trying to put me at the shooting when he knows goddamn good and well that he told the cops it was somebody else? And then these fucking guards treating me like I'm some kind of animal. Can't you see, can't you understand what a big joke this whole fucking thing is? And you expect me to keep going on with it? What's wrong with you, little brother? How long is it going to take before you wake up, before you open your eyes and stop being a pawn for them? How long are you gonna keep letting yourself be used by the white man's evil system?"

Now it was I who didn't answer. We sat in silence. After a while, I looked at my watch. It was long past the five minutes that Judge Wilson had allotted me. A moment later the iron door's lock clicked loudly. The door opened and one of the deputies said, "The Judge wants to see you in his chambers, Mr. Rue-ez." I stepped out into the courtroom. There were several deputies and guards there, but no jurors.

In his chambers Judge Wilson asked, "Well, Mr. Rue-ez?"

"He's not going to get dressed, Your Honor."

"Deputy, I want you to put leg irons on Mr. Mims. Take him out of the holding cell, put him in the chair he's been sitting in and bolt him to the floor."

"Yes, sir. But the guards say he's been telling them that he's not going into the courtroom anymore."

"I don't care what he's told the guards. I want him in that chair bolted down to the floor. I don't care if you have to drag or carry him out of that holding cell. I want him in that chair, dressed as he is, but with leg irons and bolted to the floor. Am I understood?"

"Yes, sir."

I returned to the courtroom. Richard Rodriguez was sitting quietly next to his Public Defender dressed in khakis and a white shirt. There were four guards and five armed deputies in the courtroom but no one else. The deputies went to the iron door, unlocked it and entered the holding cell, and after a brief, loud struggle, they emerged carrying a writhing, squirming, shouting, cursing, giant of a black man in white coveralls and bare feet. They thumped him down in his chair, and while three of them held him down, two chained him to the iron ring in the floor. When they stepped away from him, he tried to stand but winced and slumped back down on his chair and sat with his chin on his chest.

Judge Wilson came out onto the dais and once seated said, "Mr. Mims, you have refused to dress as your co-defendant, Mr. Rodriguez, is dressed in civilian clothes. You have refused to come out of the holding cell necessitating a forced removal from the holding cell by the deputies. In my chambers I could hear you cursing and shouting as the deputies carried you out of the holding cell. I have ordered that leg irons be kept on you and that you be shackled to the floor. We will proceed with the trial as you now appear and will complete it in this manner unless you have a change of mind and wish to do otherwise. But let me admonish you. If I hear one peep out of you, if you make any further disruptions once the jury is present and the trial is in session, I will have you gagged and cuffed. Do I make myself clear?" The two stares could not have been more hostile, more intense. "Good. I'm glad we understand each other. Guards, you may return to the jail. I'm confident that the five deputies can handle matters here. Mr. Bailiff, bring in the jurors."

I didn't turn to watch the jurors enter, but I could feel their reaction as they came. Silent, slow to reach the jury box, probably surveilling the courtroom. They must have heard Mims from outside. When they reached the jury box, reached my view, their attention was focused solely on Mims. As they seated themselves, they were eying him carefully, studying that sullen, angry, black face, those stark-white coveralls, his black, bare feet, and the chains.

"Good morning ladies and gentlemen," Judge Wilson said, nodding solemnly, "I'm very sorry for the delay. Mr. District Attorney, please call your next witness." As if nothing had happened. In my mind, Mims was repeating, "Can't you see, can't you understand what a big joke this whole fucking thing is?"

The first witness of the day was the arresting officer. He testified that he had stopped Rodriguez and Mims' vehicle just south of Morgan Hill for excessive speed. Rodriguez was driving and Mims was sitting in the front passenger seat. As he looked for his citation book, he noticed that Mims kept looking nervously back at him. At that point he thought there were two suspicious black men in the car and he radioed for assistance and was more deliberate in approaching the vehicle. He asked for Rodriguez's driver's license and Rodriguez handed him one, but the tension in the vehicle disturbed him and seeing Rodriguez, he recalled a radio alert for a white or Latino man and a black man fleeing the scene of a fatal shooting in San Jose, and he became very suspicious. He told Rodriguez that he had stopped him for speeding and wanted to check the status of his license. He returned to his car and radioed for more assistance, saying that these two men might fit the description of the fleeing killers. When another patrol vehicle arrived, the two officers went to the suspect vehicle but the occupants were now hostile and uncommunicative. As soon as more officers arrived, Rodriguez and Mims were ordered out of the vehicle, and a search was made which revealed a stockpile of guns and ammunition. Some of the guns and ammunition matched the descriptions of those that had been used at the Rose Garden slaying. Rodriguez and Mims were placed under arrest.

The next witness was a pathologist from the Coroner's Office. He had examined the body of James Carr and established the cause of death as bullet wounds to various parts of the body. He then posted a large drawing he had made of the victim's body on a courtroom bulletin board. He placed the numbers one through forty on the drawing and said that each number represented the entry point of a bullet into Mr. Carr's body. Then with a pointer in one hand and his report in the other, he traced bullet by bullet the path each bullet had taken and the damage it had caused. When he was finished, the jury was aghast and Judge Wilson declared a 15 minute recess. Outside in the hallway as I made my way to the men's restroom, I avoided the jurors' eyes.

When I returned from the restroom, I saw the jurors sitting outside the courtroom. Rather than pass through them again, I decided to remain at the other end of the hallway, out of their view, until I could see them returning to the courtroom. Some minutes later, as the last of them entered the courtroom, I started down the hallway. When I entered the courtroom I noticed that all the jurors were seated and I hurried to take my seat at the counsel table. Only then did I see that while the District Attorney, the Public Defender and Rodriguez were seated, Mims' chair was vacant. I took my seat and as soon as I did, the bailiff rapped his gavel and said, "Please rise!" And Judge Wilson appeared. As soon as he was settled he said, "Deputies, bring out Mr. Mims."

The deputies went to the iron door, unlocked it and entered. A fierce struggle ensued with men grunting and Mims shouting and cursing. Then the deputies reappeared, carrying that giant of a man in a prone position, kicking, writhing, cursing and screaming. There were whimpers from the jury box where the jurors sat stunned and wide-eyed. The deputies sat Mims down so hard that there were "oow's" from the jurors. Then they shackled him to the floor and Mims slumped in his chair, perfectly still and quiet.

Unperturbed, Judge Wilson turned to the District Attorney and said, "Call your next witness."

He was the ballistic expert from the District Attorney's Crime Lab who had examined, tested and fired the guns and ammunition found in the suspect's vehicle and had compared those bullets with the ones found at the scene of the shooting and those taken from the body of James Carr. He was a distinguished-looking man in his 50's who began listing his credentials and work experience. At that point Judge Wilson saw that some of the jurors were still shaken by what they had seen moments before.

"Just a minute, sir," he said to the witness, and then turning to the jury said, "Ladies and gentlemen, this trial has to proceed to completion. Now there may be aspects of it that may be upsetting to you but that's to be expected in these types of cases. So let's pull ourselves together here and get on with the necessary business at hand.... You may continue, sir."

The witness continued citing his work experience for a few more moments, when Judge Wilson stood and said, "This court will be in recess until two o'clock this afternoon," and left the courtroom.

Two of the jurors were still visibly upset. It was 11:15 and it was going to be a long luncheon recess. For once, I thought, James Wilson was at a loss about what to do. It took me a while to sort through all that had happened that morning until my mind stopped, wouldn't budge from something that Mims had said to me earlier in the holding cell. "...that sorry motherfucker yesterday, trying to put me at the shooting when he knows goddamn good and well that he told the cops it was somebody else...." That was the closest Mims had ever come to denying that he was one of the shooters. And in light of all the witnesses' difficulty in identifying him, except for Betsy Carr, it made sense. I told my secretary that I was not to be disturbed, that I was not in for anyone. Then I scoured through Mims and Rodriguez's notebook and daily expenditures for any sign of a third person. I found one in a motel receipt for a stay in Los Banos the night before they arrived in San Jose. I must have looked at that receipt a dozen times before, without ever noticing the entry alongside the designation at the upper right hand corner: Number of Parties, 3.

I called Los Banos. The motel owner remembered the night. "Because it was late and I only had one room left with a double bed and these three fellows came in. Two Neegrows and a Messicun. Said they'd been driving all day. Didn't look like they had much money. And when I told them I only had one room with a double bed, but that I might could put a cot in there for two dollars extra, they jumped at it."

"Do you remember what they looked like?"

"Not really."

"Nothing at all?"

"No, except that one of the Neegrows and the Messicun were about the same size and the other Neegrow was a lot bigger."

"Bigger?"

"Yeah, taller, bigger build, you know."

"Are you sure?"

"Yeah. I'm sure."

I was elated. I paced around my office trying to decide what to do and how to do it. I had to talk to Mims, that before anything. I drove as fast as I could to the jail, before they sent him back to the courthouse for the afternoon session. But halfway there, I realized that even if I could show that he wasn't one of the two shooters, he still could be convicted of conspiring to do what they did and in most conspiracies, a co-conspirator was deemed as guilty as the perpetrators. And, as often happened when I practiced criminal law, another of the few exhilarating feelings I experienced about a case vanished as quickly as it had appeared. I slowed down. What was the point? Another futile act, another futile effort? No, because despite being found guilty of all the same charges as the perpetrators, it was not unusual for a co-conspirator to receive a lesser sentence. I had to talk to Mims.

He was sitting in a jail holding cell, barefoot and in his white coveralls. When the guard let me in, he looked up quizzically but said nothing.

"Leroy, I think I can prove that you weren't one of the two men who shot James Carr."

"What?"

I had a copy of the motel receipt in my hand and I showed it to him. "Here. Look. This shows that the night before you arrived in San Jose, three of you registered in a Los Banos motel. I've talked to the owner there and he said that there were three men that registered there that night. Two black men and a Mexican. One of the black men was about Rodriguez's size. That's exactly what the witnesses have been saying. The motel owner said the other black man was much bigger. That had to be you."

Mims was watching me. When I stopped and waited for a response, he said nothing. Instead, he continued looking at me, calmly, evenly for several moments before he said, "I don't want you telling anybody about that and I sure as hell don't want you telling that Judge that or bringing it up in court." Now his look was stern, strong. So strong that I remained silent.

"I know where I'm at and I know what's coming to me. I've accepted that and I'm O.K. with that. But if you start messing with things, you're gonna fuck everything up. You're gonna hurt people that don't need to be hurt. And you could end up hurting yourself. I mean it. I'm not bullshitting you. You could end up hurting yourself real bad."

I tried explaining that as his attorney, I was duty bound to raise every legitimate defense on his behalf, that even if he were convicted as a co-conspirator, he might receive a lesser sentence. But he would have none of it. He simply looked away and shook his head until I left.

I didn't know what to do. His concern that I might implicate others didn't bother me. If someone else did the shooting, he deserved to be implicated. His warning that I might end up hurting myself, I didn't take seriously then. In retrospect, I probably should have taken it much more seriously. But if there was a real possibility that I could lessen Mims' sentence, then I felt I had to raise the issue.

At ten minutes of two, I knocked on the courtroom door. When the bailiff answered, I said, "Tell the Judge that I need to see him and the other attorneys in his chambers before we start this afternoon."

Judge Wilson did not appreciate my request. He already had his robe on and was standing at the side of his desk that was closest to the dais' door. Only he, the District Attorney, the Public Defender and I were in his chambers. "What is it Mr. Rue-ez?" irritated, already far behind the time he had scheduled for this case.

"I think I've just discovered conclusive evidence that Leroy Mims was not one of the men that shot and killed James Carr."

Now he was even more irritated. "Well, present it in court. That's what attorneys are supposed to do, aren't they."

"Yes, except that my client has ordered me not to do so."

"What!" the District Attorney piped in.

But I had taken Judge Wilson by surprise too. He paused. He thought. He looked at me again, still annoyed. But he moved back to the center of his desk and sat down. "What is this again? Explain this to me, please."

I repeated myself.

"Yes, I heard you the first time. But give me some details," his fingers motioning from his cupped hand.

"The night before they arrived in San Jose, Mims and Rodriguez spent the night at a motel in Los Banos. But there was another man with them. Another black man. One that fits the description that yesterday's last witness gave the police and explains why almost every witness has had a difficult time identifying Mims but not Rodriguez."

"How do you know this?"

"Well, here's a copy of the motel receipt that clearly shows three persons were in the party that night, and I've spoken on the phone to the motel owner in Los Banos, the man who registered them into the motel that night."

"When did you learn this?"

"Just today, Your Honor."

"A little late, isn't it, counselor?" the District Attorney offered. "You've had the discovery for weeks."

"And you had it a couple of weeks before I did. Why haven't you called it to anyone's attention?" I answered.

"Gentlemen! I won't have any bickering in here between the attorneys. If you have something to say, address it to me."

"This is just a red herring, Your Honor. Defense counsel is simply trying to disrupt these proceedings before the jury readily convicts his client."

"This is not a red herring, Your Honor. As many times as I've gone over the discovery, I just happened to notice the entry today and called the Los Banos motel."

"What difference does any of this make, Your Honor? Mims at the very least is a co-conspirator. I've certainly established that. He's guilty of all the charges regardless of whether he's a perpetrator or not."

For the second time that day, Judge Wilson did not have a ready answer. He turned in his swivel chair and looked out the window. He turned again and stared at the wall. He tilted his chair back and looked up at the ceiling. He was not a man of indecision, but this one took him several minutes to decide.

Finally he said, "You say that Mr. Mims told you not to raise this defense?"

"Yes, Your Honor."

"This is his case and you are his attorney?"

"Yes, Your Honor."

"Well, the representative should always do as the represented requests. Shouldn't he?"

"...Not always, Your Honor."

"Well, I think that Mr. Mims should be accommodated. I'm going to let him have his way. Alright, gentlemen, that will be all. Let's proceed with the evidence."

The prosecution concluded its case the following afternoon. Neither Rodriguez nor Mims testified, nor called any witnesses on their behalf. The jury deliberated that afternoon and decided the case in less than an hour. Guilty as charged, on all counts. Three weeks later, Judge Wilson sentenced Mims and Rodriguez to life sentences in the state prison.

Chapter 8

Over the more than thirty years that I practiced criminal law, I represented more than a thousand individuals in criminal cases. Yet, I was never hired by a white defendant or his family to represent him in a major felony case. Court-appointed, yes, but never privately retained. Nor did I expect to be. After all, I was a "Mexican lawyer," and defendants in those situations who could afford private counsel wanted white lawyers. A "Mexican lawyer" was too much of a risk for those serious cases. In fact, it wasn't until the last two or three years of practicing law that I was privately retained to represent white defendants, though never in a major criminal case. Those white defendants came to me on the recommendation of other white lawyers. I very much appreciated their referrals, not so much for the money as for the validation. But then, I doubt that Clint White, the black Oakland lawyer who was by far the best trial lawyer I saw, ever had a white client.

Today, there are but a handful of names and faces that I can readily recall from all those cases. One of those will always be Hugh Schade, M.D., another court appointment. When I first met Hugh Schade, he was no longer a medical doctor. He had already been stripped of his license to practice medicine by the Medical Board of California. At that time Schade was being charged with more than 50 counts of over-prescribing controlled substances to his patients. He spent a great deal of time educating me about his medical practice, reconstructing his care of patients whom he had treated for months and years, and discussing chronic pain with me and two medical doctors that were supportive of him. The preliminary examination took several days and the jury trial consumed more than three grueling weeks. But after all that time spent together, I didn't really know Hugh Schade. What I remember most about him was the manner and air with which he said over and over again throughout all those days and months: "I did nothing wrong."

Hugh Schade was a proud man with a proud look. There was arrogance in that look, almost as if he was enduring all who could not, or would not, understand what he was trying to do in his medical practice. There was pain in that look too: Hugh Schade felt that he was being unfairly persecuted. His was a quiet voice. He never once raised it in protest, never cursed, never blamed. All he said, time and again, was, "I did nothing wrong."

He was not a handsome man, but he carried himself with much poise and dignity. Red faced, big-nosed, with rimless glasses that made him more officious looking than he needed to be. He had a large forehead beneath closely cropped brown hair. He stood five-foot nine-inches tall, and seemed to be an exceptionally, physically fit fifty-year-old man.

When the call came advising me of the court-appointment, I was told that "Doctor Schade" was out of custody, that the Medical Board had already taken his license, and that his office had been closed. I was given his home phone number and I called him, introducing myself, telling him that I had been appointed by the court to represent him, and then setting up an appointment for him at my office. I worried that I wouldn't be able to convince "Doctor Schade," and myself, that I was capable of being his lawyer, that it was alright for him to be represented by a Mexican lawyer. I feared that he probably thought that the court had appointed him a Mexican lawyer because that's all he deserved. I consoled myself by thinking that he couldn't have been much of a doctor if he had more than fifty counts of over-prescribing controlled substances to his patients. He had to be a fat, greedy, drunken or drug-addicted slob. Mine was a small office in a converted house far from the downtown, high-rise offices of the prestigious law firms. I was convinced that when he saw my office, that it would reconfirm his fears about being represented by a Mexican lawyer. To hell with him, I repeated to myself. How much of a doctor could he have been if he couldn't afford one of those downtown lawyers? Or any lawyer, for that matter? Whatever our first meeting was like, within a week, this brown-skinned Mexican and that red-faced German became and remained committed to each other in the months that followed, to and through a difficult jury trial.

Dr. Schade's specialty was internal medicine. He had, in fact, had a successful medical practice for some 15 years before he became interested in chronic pain. His interest began with treatment of patients who had had three and even four back surgeries, each successive surgery achieving nothing, except at times, to increase the pain. He prescribed narcotics to alleviate the pain. The narcotics didn't cure the pain; they simply gave the patient temporary relief. When the pain returned, the patients returned and Dr. Schade prescribed more narcotics. The word spread among those similarly afflicted. Gradually, his patients were becoming more and more chronic pain patients and Dr. Schade was prescribing more and more narcotics. The word also spread to other physicians, pharmacists, junkies, and finally to the Medical Board.

The Medical Board of California is the State agency that licenses medical doctors and disciplines those who violate the law. One of the Board's principal services is the investigation of complaints against physicians. Among other things, the Board investigates complaints of mis-prescribing or over-prescribing drugs. The original complaints against Dr. Schade may well have come from other physicians who had heard enough times from their patients that Dr. Schade was prescribing controlled substances that they were reluctant to prescribe. On the whole, physicians had a healthy respect for the Medical Board which could both license them and take away their license. Then too, there were reports pharmacists were required by law to send to the Board showing the amounts of controlled substances prescribed by individual doctors. It was only a matter of time before those reports showed that Dr. Schade was prescribing far more controlled substances than his peers. And unfortunately it wasn't long until drug addicts heard that if they had enough money to pay for a medical visit and could come up with a plausible story of chronic pain, there was a doctor who would write them a prescription for the drugs they needed. Nor was it long after the Board's investigation of Dr. Schade began, that its investigator, working with the police, put together an undercover operation whereby known drug addicts were sent to Dr. Schade to obtain prescriptions for their "chronic pain."

In those first days representing Dr. Schade, I looked for any sign of a sleazy doctor prescribing as many narcotics to as many patients as he could for money. I saw no such signs. In fact, the opposite seemed true. He usually wore a business suit, one of three off-the-rack, narrow lapel suits which were perfectly pressed and clean, and if not threadbare, at least well worn. Under it was always a heavily starched, inexpensive white shirt and a long, thin tie that had long since gone out of fashion. Occasionally, he switched to a sport coat and slacks, a woolen tweed sport coat that showed wear at the elbows. Shirley, his devoted wife of some thirty years, wore simple, inexpensive dresses and jackets. They drove a small, economy two-door sedan that they had owned for years, which also was very neat and clean. I never visited their home but I knew it was located in an old, middle-class neighborhood in San Jose. Clearly, Dr. Schade had not made a great deal of money practicing medicine. Yet from the first day I met him, I found him to be a very intelligent, competent, thoughtful person. He too was a sole practitioner, and as we began reviewing his medical records, I immediately saw that his files were more complete and better organized than my own.

"So why did you prescribe narcotics in this case?" I asked many times.

"Because the patient told me he was in chronic pain."

"Why did you continue prescribing narcotics for so long a period?"

"Because the patient continued telling me that he was in chronic pain and I believed him."

"Did you ever doubt that he might be in chronic pain?"

"I might have. But how can one really know?"

"But if you had some doubt that he might be in chronic pain, why did you continue prescribing narcotics?"

"If the patient continued saying that he was in chronic pain and I felt that it was more likely than not that he was, I continued prescribing the pain relievers.... Look, when I was sitting in the examination room with the patient, I was a doctor, not a detective or an investigator or a District Attorney. I believed what he or she said, and I gave them a prescription to help them with their pain."

"But you had to be aware that you were prescribing narcotics a great deal more than other doctors."

"I was aware of that, but at some point it didn't matter anymore."

"You knew that other doctors were very reluctant to prescribe those drugs. You've told me that. Several of your patients told you that."

"I can't speak for what other doctors did or didn't do, or were reluctant to do. I can only speak for myself. I thought and still think I did the right thing. I did nothing wrong."

Within two weeks of my appointment, a preliminary examination was held in the Municipal Court. In felony cases, preliminary examinations were held to determine whether there was probable cause to send the District Attorney's charges to the Superior Court for further proceedings and trial. It was akin to a court trial except that the judge decided only whether there was sufficient evidence to send the case on to the Superior Court. Many times it was the first opportunity the defense attorney had to see what evidence the prosecution actually had. That was the case for me then, especially given the great number of charges alleged in the complaint against Dr. Schade. His preliminary examination took three days to complete. The prosecution's expert and principal witness was a professor of medicine at the University of California's School of

Medicine in San Francisco. He testified at length that in his expert opinion, Dr. Schade had over-prescribed controlled substances on many occasions to many of his patients. Of the fifty plus counts that were alleged in the complaint, after the preliminary examination, Doctor Schade was held to answer on forty four counts in the Superior Court.

It wasn't long after I began working on the case that I learned that Dr. Schade was something of a pariah in the San Jose medical community. Many doctors wanted nothing to do with him. They believed that he had gotten what he deserved. In their minds, there was absolutely no reason, no excuse, for the large number of narcotic prescriptions he had written for so many patients over such a long period of time. Two doctors did quietly come forth and offer their assistance. They too believed that in cases of chronic pain, there was nothing more a physician could do other than prescribe narcotics. They pointed to at least one article written by a professor of medicine at Stanford's Medical School which said exactly the same thing. But they didn't want to become openly involved in Dr. Schade's case. They didn't want to draw attention to themselves, especially not the attention of the Medical Board, possibly jeopardizing their own licenses to practice medicine. I did subpoena the Stanford professor to testify at Dr. Schade's trial.

In preparing for trial, we attempted to contact all 44 of the alleged victims. Of those that we were able to contact, most said that they did not want to talk to me or Dr. Schade about the case, that they had already spoken to law enforcement and had been subpoenaed by the District Attorney's Office to testify at the trial, and felt that was enough. Four of the alleged victims agreed to talk to us. One still stands out in my mind.

She was a woman in her early fifties who lived in Los Gatos, an affluent suburb of San Jose. Dr. Schade and I drove out to her home one afternoon. It was a large, impressive house although not in the least bit ostentatious. She was expecting us and met us at the door with a warm, cheerful smile. She was bright, well-spoken, pleasant, and obviously had a great deal of respect and affection for Dr. Schade. We sat at her dining room table for more than an hour as she told of her surgeries and medical care. She had been an avid gardener and several years before had a small tree taken out of her backyard. But a stump had remained and in time its roots became more and more bothersome. She decided to remove the stump herself. Pointing to a spot in her backyard, she told us how she had dug around the stump with a shovel until she was deep enough so that she thought she could begin prying the stump upward. She pried and pried until she felt a sharp pain in her lower back. The pain was so excruciating that she lay on the ground for a long while unable to walk without increasing the pain. At the hospital, she was diagnosed with a herniated disc in her lower back. Surgery was recommended and in the weeks before the surgery, she spent much time in bed hobbled by pain that could be brought about unexpectedly by any movement as she went about her daily life. The first surgery seemed to have alleviated the pain until she stopped taking the post-operative narcotics that had been prescribed. Then the pain seemed to be sharper and more frequent than before. A second surgery changed nothing, and a third yet again increased the pain and its frequency. Her only relief came with the prescribed post-operative drugs. After each operation, the surgeon prescribed pain-killers for longer periods of time. But after several months of prescribing controlled substances, he was reluctant to continue. He talked of yet another surgery and she was panic stricken. Not wanting a fourth operation, she went to other doctors, describing her history of chronic pain and asking for pain killers. Some suggested that she had become addicted to pain killers. They wouldn't believe or didn't want to risk believing that she was in chronic pain, and would not prescribe more drugs. But one mentioned Dr. Schade whom she sought out. He examined her and believed her, and for more than a year prescribed controlled substances for her. The drugs allowed her to be pain free much of the time and to resume her daily activities.

As she spoke and answered my questions, Dr. Schade sat quietly aside saying nothing. He just sat and watched with an officious, arrogant look on his red face. I couldn't help but think that he was feeling vindicated, that he was saying to me, "See, this is what I do. This is what needs to be done. I have done nothing wrong and I was not afraid to do it."

Before we left, I asked her if she was still in pain and how she had been coping with it since Dr. Schade's arrest. She said that a doctor who was a friend of a family member was prescribing pain medication for her. But she added that he was very nervous doing so and had made her promise not to divulge his name to anyone. She also said that she had been subpoenaed to testify at Dr. Schade's trial and that she had been interviewed by an investigator with the Medical Board. She told him everything she had told us, but she had the impression that he didn't believe her, didn't believe the chronic pain she had endured for so long. Like some of the other doctors she had visited, she felt that he thought she was just a drug addict.

The other former patients we interviewed had similar stories. Years of chronic pain and surgeries that never remedied the pain and sometimes worsened it; and longer and longer periods of prescription drugs for the pain until no doctor, except Dr. Schade, would prescribe pain medication for them. They all clearly appreciated the help Dr. Schade had given them.

Because the trial was estimated to last three to four weeks, Dr. Schade's case was transferred to a courthouse annex near downtown San Jose, and Judge James Wright, a retired judge who was sitting pro tem, was assigned to hear it. Jim Wright had been a running back for the University of Santa Clara Broncos football team that played in the 1937 Sugar Bowl. Nearing 70, his body, though thicker, still suggested the athleticism that was once there. Sturdy, erect, with a keen mind and sharp, blue eyes, he was still a very handsome man. White, wavy hair and a California tan, which together with a clean, warm smile, made his wrinkles irrelevant.

I had appeared just briefly before Judge Wright prior to his retirement. For years, he had been a partner in an old, prestigious San Jose law firm with no experience in the criminal courts that I was aware of. After his appointment to the bench, he served primarily in the Civil Division. It was just after I went to work for the ALRB in Sacramento that he began serving in the Criminal Division of the Superior Court. In 1981, I made a couple of appearances before him that took at most two minutes. But they left me with the impression that he was a stern, difficult judge. To my surprise, lawyers in the Public Defenders Office and in the private bar thought highly of him as being courteous, affable and completely fair, but expecting that you came into his courtroom fully prepared to try your case. Deputy District Attorneys had the same opinion. So I was not disappointed when I learned that we had been assigned to Judge Wright for trial.

As we approached the trial date, I had spent far more time with Dr. Schade than I had spent with any other client. But Hugh Schade was still a mystery to me. At that stage in the case, most of my clients were either very nervous, fearful, self-pitying or full of protestations of innocence. Hugh Schade was calm, stoic and seemingly at peace with himself. Often he had a faraway look in his eye that seemed to say that he was above it all. "I did nothing wrong," he would repeat. "They told me they were in chronic pain. I believed them and prescribed what I felt would give them some relief and make their everyday lives better." Whatever his peers or the Medical Board or the District Attorney believed mattered not in the least to him. Nor did the great number of felony counts that he was charged with and that we were about to try. Nor did the pages of police reports in which some of the alleged victims admitted that they were addicted to drugs, and having heard of Dr. Schade, had gone to him and told him of a trumped up physical condition that was causing them chronic pain, after which Dr. Schade had readily prescribed controlled substances for them on numerous occasions.

Facing 44 felony counts, 99.9% of my clients would have at least asked, wondered about, a plea bargain. A lesser sentence, probation if they were to plead guilty to one or a few of the charges. Not Hugh Schade. A plea bargain, a guilty plea was never a consideration. We were destined to go to a jury trial from the very beginning.

Judge Wright made a lasting impression on me during the jury selection process at the very beginning of the trial. As the first twelve prospective jurors were seated, he began by asking if there was any reason why they felt they couldn't sit as jurors on the case. He had already told them that the case was estimated to take three to four weeks to try. As was to be expected in a case of that length, several hands went up. The first had to do with work schedules and vacation plans. Then one man stood up in the back row of the jury box. I can still picture him. He was a hefty, pot-bellied man in his sixties. The exchange went something like this.

"Yes, sir?" Judge Wright said with a brisk but engaging smile.

"Well sir, Your Honor, I just don't really believe that I can sit on this case."

"Why is that?" Patient, attentive, inoffensive, while everything about him exuded strength, firmness, and determination.

"Well, you see Judge, I'm 61 years old, soon to be 62 and getting near to retiring and I can tell that the older I get, the less able I am to do what I used to be able to do. And to sit here for three or four weeks and watch and think about this case is more than I think that I can handle."

Judge Wright bowed his head, thought for a while and then came up with that wonderful, sparkling smile and gently said to a man who was probably five years younger than him, "Mr. Williams, I understand your concern, believe me. I'm not a youngster myself. But you know, aging, like so many other things, is a matter of the mind, and just listening to you and observing you, tells me that there is nothing about you that will prevent you from sitting here and listening to this case and deciding it fairly and impartially. Nothing, except perhaps, you're telling yourself that you can't do it. So, come on now, you and I both know that you can do it. I'm not going to excuse you. Simply because I'm convinced that you're fully capable of being a good juror."

Subsequently, it was either the District Attorney or I who excused Mr. Williams from serving as a juror.

It was customary during jury trials for a judge to declare a 15-minute morning and afternoon recess once the court had been in session for an hour and a half or two hours. But that first morning, Judge Wright did something I never saw another judge do, and he continued to do it throughout the three and a half weeks that we were in session. Every hour, almost to the minute, no matter at what juncture we might be in the trial, he would rise, smile and say, "Excuse me for a moment, please. And please remain where you are." Then he would step away from his desk and put his hands on the back of his hips, extend his chest and stretch for ten or fifteen seconds. Relax and then repeat the stretch. He was a sight to remember. Standing above us in his black robe, big, strong, white-maned and handsome, stretching. Then he would step back to his desk, sit, smile and say, "Thank you. Now may we please continue." It was some time before I came to appreciate what impact those stretches would have on Dr. Schade's case.

Once the jury was selected, the testimony began. But for reasons never mentioned, and known only to herself, the District Attorney called only 33 of the 44 alleged victims to testify. The woman Dr. Schade and I had interviewed in her Los Gatos home did not testify. Several of the witnesses called testified to years of chronic pain and medical treatment, including surgeries, with no relief except for the medications Dr. Schade had prescribed. Others said that they were drug addicts and when they told Dr. Schade that they were in chronic pain, he readily prescribed controlled substances. In the latter group, some were part of the Medical Board's undercover operation.

The District Attorney used as her expert and principal witness the same medical professor from the University of California's Medical School in San Francisco that she had called at the preliminary examination. He unequivocally stated that it was his expert opinion that in all of the 33 cases before the jury, Dr. Schade had illegally over-prescribed controlled substances. In preparing the case for trial, I had learned that the Medical Board and District Attorneys in other counties had used the same professor as their expert witness in similar cases. As a result, I was able to obtain copies of his prior testimony in other cases. What I found was that at times this medical professor's standards and interpretation of the facts varied noticeably; yet, he was always able to conclude that in his expert opinion the physician was guilty as charged. He testified in Dr. Schade's case for three days, much of it under cross-examination. It was a cross-examination that I believe he never forgot.

We called three witnesses for the defense. The first was the Stanford Medical Professor who had written on the subject of chronic pain. He testified that when a patient was in chronic pain, controlled substances were the only medications that could give any relief. The issue, he said, was whether the patient was indeed in chronic pain. The second witness was one of the two doctors who had come to Dr. Schade's assistance when we were preparing his defense. He also testified that narcotic medications were the sole treatment that would give chronic pain patients relief. I didn't subpoena him. He came, I think, out of a matter of conscience. But he was so concerned about what the consequences might be for testifying, that he was a terrible witness. He may not have hurt Dr. Schade, but he didn't help him. Then there was Dr. Schade.

Throughout the trial, Dr. Schade was as he had always been: implacable, unperturbed, sitting upright, chin-up, red-faced, eyes focused on the witnesses, the judge, the jury when the situation called for that, without a hint of anger, fear or remorse but rather, gracefully, calmly, evenly. "I have done nothing wrong." Nothing seemed to phase his imperious countenance. On the other hand, I was my usual emotional mess, fighting and clawing as much for my own identity as for his.

The courthouse annex was in a converted building that was situated in what had once been a residential neighborhood, but now was being redeveloped to become part of downtown San Jose. The area surrounding the courthouse annex was pretty much deserted and very suitable for the walks that Dr. Schade and I took every morning and afternoon during the court's 15 minute recesses.

I can still see us walking, the afternoon walks in particular, because by then we had been through three-fourths of another grueling day- he, upright, red-faced, stoic, in that stiffly starched white shirt and that spotless, neatly pressed worn suit, looking off into the distance as if there was absolutely nothing to be concerned about. And me inwardly raw and exhausted, scraping for every ounce of energy that I had left, hoping that I would have enough left to get me through the rest of the afternoon, to appear composed for just another hour and a half, so that he and all of them wouldn't see what a mess I really was.

I was sleeping no more than five hours a night, sometimes four, sometimes less. After court each day, as a sole practitioner, I still had to return to my office and run the rest of my law practice. When I got home at night, the children had gone to bed and often my wife too. Five hours was what sleep I set the alarm for, believing that I could fully function the next day on that amount of sleep. Many nights I couldn't even sleep five hours. Some nights I didn't know if I had slept at all because my mind was racing the entire time, replaying the day and taunting me with worries and fears of the day and days to come. No matter, I was out of bed five hours or less later. Showered, shaved and dressed, I headed for San Jose. There I would have breakfast at a diner that opened at 6:00a.m. Then to my office to first make certain that I had made all the necessary preparations for my secretary to deal with yet another day of my absence. Then to prepare for another day of testimony, another day of cross-examination, another day to argue the law, to argue the admissibility of evidence. When I arrived at Judge Wright's court around 8:45, I was already exhausted. But exhaustion was my state of being then. From 9:00 to 12:00 and then again from 1:30 to 5:00, I was constantly plagued by the fear that I wasn't appearing composed, or that I didn't know what I was doing, all too afraid that I would stumble or bumble and be the Mexican lawyer they all expected. Still, I needed to concentrate on the witnesses and their testimony, looking, hoping for whatever misstep, opening they might give me for cross-examination. I also had to watch Judge Wright and the jurors, especially for their reactions to parts of testimony that I felt were important. Lastly, most importantly, I had to lift myself, preen myself, hone my mind as best I could to its highest edge and try to keep it there through cross-examination after cross-examination.

Saturdays meant a full day at the office trying to preserve the practice I had and develop new business in spite of my weekday absences there. I spent hours making and answering phone calls, all too often trying to calm my clients' worries and fears about not having been in court with them in the past week or wouldn't be in court with them in the coming week. Then too, there were those who felt they needed to talk to me, some "desperately," during the week when I had been unavailable. My secretary had been sure to make Saturday appointments for potential new clients who had phoned or come into the office. She knew as well as I that new business was her salary to come as well as the office's future overhead and food and shelter for my family. All too often, those Saturday phone calls and appointments were torment as I struggled to pull my mind away from Dr. Schade's case and listen to them.

Sundays, I forced myself to remain at home. But it would have been better if I hadn't. Because I worked on Dr. Schade's case there too, resenting any noise, however slight, or any interruption from the other five members of my family. My mind and feelings only had space and time for Dr. Schade's case. By mid-morning, my negative presence would not have been missed, applauded instead, had I gone to San Jose.

Almost without exception, this was what my jury trials' experiences were like for all the years that I practiced criminal law. Thus I have never been able to watch a Hollywood or television courtroom drama. I have always turned the television off or left the room. In a theater, if I was with someone and couldn't leave, I would close my eyes and try to sleep. Those productions never bore any resemblance to what my experience had been. Of course, Hollywood and television producers are in the business of making money. Within that parameter, my courtroom experience was not relevant.

Dr. Schade testified in that calm, soft-spoken, clear-eyed manner as if he had nothing to hide, nothing to fear. "They told me they were in chronic pain. I believed them. And I prescribed the medications that I felt would give them relief from that pain."

The jury deliberated over the course of two days. They returned a verdict of guilty on 17 counts and not guilty on 16 counts. Once a guilty verdict was returned by a jury on felony charges, it was customary for the trial judge to remand a defendant into custody if he was out of custody, pending a sentencing hearing. I was surprised when Judge Wright said, "Doctor Schade, you are ordered to return to my courtroom with your attorney four weeks from now for sentencing. In the meantime, I am ordering you to go to the Probation Department so that they may prepare a report for my review. That will be all. This court is now in recess."

I had fully expected Dr. Schade to be sentenced to state prison and therefore he would have been remanded into custody until the sentencing date. As we left the courtroom, I was puzzled. All I could deduce was that Judge Wright didn't think that Dr. Schade was a flight risk. My quandary was resolved a week later when, as I was walking through the courthouse, Judge Wright's bailiff called to me and said, "Mr. Ruiz, the Judge would like to see you."

I walked into the Judge's chambers to find him standing near his desk in his black robe extending his hand. "How are you, Mr. Ruiz?"

It seemed as if he was truly interested in how I was. "I'm fine Judge. And you, sir?"

"I'm fine," as he shook my hand. "But please, sit down. There's something I want to talk to you about."

I took a seat and he moved behind his desk, sat and then brought his cupped hands to his chin and looked aside for a better way to begin. Then, "You know, Mr. Ruiz, I don't want to send Dr. Schade to prison. On the other hand, I've heard all the testimony in the case, including his, and I believe there was some wrong-doing on his part. Neglect perhaps, arrogance too, maybe. I don't know. But I'll get to the point. Will you please tell Dr. Schade for me that when he goes to the Probation Department for his interview, if he'll admit to some wrong-doing on his part, I won't sentence him to prison. Instead, I will place him on probation."

I sat there stunned, filled with admiration for that old running back and his perception, understanding, courage and decency to call me in like that and personally give my client the option for probation even before he went to the Probation Department for his interview. He did something that no other judge had ever done or would ever do in all the sentencing matters I had had or would ever have.

"Thank you, Your Honor. I can't tell you how much I appreciate this."

I set up an appointment with Dr. Schade for that same afternoon. When I told him what the Judge had said, he replied, "But I did nothing wrong."

"Hugh, listen to me. Be reasonable. You're facing prison. You've got to go into that Probation Department and tell them something like, 'I know now that I should have been more careful, more select in who I prescribed for. I can see now how I erred, how I was wrong.'"

"I did nothing wrong."

"Hugh, if you don't want to think about yourself, then think of Shirley. She's a very sick woman. She'll be alone. You'll probably be gone for a very long time. Who's going to look after her when you're gone?"

"I did nothing wrong."

We must have gone on for more than an hour with longer and longer periods of silence. But in the end, it was always that same stoic, soft-spoken sentence. "I did nothing wrong."

He said that too, to the Probation Department. And Judge Wright sentenced him to the state prison for the minimum sentence of 32 months.

Two plus years later, I received a call from a clerk of the Superior Court. "Ron, I think you should know that Dr. Schade is out of prison now."

"Oh." I was neither elated nor disturbed. Shirley was dead and Hugh Schade's release didn't seem to matter.

"I think you should also know that he's filed a civil suit for damages against the County."

"For what?" My indifference must have gone something like, That crazy son-of-a-bitch. It doesn't surprise me.

"It has to do with the court-appointed representation he got in court."

"What!"

"Yes, and he's named you and a bunch of other people as defendants."

"What!" I burned with anger.

It took me a few days to locate Hugh Schade. He was working as an aid in some doctors' offices. I waited for him until he came out for lunch. When I first saw him at a distance, he looked the same: red-faced, erect, chin-up. But when he got closer, there was a sadness to him in his face and in his body too.

"Hugh, why did you sue me?"

"I didn't sue you, Ron."

"Like hell! You filed a law suit against the County, didn't you?"

"Yes."

"And you named me as a defendant."

"No."

"Hugh, the complaint was read to me by a court clerk."

"There must be some mistake, Ron. You know I would never sue you."

"That's not what the clerk said."

"Believe me that has to be a mistake and I'll see that it's corrected."

A week later, an amended complaint was filed and I was not named as a defendant. I never saw, heard from, or spoke to Hugh Schade again.

Chapter 9

The phone rang. It was mid-afternoon, early June, 1992. I had just returned from court. The receptionist said, "It's Tom Kelley. Do you want to talk to him?"

"Yes, put him through, please.... Hello, Tom?"

"Hi, Ron."

"What's up?"

"Well, I've just learned that the D.A. indicted multiple defendants in a death penalty case against the *Nuestra Familia* prison gang."

"Whoa!"

"Are you interested?"

"Yeah. But tell me more."

"Well, apparently the D.A.'s Office and the State Attorney General's Office have decided that they're going to wipe out the *Nuestra Familia* prison gang."

"How do they plan to do that?"

"By indicting 21 of its members in a death penalty case."

"Twenty-one? You've got to be kidding."

"No, there's nothing funny about this. They're determined to wipe out the gang."

"I don't think there're twenty-one N.F. gang members here in San Jose. Or are there?"

"I don't know. But what they're doing is filing on known gang members who are now in prison throughout the state."

"And bringing them down here?"

"Yeah, on a conspiracy charge involving, among other things, six murders in San Jose in the past two years."

"Who's got the case in the D.A.'s office?"

"Charlie Constantinides."

"Probably their best."

"Yep. And he's got this hot-shot from the Attorney General's Office helping him, who's supposed to know all about prison gangs."

"Oh."

"You still interested?"

"Yeah."

"Well. Why don't you come over to my office and I'll go over what I know about the case with you, and you can pick out the defendant you want to represent. O.K.?"

"I'll be there in about half an hour."

"Good."

Tom Kelley was the Director of the Conflicts Office, a Department created by the Santa Clara County Board of Supervisors a few years before with the advice and counsel of Judges, the District Attorney and the Public Defender. It was designed to select and oversee the work of court-appointed private attorneys in criminal cases having multiple indigent defendants because under California law, the Public Defender could represent only one defendant in multiple indigent defendant cases. The private attorneys worked as independent contractors on an hourly basis, which varied based upon the gravity of the crimes. Tom had been a well-respected criminal defense attorney who had been appointed to the position by the Superior Court Judges. Tom and I had been friends for several years.

I was at Tom's office within half an hour, but from the moment I finished speaking with him on the phone until I got there, the uppermost thing in my mind was the *Nuestra Familia* prison gang, the N.F. as I had come to know it, and the impending death penalty case. Although Mexican-Americans made up less than 20 % of California's population, we were the largest racial group in the prisons, followed by the blacks and then the whites. That fact had always bothered me. We were not born that way. We did not come out of our mothers' wombs that way. Those thoughts had run through my mind countless times when I saw day after day that the vast majority of criminal defendants that were brought into court in Santa Clara County were Mexican-Americans. I can still recall going into homes in the run-down *barrios* of East San Jose and seeing family photos hanging on the front room walls of men in prison denims or rows of young men in white T-shirts and blue denim pants standing and kneeling in the prison yard for a group photo. I can still hear the animated voices of little, brown youngsters in those rooms saying, "That's Papa when he was in Folsom. And that's Uncle Johnny when he was in Soledad. And that's our brother, Bobby, the guy in the middle, in the front row. He's in…"

From the largest racial group in the California prison system had been spawned the two biggest, most powerful, ruthless and dangerous prison gangs: the Mexican Mafia and the *Nuestra Familia*. The Mexican Mafia was based in Los Angeles and its members were known as *sureños* (southerners). *The Nuestra Familia* was San Jose based and its members were called *norteños* (northerners). The two gangs were bitter rivals and a huge problem for prison officials.

I had become aware of the *Nuestra Familia* not long after its inception mainly because of my former client, Hector Padilla's, role in the birth of the N.F.

Nuestra Familia, Our Family. In some ways there couldn't have been a more fitting name. Once you became a member, you were, according to the gang credo, part of the family for life. If you tried to leave the stated penalty was death. It was not unlike a paramilitary organization, from the mandatory daily exercises to following the commands of your superiors as handed down from on high. Failure to follow those orders could result in beatings, humiliation, and even death. The killing of errant members seemed exceptionally brutal. The gang ran your life inside the prison and, once you were paroled, outside the prison. But prison life in California was hell and the gang gave you protection and purpose. Black and white inmates were your natural enemies, and for reasons which to me defied all logic, so were the *sureños*. Once outside the prison walls, you were expected to follow orders and raise funds by whatever means necessary: robberies, burglaries, drug sales or by "taxing" other drug dealers, to make life easier for your fellow family members in and out of prison.

I had asked some of my former clients why they had joined the N.F. The answers went something like this. "When you drive up to the joint the first time, man, your paperwork's already waiting for you. And the clerks handling and looking at your paperwork in those offices up there in the joint are all cons. They run those offices. They've read all that shit about you that these people out here, the probation reports, the police reports, the D.A.'s two cents, have sent up there. So when you step inside that joint for the first time, them cons know more about you than your old lady does. They know where you're from, what you've done and where you been. And they've already told their friends inside. It's like everybody's expecting you in there. And sure as shit, somebody's gonna come up to you and say, 'What do you claim, *ese?*' They already know I'm from San Jo, so I can't go around saying I'm a *sureño*. And I sure as shit ain't gonna say, 'I don't claim nothing,' 'cause that just makes me fresh meat. I'm just crucifying myself that way. 'Cause I already know that if I say that, I'm gonna get punked, beaten, robbed and turned into a pussy. So of course I said, 'I claim San Jo, man. I'm a *norteño*.' And the dude says, 'Good, brother. Now let me tell you where it's at.' And that's it. That's all there is to it. I'm one of them. I'm one of the *Familia*."

Early on in my career, I had been introduced to the ravages of rapes on male inmates at the county jail. One of my clients and four of his cellmates raped a young, white boy in their dorm-like cell. They had threatened to kill him if he told, even though the boy didn't want anyone to know. But they had left him in such a condition that he was taken to the infirmary where the nurses soon saw what had happened. I watched some of the court proceedings in that case. It all left me with such a revulsion that it was difficult for me to get near my client for the duration of the case I was representing him in. I asked some of my other clients about it. "It happens all the time, man. It's part of the package. And this ain't nothing compared to what goes on in the joint. You better have some back-up when you get there, or you're going to have a steady diet of being punked." Once I overheard cops talking about a male victim of a robbery. "They beat him up pretty bad. We think they fucked him too. But that's not something any man wants to talk about." And soon, I became aware of the snide remarks some jail inmates would make about another inmate. "You know what he was when he was up in the joint, don't you? Look at him. Nothing but a fucking punk."

They were all reluctant to talk about it. But two 22-year-olds locked up in an 8x10 cell day and night for months and years — is it so improbable to find both a "punked" and a "punker"?

I had nightmares of being sent to "the joint" and I'd wake in a cold sweat. Often I would ask myself: If you were ever up there and someone asked you, "What do you claim?" I'd say "San Jo." No doubt about it. Then I too would be one of the family.

This was some of the mental baggage I was carrying when I made my way to Tom Kelley's office on that August afternoon. And I was also very much aware that the vast majority of prison inmates came from the lower economic class: poor Mexican-Americans, poor blacks, poor whites. Most of them were poorly educated and would have had a difficult time finding a place in mainstream America. For so many, alcohol, drugs and crime must have seemed like a better, easier alternative, at least in the beginning. Then they were in prison, their ultimate home, a home they would return to again and again.

I was aware too of the increasing number of youth gangs in the *barrio*; gangs made up of young, disenfranchised Chicano kids who did not, could not, and would never become part of mainstream American society, and therefore had created their own little societies which were not unlike the gangs that their fathers, brothers, uncles, cousins and friends belonged to in the California prisons. They called themselves The Northern Structure or *La Raza* gangs. For them, Juvenile Hall, the County Jail, and California's prisons were already just another part of life. And the public and the legislature were responding each year with bigger, harsher prison sentences which were dramatically increasing the prison population as well as swelling the size of its largest racial component and its two gangs. To adjust for this, there was a building boom of new prisons, billions of dollars spent on 21 new prisons, unlike anything California had ever seen. Not only were the sentences longer, but the recidivism rate for paroled convicts was nearing 70 %. What was clear to me on that June afternoon, and what I foolishly thought should be clear to everyone, was that the prison system itself was a big part of the problem. It was churning out new, hardened, life-long criminals almost as fast as fresh blood came in.

Tom was waiting for me. On his desk was a list of 21 names. "Know any of these guys?'

"No, not by those names."

"So you haven't represented any of them?"

"If those are their true names, then no, I haven't represented any of them."

"Well, these are the 21 they've indicted. Thirteen are facing the death penalty. It'll be the biggest death penalty case ever, anywhere."

"Where are they now?"

"In different prisons around the state."

"Where are they going to house them for this case?"

"In the county jail here. I'm told that the Department of Corrections is already renovating the third deck of the old jail."

"Twenty-one gang members and 13 facing the death penalty. That's going to take a lot of work and a long time."

"Two or three years, maybe longer, and more work than you've ever seen in any one case.... Still interested?"

"Yeah, but where are you going to get 21 lawyers, at least thirteen of whom are qualified to try a death penalty case?"

"I'll probably have to recruit some from adjoining counties, Alameda County mostly. So take your pick," pointing to the list. "You're the first attorney to come in. Take whichever one you want."

"What do you know about them?'

"What I've been told is that the gang is run by a table of three. The head of that group is Vicente Arroyo. He's the leader. His is the first name on the list. The second in command is a Pinky Hernandez. His name's the second on the list. The third is somebody they call Brown Bob. His name's not on the list."

"Are they going to file on him?"

"I don't think so."

"Why not?'

"Because they said they wouldn't be filing on anyone else."

"That might not be so good for him when some of his friends find out."

"That occurred to me too."

(In fact, Brown Bob was shot and killed two years later as he worked on his car in his garage at his home outside of San Jose by three unknown assailants.)

"And the other names?"

"Some of them are captains or sergeants, I don't really recall which. But most of them I guess you would just call soldiers.... Well, take your pick."

I wasn't quick to choose. A year or two before, I wouldn't have hesitated, I wouldn't have given it a second thought. I would have immediately chosen Arroyo, the leader of the gang. Ego of course. Then I would be recognized throughout the legal community and beyond as representing the key defendant in the most serious of criminal cases. There was my mantra too. If I called myself a criminal defense attorney, then I had to be willing to represent any criminal defendant no matter how heinous the charge might be. And at that moment, Vicente Arroyo stood to be the most heinous of the 21.

Tom said, "Take your time. Think about it. I'll be back in a minute."

Something had happened to me in that past year or two that I couldn't explain and was having more and more difficulty dealing with. Anxiety, a momentary, repeating fear that I would no longer be able to do what I had been doing for 26 years, had begun to plague me. I was in court almost every day of the week. When my client's case was called, I would stand and identify myself and tell the court what we intended to do at that juncture of the case. That normally took no more than a minute or two. But for some reason, I had begun fearing that I wouldn't be able to perform that minuscule task. So much so that I had begun writing down what I was going to say in those first, brief moments, and then covertly reading from those notes when the case was called. Once I got beyond that introductory stage, I had no problem dealing with whatever else had to be done. Only in those first minutes did the fear grip me. But more and more, I now found myself thinking, worrying that maybe the fear would soon extend beyond those first moments to such an extent that I would never be able to practice law again, at least not in a courtroom.

When Tom returned, I said, "I'm going to take Pinky Hernandez."

He looked at me surprised. "Really?"

"Yeah, this case is going to take a lot of time and work, and there'll be problems and hassles coming from every direction. So why saddle myself with the big dog? I just don't need it."

"Well, O.K., I guess I understand that."

"Yeah. Let me know when I can start getting some of the discovery and when the first court date is, will you?"

"Sure."

With that I turned and left.

I walked downstairs, walked half a block, then stopped, turned around and headed back. I was losing my self-respect. I was running away from the biggest challenge of my career as a criminal defense attorney. I walked upstairs and back into Tom's office. "I've changed my mind, Tom. I want to take Arroyo instead."

It wasn't long before I realized that the case had been in process for months. The District Attorney and the State Attorney General had elected to use the County Grand Jury to obtain an indictment. Those proceedings were secret and the court had ordered all witnesses as well as everyone present not to reveal anything that had gone on there. The prosecution had presented 150 witnesses over some six weeks. Their indictment was a foregone conclusion.

The Grand Jury issued an indictment accusing 21 members of the *Nuestra Familia* of a conspiracy to commit murder, extortion, intimidating witnesses, sales of drugs and other crimes. Thirteen were charged with murder and could face the death penalty. Nine were charged with multiple murders. On June 2,

1992, 18 of the suspects were arraigned in a secret early morning court session before Judge Kevin Murphy.

At that time, the County jail was administered by the Santa Clara County Department of Corrections, situated in two buildings: the old, three-story structure and a recently built eight-story building on what had been a parking lot directly in front of the old jail. The third deck of the old jail was then being renovated to house the N.F. defendants. Those renovations were not completed until late August, so that for the first several court appearances, the defendants were bused from San Quentin Prison 65 miles away where they were being temporarily held.

From the time I left Tom Kelly's office until I made my first appearance in court, the N.F. case was constantly on my mind. As much as anything, I wondered about Vicente Arroyo. Who was he? What was he like? I had known nothing of the leadership of the *Neustra Familia,* but I knew enough about the gang to think that whoever the leader was, he wouldn't be your run-of-the-mill inmate. He had to be a skilled survivor. Cunning, manipulative, street-wise, people-wise and intelligent enough to have survived his way to the top of a gang that had so little regard for human life. How would I deal with him? That question nagged at me. I had no answer. I would have to wait to see who he was.

A week later, Tom Kelly called. "Ron, the identification of counsel and further arraignment has been set for 4:00 Wednesday afternoon in Judge Murphy's courtroom. Judge Murphy has asked that the attorneys arrive early, no later than 3:45, because security will be extremely tight. Every attorney will have to go through the metal detector and will be pat searched before entering the courtroom. You should have a Bar card and driver's license with you for identification. There's going to be at least 18 defendants and 18 defense attorneys plus the prosecutors in the courtroom. Seating is going to be limited and assigned. My guess is that there'll be plenty of media and spectators. Everybody's going to be thoroughly searched and screened. The security's going to be unbelievably tight."

"Why?"

"Well, for one, the number of defendants and who they are. Then they're really concerned about outside gang intervention, either from the brothers in the N.F. or the Mexican Mafia, either to help or to hurt."

"So Murphy's got the case?"

"Yeah. These guys aren't going to catch any slack from Kevin. My guess is that he volunteered to take the case."

"Probably."

Kevin Murphy was then one of the toughest judges assigned to the Superior Court Criminal Division. When he handled the Violation of Probation Calendar, defense attorneys winced as they learned that one of their clients was going to be arraigned for violating his probation before Judge Murphy. Most felt that it would have been better had their clients been sent to prison initially by the first sentencing judge rather than being placed on probation, only to return for a second sentencing before Judge Murphy. Now their clients were going to prison, but probably for a much longer time than the original judge would have given them.

In June of 1992, I had been appearing in the Santa Clara County criminal courts for 26 years. Some of the attorneys I had practiced with and against were now judges. Kevin Murphy was one. He had been a Deputy District Attorney for several years before becoming a judge and I had appeared in court against him numerous times. He was rigid, tough, but fair and well-prepared. I believe there had been a mutual respect then and that there still was between us. His sentences could be as harsh as Judge James Wilson's, but there was a distinct difference in the way the two judges dealt with me. To Judge Wilson, I was an obstructionist, an irritable, naive, bleeding-heart liberal. To Judge Murphy, I was a competent, defense attorney doing the work that was expected of me by the judicial system. That is not to say that he gave me or any of my clients any favors, but he was always as courteous and accommodating as he could be. And I always felt that within his standard, he would be absolutely fair and follow the letter of the law. In some ways, I thought that he was as good a judge as Vicente Arroyo could have in that case.

The identification of counsel and further arraignment was to be held in the Superior Court located next to the jail. This court was part of a four-building complex that housed five Superior Court Departments, the main branch of the Municipal Court, and the main Jail. The five Superior Courts were located in the center T-shaped building, the four-story building on its right had the Municipal Courts, and the two buildings on its left were the County Jail. The courts were connected to the jail by underground tunnels. The parking garage across the street faced the entrance to the Superior Court.

That afternoon, I arrived at the garage just after 3:30. As I started to cross the street, I stopped and looked again at what I thought I had seen atop the roof of the Superior Court building. No, I wasn't mistaken. There were numerous Sheriff's deputies armed with automatic rifles standing every twenty feet apart on it. I stood there for several moments. In 26 years, I had never seen anything like it. As I started walking again, I stopped at the sight of armed deputies on the roof of the Municipal Court building too. I couldn't see the jail but I imagined there were armed deputies on those building as well. Tight security? Tom Kelley had not been exaggerating.

I crossed the street. There were armed deputies outside the courthouse and an increased number of deputies at the metal detector just inside the entrance. They were carefully scrutinizing everyone and everything. I knew most of them by sight, if not by name, but they were tight-lipped, somber, tense, and determined that everyone would follow the new screening instructions. Judge Murphy's courtroom was off to the left of the metal detector station, and that part of the building had been cordoned off to everyone except those somehow connected to the further arraignment. Outside the courtroom door, there were several more deputies posted, screening, once again, everyone that was about to enter the courtroom, asking our names, even though some of them knew us, and for identification and for the names of the defendants we were representing.

The courtroom itself was 100 feet deep, 40 feet wide, with a 15-foot ceiling. Two large doors admitted people in from the hallway onto a center aisle. On either side of that aisle were rows of seats capable of seating 80 people. A railing divided the courtroom. Along the railing inside the divide, were a few chairs for attorneys. Along the left wall was a jury box that began about 10 feet from the railing and ran some 20 feet toward the judge's dais at the front of the courtroom. The jury box had two rows, each with seven seats, in front of which had been placed seven chairs. Two eight-foot counsel tables were on either side of the courtroom facing the dais. Below the dais was the court clerk's desk. Judge Murphy always entered the courtroom from his chambers through the door in the wall behind the dais.

I had been in that courtroom hundreds of times but it had a very different look that afternoon. There were some 20 armed deputies in the courtroom beginning with one on each side of the two doors, and then another and another, about 10 feet apart along the back walls and side walls up to the railing. Inside the railing, there were more armed deputies on the opposite wall facing the jury box and one on either side of the judge's dais. They had to have been the biggest, burliest deputies in the Sheriff's Department.

At first, only the attorneys were being allowed into the courtroom. But when I entered, I saw several, casually dressed, plainclothes deputies sprinkled throughout the remaining spectator section. Most of the attorneys took seats in the first two rows behind the railing on the left side of the courtroom closest to the jury box where the defendants would be seated. For several minutes only the attorneys and the deputies were in the courtroom. Then slowly, others were ushered in and assigned seats. Some of those were media people, and some were strangers. When all the seats were filled, the doors were locked and we waited, I anxiously, for the entry of the defendants. They would have been brought over from the jail through an underground tunnel, up the stairs to the holding cell behind the steel door next to the judge's dais. We waited.

I had no idea what Vicente Arroyo looked like. I had not seen any photographs nor had I been given a description. But I thought short, dark, husky. Finally, at some predetermined signal, a deputy went to the steel door with a huge key in his hand and we heard the crunching of the iron lock, and the door opened.

They entered one by one, slowly, their leg irons clanging on the concrete landing, their hands in cuffs that were locked to waist chains. They wore blood-red jail garb signifying that they were dangerous. Despite the chains, they moved with a swagger and cocky, defiant, uplifted heads as they filled the jury box. Once they were seated, they looked out at the audience boldly, arrogantly. They were a surly, cocksure bunch, short, dark, muscular and mean-looking. I tried to pick out Arroyo but couldn't. As I watched them glare out at us, their looks reminded me of the looks I had seen in the eyes of big, caged animals, and I wondered how long it had been since they had been in public.

Then the court reporter and the court clerk came out and took their places under the dais, signaling that Judge Murphy would soon be out. I waited, tensing more and more by the moment. The door in the wall behind the dais opened and a black-robed figure that I assumed was Judge Murphy stepped out, turning his back to us to close the door as the bailiff said, "Please rise. The Superior Court of the County of Santa Clara is now in session, the Honorable John Garibaldi presiding." I was surprised and disappointed. I did not have the same regard for Judge Garibaldi that I had for Judge Murphy. But one of the other lawyers mumbled, "It's Murphy's case. Garibaldi's just filling in today. Murphy had something else to do."

A roll-call was taken, and it turned out that Arroyo was seated in the top row closest to the railing. He had been the first one out of the holding cell, either by court or security design, or because of deference paid to him as their leader by the other defendants. I could not have anticipated what I saw when he stood. He was five foot five at most, muscular, but not at all like the typical body builder of today. Rather, he was a thick, block of a man, from that broad chest whose width seemed to match half his height, to the bulging thighs that stretched what should have been loose-fitting jail pants. His head was immense: picture the heads one sees of men in political cartoons with small trunks and pencil-thin legs, except that Arroyo's head sat on an enormous trunk supported by elephantine legs. His face was brown, darkened even more by a big, black, bushy moustache that ran down either side of his upper lip, and thick, black eyebrows and a swab of coarse black hair. His nose was round, his nostrils wide, wide enough to sustain his big trunk. His eyes were black and deep-set with seemingly little movement, but missing nothing.

After a few introductory remarks by Judge Garibaldi, defense counsel began voicing their concerns and objections about their inability to communicate with their clients who were being held in San Quentin Prison 65 miles away. In multiple defendant cases it was inevitable that whenever one defense counsel raised a point, other defense counsel were sure to follow, seldom adding much more. It was ego, human nature, everyone had to be heard, no one wanted to be outdone. With 18 defense counsel and three prosecutors and all the media coverage, this case was going to be a nightmare. That is not so say that I had never been guilty of that same petty vice, but after 26 years, I was tired of it.

As defense counsel after defense counsel rose to reiterate how difficult it was for him to communicate with his client, it occurred to me that this would be a good time for me to tip-toe up to my client, and whispering, introduce myself. Carefully I made my way to his side. His head was turned to the Judge. I tapped his arm. He half-turned and I whispered, "Mr. Arroyo, my name is Ron Ruiz. I'm the attorney who's been appointed to represent you in this case and I..."

With little more than a glance at me, he held up an open, cuffed hand and said in something more than a whisper, "We can talk about this later," and turned back to Judge Garibaldi.

I stood there flushed and embarrassed and dismissed before all the attorneys, the media, the deputies and spectators in the room. After several moments I returned to my seat, crestfallen.

Now the defense attorneys were complaining about the volume of discovery we had yet to receive and the size of the grand jury transcript. I sat there only half listening, warm with embarrassment. There was actually very little for the defense attorneys to do that afternoon other than identify ourselves and who we represented for the record. After Judge Garibaldi had heard from everyone, he continued the case to August 26 for hearing, citing the 15-volume and 3500 page grand jury transcript and the defendants' housing at San Quentin as reasons.

I left the courthouse and parking garage as quickly as I could, wanting to avoid any questions or comments about my brief meeting with Arroyo. I felt humiliated: to have been dismissed like that in such a big case before all those people. When I reached my office, my secretary was gone and I sat sulking, not reading my messages or answering the phone. Finally, as I prepared to leave, I saw the copy of the indictment that had been given to me in court. As I started to read it, the gravity of the case overtook me. It said that the 22 counts of crimes alleged therein were the result of the *Nuestra Familias's* latest push to increase its San Jose "regiment" and fatten its treasury with drug profits. It then went on to set out the case against the defendants.

It alleged that increased gang criminal activity began in San Jose in April, 1990 when Louie "Dumptruck" Chavez, an unindicted co-conspirator, was paroled from Pelican Bay State Prison with a "hit list" of people the gang wanted killed, along with orders to revitalize the San Jose chapter and accumulate money in its "bank." Vicente "Chente" Arroyo and Joseph "Pinky" Hernandez, then members of the ruling "Mesa" had issued the orders. The indictment identified Ronald "Lucky" Shelton as the leader of the San Jose regiment, a man handpicked by the ruling Mesa. He assumed control during a summer 1990 meeting. Chavez became his second in command, but soon fell out of favor and was replaced by Bobby "Silent" Lopez.

The indictment also alleged that the gang ordered and carried out six killings in San Jose, as well as two botched killings. Tony "Little Weasel" Herrera, a 34-year-old laborer, was the first to die. He was shot eight times in the head and neck on November 20, 1990. The gang apparently suspected Herrera of leading the police to a prospective member who had been arrested on drug charges the previous day. A week after Herrera's death, gang leaders at Pelican Bay received a coded message saying, "Little Weasel is peddling daisies."

Drug dealer and aspiring boxer, Larry Valles, 28, died next. On April 15, 1991, Shelton and Lopez allegedly shot him in the head, neck and chest when he refused to pay them 25 percent of his drug profits. On June 26, 1991, Elias Rosas was chased by three men and stabbed to death for disrespecting the *Nuestra Familia*. On July 28, 1991, for reasons that remained unclear, Herminio "Spankio" Serna and his cousin, Martin Serna, shot Marcos Baca in the head at an elementary school.

On August 28, 1991, Lopez's girlfriend, 21-year-old Sheila Apodaca, was shot after she threatened to implicate Lopez in two past murders unless "he treated her in a manner she thought was appropriate." A day later, Ray "Chocolate" Perez, suspected of using heroin and having a romantic affair with Shelton's girlfriend, was shot to death.

The indictment also alleged that on May 23, 1991, Leo Cano slashed fellow Santa Clara County jail inmate, Gabriel Coronado's throat with a razor. Coronado, an admitted member of the rival Fresno based F-14 gang, survived. On September 22, Robert "Fat Cow" Jasso was shot several times in the head at a bar where he worked as a bouncer. He survived, putting a lie to the coded message to Pelican Bay that "The Fat Cow is out to pasture."

When I finished reading the multi-paged indictment, my humiliation and sulking had disappeared.

Late the following afternoon, Tom Kelley called again. "I've got the 15 volumes of the grand jury transcript and some discovery here for you, Ron. There's quite a bit here for all the lawyers, so I'd like you to come over for it as soon as you can. You better bring your car. There're five boxes here for you."

Under the case law, the prosecution was required to turn over to defense counsel prior to trial, any and all evidence it had in its possession that could either incriminate or exonerate a defendant.

When I arrived at Tom's office, he led me to a room in which there were stacked what must have been at least 90 banker boxes filled with paper.

"Whoa," I said when I saw the boxes.

"Two of the boxes in that stack are your copies of the grand jury transcript. Three of the boxes in that other stack are part of your discovery."

"Part of it?"

"Yeah, and I'm told that there's a lot more to come."

"What's in that discovery?'

"Copies of letters, that's all. For years now, the prison authorities have been opening and copying all incoming and outgoing mail for the suspected NF gang members."

"Why so much?"

"Well, through these letters they're hoping to show extensive gang participation and prove all their conspiracy and substantive charges."

"They need three banker boxes full of letters?"

"They tell me there's more to come."

"Where are the police reports, the offense reports?"

"They're coming."

Each banker box was heavy enough to require me to make five trips to my car. I had planned to review the offense reports as quickly and thoroughly as I could and then drive up to San Quentin and see Arroyo for as many discussions as I could before the next court date. That was going to have to wait.

A few days later, Tom called again. "I've got more discovery for you. Bring your car. It's five more boxes."

In his office I asked, "What are these about?"

"More letters and…"

"More letters!"

"Yes. And some investigative reports."

"The offense reports?"

"No, the prisons have been investigating these guys for years while they've been in custody. These are some of those reports."

"Some?"

"They say there's more to come."

"What about the offense reports?"

"There's quite a bit of those. Six homicides and 16 other felonies. Not to mention the underlying prison priors that they'll use to get the death penalty. More homicides are involved in those prison priors, and there are offense reports tied to those as well. It's going to be a mountain of work."

The ten boxes were an eye-sore in my already cramped office, taking up a good portion of one wall. And there were more to come. Every time they caught my eye, I would ask myself, How many more? Sometimes I would answer, Too many more. I had once had a case that brought with it 13 banker boxes. That case had made me limit the number of new clients I was taking as well as requiring me to work 70 and more hours a week. I already had ten banker boxes of discovery and we were just beginning. And it was probably going to take at least three years to try this case through a jury trial. Was I exaggerating? No, Tom had said that some of the other defense counsel had already asked for a second court-appointed attorney to help them, and the court had granted their request. But I didn't want a co-counsel. What then? Should I stop taking new clients? And what would I do with the clients I already had?

Three days later, Tom had four more banker boxes for me. More letters and now "rap" sheets and prison file records on each of the defendants, but still no offense reports.

"Tom, I'm in a quandary. I'm not even half way through the grand jury transcripts and I'm having a hell of a time making any sense out of that first box of letters. It seems like I'm working day and night, what with my present cases and court commitments, and trying to make time to go through these boxes. I find myself reluctant to take on new clients. And these boxes keep coming, and Arroyo's facing a death penalty. What do you think?"

"I think there's going to be a lot more boxes coming."

"How many more?"

"I don't know. Maybe four or five times more."

"I'm a sole practitioner. What do I do? Close my office?"

"You may have to."

I had closed my office when I had gone to Sacramento to work for the ALRB. That was not something I was ready to repeat. The closing process was an ordeal in itself: dealing with the clients and the prospective lawyers that would replace me, refunding fees, some that I had already earned and some that I had already spent, negotiating with the other lawyers for a fair fee, taking into account the work I had already done and what there was left to be done. Then, when the case was over, as my term in Sacramento had been, I would have to reopen my practice again, start from scratch as I incurred once again all the costs of opening a new office. Once the office was closed, where would I work? In Sacramento, I had gone to a stately, ready-made office. If I closed my office, my only income would be what the court would pay me. To make ends meet, I would have to work at home. But where in our home? This case could easily take up two rooms and be a disruption for everyone. No, I wasn't ready to close my office.

But a week later I had ten more banker boxes and decided to close my office. I was stretching myself so thin that I wasn't much use to anyone. The latest boxes had some of the offense reports but the volume of paper was so great that I still didn't have a sense of the case itself, or any defense; and three weeks had passed since the last court date and I had yet to see Arroyo. And Tom had said there were more boxes coming. Once I made that decision, I began making arrangements to transfer my cases, and to meet with my clients and other lawyers. But I had to see Arroyo.

Two days later, I drove to San Quentin Prison. The prison is located just across the Golden Gate Bridge and sits on the edge of San Francisco Bay below San Rafael. It was opened in 1852 and is the oldest of California's prisons. Ironically, it can provide its inmates with some of the best views of San Francisco and the surrounding bay. I arrived at the prison before 9:00a.m., and once I worked my way through the line of people at the identification hut, I passed through the prison gates about 9:30. I was directed to a two-story, brick building weathered by many years of fog, wind, sun, rain and salt air. Inside, I was ushered into a waiting room outside a channel of visiting cubicles. I took a seat and waited, knowing there would be a wait, and knowing too that when visiting a prison inmate, the more insistent an attorney became about the visit, the more deliberate the guards became and the longer the wait.

I had brought along some reading material but was too tense to read. Before coming, I had decided two things. First, to limit the discussion to the allegations in the grand jury indictment, a copy of which Arroyo had, and not to venture into any of the discovery materials in the banker boxes and the grand jury transcript. Secondly, I would not allow myself to be humiliated by him again as I had been in court. But the longer I waited, the more determined and tense I became. I finally reached a point where I promised myself that if he humiliated me again, I would withdraw from the case.

Near 11:00, a guard walked down the corridor and stood next to one in a series of doors to the cubicles and said, "Mr. Ruiz, your client is ready to see you." My heart raced and I tensed all the more. I went to the door and he unlocked and opened it. Once I entered, he closed and locked it again. It took some moments for my eyes to adjust to the lighting in the 4'x6' space, but once I took my seat next to the glass on the back wall, I saw him. That immense head, that bush of a moustache and those black eyes that seemed only to stare. There was a telephone receiver hanging on a wall. I picked it up and held it up, and he picked his up as well. Then I spoke into it.

"Mr. Arroyo, I'm Ron Ruiz and I've been…"

"I know who you are," direct, gruff.

I clenched my teeth. It was not going to happen again. "You're facing the death penalty, Mr. Arroyo. We better start talking about your case."

"What's there to talk about!" loud, angry. "I don't know a damn thing about this case! I've been locked up in Pelican Bay, in the SHU. You know what the SHU in Pelican Bay is like? I've been up there for three years. Ever since they built that shit hole place. I've been in solitary confinement for three years. I've seen nobody, no one. You know what that place is like? When I got there from Corcoran, they told me that it had been built especially for people like me and that I was going to rot there."

He paused, looked down, as if in disgust. As I watched him, I saw and felt a strength in him that I had not seen in anyone before. His anger I had not expected, but somehow I didn't feel it was directed at me.

He looked back at me and began again, calmer, steadier, yet forcefully because, as I was to learn, as often as not, there was an intensity in his words even when he was speaking softly. "Look, about a month ago, they woke me up in the middle of the night and put me in one of their little planes. It was the first time I had been out of the SHU in three years. Then they flew me down here. I kept asking them where they were taking me and why. All they kept saying was, 'Shut the fuck up, Arroyo, you'll know soon enough where you're going.'

"Once I'm here, they put me in the hole. When I ask them what's going on, they don't answer. A couple of days later, they put me on a bus with a bunch of other guys. Everybody's chained up. The only guys I know on that bus are Pinky Hernandez and *Huevo*, the bald-headed guy. The rest of them I've never seen before, never laid my eyes on them or talked to them, nothing. Pinky I know real good. We go back a long ways. We were road dogs on the streets and cellies at Corcoran. So on the way down to San Jose, I ask Pinky what's going on. And he tells me, 'I don't know, Chente, except some of these guys are saying this gots something to do with some murders in San Jo.' When we get down to San Jose, there's cops and armed guards everywhere. Cop cars following us and in front of us. Cops up on the roofs. They take us into court and there's more cops in there than most towns have on their police force. Then that judge starts talking about the death penalty and I just go, Oh! That's all I know. You tell me."

I searched for a beginning. "Mr. Arroyo, I..."

"Please. My name's Vicente Arroyo, but everybody calls me Chente. So just call me Chente, O.K.?"

We sat in silence for a while, he looking at me and I looking at him. His look was neither hostile nor threatening, but it was unwavering. It was a look he would always have, as if he were studying you, waiting for you to weaken, or perhaps inevitably betray him. It was unsettling too, but I tried hard not to show it. To break that look I said, "I think we should talk about the indictment. They gave you a copy the first time you were in court, didn't they?"

"Yes, they did."

"And you've read it?"

"Many times."

"You're saying you don't know anyone listed in that indictment except for Pinky and Huevo?"

"That's right."

"You don't know Louie 'Dumptruck' Chavez?"

"No, I've never met him. I don't know him and I've never talked to him."

"Did you ever give him or have sent to him a 'hit list' of people you wanted killed in San Jose?"

"No, that's ridiculous."

"You never issued any orders about people you wanted killed in San Jose?"

"No, never."

"Do you know a Ronald 'Lucky' Shelton?"

"I know who he is now. But I didn't know who he was until we were on that bus heading to San Jose for court the first time."

"Did you hand-pick him to lead the San Jose regiment?"

"Come on. How can I pick somebody I don't even know to do anything?"

"How about Bobby 'Silent' Lopez, do you know him?"

"Same thing. I know him now but I didn't know him until they put me on that bus going to San Jose the first time."

"That was June of this year?"

"Yes."

"Never had any communication, letters, wires, anything before that day with either him or Shelton?"

"That's right. Never."

"Tony 'Little Weasel' Hererra. Did you know him?"

"No. I've never known him or known anything about him until I saw his name on that indictment."

"Did you order him killed?"

"How could I or anyone order someone killed that they didn't even know existed?"

"And Larry Valles, the boxer who was shot and killed by Lopez and Shelton, did you know him or anything about him?"

"No, not until I read his name in the indictment."

"Did you order him killed?"

"Please," as if insulted.

"Elias Rosas, the man who was stabbed to death by three men for disrespecting the *Nuestra Familia,* did you know him or anything about him before you read his name in the indictment?"

"No, and I didn't order anybody to kill him."

"And the three men that did the killing?

"I don't know who they're talking about."

"The cousins, Martin and Herminio 'Spankio' Serna. You know them?"

"Martin Serna I've never known. Spankio I know now because I met him on that bus to San Jose."

"Ever have any kind of communication with either one of them?"

"No."

"What about Marcos Baca, the guy they shot in the head at that elementary school, did you know him or anything about him?"

"No, and I didn't order anybody to kill him.

"And Sheila Apodaca, Lopez's girlfriend, did you know her?"

He didn't answer for several moments. Instead, he looked back at me with a wry, closed smile. "Look, if I don't know Lopez, how am I going to know who his girlfriend is? And why would I order someone killed that I didn't even know existed?"

Now it was I who stared back at him, confused, non-believing. His answers and questions to the indictment had me baffled. I didn't, couldn't answer for several moments. But those big, dark eyes set in that immense head, were watching. "Did you know Ray 'Chocolate' Perez, the guy that was shot and killed because he was suspected of having an affair with Shelton's girlfriend?"

The wry smile appeared again and he shook his head several times before saying, "No, and how would I know that that man was fooling around with the girlfriend of the man I don't even know?"

I stopped. I avoided his eyes but I could hear his breathing through the receiver, heavy, strong. I had to sort through my thoughts.

"You say that you didn't know Shelton or Lopez until you got on that bus in San Quentin. But did you ever receive any letters from them while you were at Pelican Bay?"

"No."

"Did you ever write to them?"

"No, never."

"Did you receive any mail while you were in the SHU?'

"Yeah, mail from my sister and my daughter."

"Any mail from other prison inmates?"

"Yes."

"Did you answer them?"

"Yes."

"Did you send out or receive any coded messages in your mail?"

"No. I'd have to be a fool not to guess that every letter I got and every letter I sent out was being read by the prison people. They could tell you a lot more about codes than I could. They were watching my every move. Do you really think I'd jeopardize myself or anyone out there by trying to get a 'hit list' past them through some secret code? How am I going to know anything about a secret code after being locked up all by myself for three years? Another thing, how many letters that were sent to me, never got to me? Or how many letters that I sent out never went out? They could censor and stop any mail they wanted to. Who would be the wiser?"

I paused again. His had been as complete and convincing, and frightening too, a denial as I had ever heard, and in a death penalty case no less. I'm not sure what I had expected to get from Arroyo on that first interview, but certainly not what he had said. The pressure to answer mounted, as did the fear that I was appearing unsure of myself. I knew what I had to ask, but was reluctant to ask it. Finally, I blurted out, "Are you the head of the *Nuestra Familia?*"

His look wrinkled. I thought I saw anger. "What's that got to do with anything?"

"It's got everything to do with everything."

"Like what?"

"If everything you've told me is true, and I'm not saying it isn't, then the only reason you're looking at a death penalty is because you're the head of the NF. Given that, we have to talk about it."

He looked away for a moment and thought. When he looked back at me, he said, "Yeah, I'm the head of the *Nuestra Familia*." At that moment, I felt I had become his lawyer.

"The indictment says there's a ruling Mesa. Is that true?"

"Yeah."

"Who's on the Mesa?"

"Me, Pinky and Brown Bob."

"Where's Brown Bob?

"I don't know."

"Is he going to be indicted?"

"I don't know."

"What role, if any, has he played in this indictment?"

"I don't know."

"You said you're the head, but you've also said that there's a ruling Mesa. How does that work?"

"We try to have everything come before all three of us and we discuss it. But no matter what, mine is the last say."

"Do you have any disagreement with me when I say that if everything you've told me is true, then the only reason you're in this death penalty case is because you're the head of the N.F.?"

"No, I think that's the way it is. But do *you* understand," looking at me as if he were looking through me, "that I had nothing to do with any of this? I've been locked up in the SHU for years and I don't know any of these guys, except for Pinky and *Huevo*, and I had nothing to do with whatever those other guys did out there on the streets. And I'm not pleading guilty to any of this. I've been around for a long time and I've seen plea bargain after plea bargain. I know what the DA's gonna come out with. 'If he cops out to some other beefs and doesn't go to a jury trial, then I'll drop the death penalty and all he'll get is a life sentence. But if he doesn't cop out, he's gonna get convicted and he's gonna get the death penalty.' I don't want to hear any of that. I didn't do anything and I'm not gonna plead guilty to anything. I want a jury trial."

I looked at him evenly and said, "I understand." There was nothing more to say. He had said it all.

The drive back to San Jose seemed to pass in a minute. I wasn't aware of the traffic, the roads, the highway, the city, the suburbs. I was consumed with replaying, dissecting, and attempting to refute, yet finding it difficult, if not impossible, to refute some of the things that Arroyo had said. For years almost all I had heard during first interviews with my clients were claims and entreaties of innocence. I soon learned only too well that once I had reviewed all of the prosecution's evidence, those assertions would crumble like sand castles. But Arroyo had raised for me some substantial questions and doubts about the truth of the charges.

First, aside from Pinky Hernandez and *Huevo*, did he in fact know any of the perpetrators or victims in the indictment given his imprisonment in Pelican Bay's SHU unit? I couldn't answer or dismiss that question until I knew more about the SHU unit and had a solid grasp of that mountain of material in the banker boxes.

Second, the "hit list" story and sequence made little sense. Louie "Dumptruck" Chavez leaves Pelican Bay in April of 1990 armed with a "hit list" of the people that the ruling Mesa wants killed in San Jose. Seven months later, on November 20, 1990, Tony "Little Weasel" Hererra was shot and killed because he was suspected of leading the police to a prospective N.F. member the day before, and apparently not because he was on a "hit list." How was the ruling Mesa to know seven months beforehand that Herrera would lead the police to a prospective N.F. member? Then, a year after "Dumptruck" Chavez left Pelican Bay with the Mesa's "hit list," Larry Valles is shot and killed by Shelton and Lopez because he refused to give them 25% of his drug profits. How could the Mesa have anticipated Valles' refusal and put him on the "hit list" the year before? On June 26, 1991 Elias Rosas was stabbed to death for disrespecting the N.F. Again, how could the Mesa have foretold that disrespect 14 months beforehand and put Rosas' name on a "hit list"? Then there was Marcos Baca, who on July 28, 1991, was shot and killed by Martin and Hermino Serna in an elementary school yard "for reasons that remain unclear." "Hit list"? On August 28, 1991, Sheila Apodaca, Lopez's girlfriend, was shot and killed after she threatened to implicate Lopez in past murders. How could the Mesa, some 16 months beforehand, have come up with the name and future conduct of Sheila Apodaca that would have warranted putting her on a "hit list"? Likewise, Ray

"Chocolate" Perez, who was murdered a day later for being suspected of having an affair with Shelton's girlfriend?

But anytime I felt a glimmer of hope rising from what Arroyo had said, reality came crushing down on them. The jury was not going to like Arroyo. They were going to abhor the *Neustra Familia,* and Arroyo was its leader. There would be those who, no matter what the evidence showed, would want to convict him and give him the death penalty simply because of who he was. Add to that the fact that during the trial they would more than likely learn about his two prior homicide convictions. What more would they need? Then too, he was obviously the oldest of this motley crew, much older than many of his very young-looking followers. I could just see myself arguing, pleading to that jury again and again that it didn't matter who Arroyo was or what he had done in past, the evidence was not sufficient to convict him. And I could see their cold-faced reactions. But Arroyo had already made it quite clear: he was not pleading guilty to anything and we were going to a jury trial. The question and fear that reverberated in my mind was, would I end up being a lawyer whose client, though innocent of the charges, received the death penalty?

When I returned to my office late that afternoon, it was in chaos. The attorney who had appeared in court for me that day on previously scheduled matters had badly mismanaged two cases. The judge in one of the cases had ordered that I appear in his court the next morning with an explanation. My client in the other case had made several calls from the jail demanding that I see him that day. I had written to several clients telling them that I would be withdrawing from their cases and that I would be referring them to new attorneys. The letters must have arrived that morning because I had received several calls from clients, family members and friends wanting an immediate appointment and explanation. A few were nasty, referring to the money they had paid me, demanding a full refund and even threatening to report me to the State Bar. Finally, there was a message from Tom Kelley telling me that he had more boxes for me. I looked over at the 24 boxes that were already stacked in my office and wondered how many more I could accommodate and still maintain the semblance of an office. Worse, I hadn't even opened the vast majority of those boxes, nor had I gotten any sense of the case from the boxes that I had opened. By the end of the day, one thing was absolutely clear: I had to close my office as soon as possible.

I spent the next week and a half making my scheduled court appearances and transferring my clients and their cases to other attorneys. Then came the matter of arranging for a new work site. To afford myself the best working conditions for everyone concerned, I had decided to build a makeshift structure on the Branciforte property big enough to contain all the expected boxes and my necessary office equipment, and far enough away from the house to keep distractions at a minimum. Once I had that project underway, I could finally turn to the discovery, which now numbered 33 boxes, full time. Time was of the essence because there was a little more than two weeks left before the next court appearance.

As I began, it occurred to me that I had to learn as much as I could about the SHU unit at Pelican Bay because Arroyo's housing there, his isolation there, was crucial to any defense he had. I had read and heard about the SHU unit. It had been billed as the state-of-the-art maximum security prison unit in the country. Prison officials from all over the nation were visiting it. But that was all I knew. I soon learned that Pelican Bay was a recently constructed prison, having been opened in 1989, eleven miles from the Oregon border in a forested area. It was designed to house what prison officials considered the most dangerous inmates in the California prison system. The prison was divided into two parts, the larger part housing "general population" inmates, like most other prisons. The smaller part of the prison was where the Security Housing Unit (SHU) was located. It was a prison within a prison, in that while it was situated inside the prison walls, it was set off from the other part of the prison by electrified fencing. The SHU was made up of several round, mound-like buildings with electronic guard controls located at the center of each mound. The inmates were housed in single cells located in compact wings that spanned out from the control centers. Each inmate was in his cell 23 hours a day and alone at all times. His food was brought to his cell. For one hour a day, he was allowed out of his cell into a small adjoining exercise yard, again alone. Every movement of every inmate in every cell could be viewed on screens in the control rooms at all times, day or night.

At first that information gave me hope, made me jubilant, because there was nothing there to contradict Arroyo's claim that he knew none of the participating perpetrators of the six murders and had not, and could not, have composed the alleged "hit list." But then it brought me despair and fear. The jury was going to despise him. They would find a way to convict him no matter what the evidence was. A twice-convicted murderer and leader of the most murderous gang in California was not going to be set free. Why had I taken on this case? Was I up to the task? A look at the 25 unopened boxes frightened me. And Tom's secretary had called again with more boxes.

Each new set of boxes added to an increasing tension and fear within me. The boxes were not labeled. There were no identifying marks on them. Each box had two neat stacks of paper that completely filled the box. Sorting through each box simply to organize it and somehow make a determination as to its relevancy to the case as well as to the other opened and unopened boxes was taking hours. But sorting was by no means a substitute for the actual reading that had to take place. Many days I felt as if I had made no progress whatsoever. And then every two or three days there were problems with the structure that was being built at my home which required me to drive out there and stay there for a while or begin the day there. When the afternoon of my second court appearance in Vicente Arroyo's case arrived, I was a mess, unsure of myself, the case and Arroyo.

Exiting the parking garage, what I saw across the street was more daunting than what I had seen two weeks before. There were more armed guards everywhere: on the roof tops, alongside the buildings, in front of the buildings. I swallowed. I wanted to get in and out of that courthouse as quickly as I could. Inside the building, the security was much greater: more guards, more pat-searching, more questioning. When I stepped into the courtroom and saw the greater number of guards along the walls, and near the dais, and the increased number of plain-clothes deputies in the spectator section, I felt sick. It was anything but a courtroom, and I kept reminding myself, reassuring myself that I would be out of there in a few minutes. All I would have to do was identify myself and my client and ask for a long continuance based on the volume of discovery and the difficulty of meeting regularly with my client while he was housed at San Quentin. To insure a smooth beginning when I stood to speak, I had written my name and Arroyo's name on the palm of my hand. The other attorneys were going to make the same request. There would be nothing else to say or do and we would be out of there shortly.

I was among the first attorneys admitted into the courtroom. Slowly the others entered. Then the media began filing in, then the familiar and unfamiliar spectators. That process took more time than it should have, and the defendants had yet to be brought in. As the courtroom filled, it became stuffy and overly warm. We sat there for long, unexplained minutes. Where were the defendants? Why weren't they bringing them in? Seconds seemed like minutes. Finally, the holding cell door was unlocked and the defendants entered. Arroyo took his seat and this time turned and nodded to me and I to him.

I expected Judge Murphy to come out at any moment. That didn't happen. After several minutes the court reporter entered from the judge's door with her machine in one hand and its stand in the other and sat on a lone chair near the clerk's desk. I was now taking long, slow, deep breaths, which wasn't expediting anything. Where was the clerk? Where in the hell was the clerk? Judge Murphy wouldn't come out until she did. What the hell was taking her so long? Then she appeared, prim and proper, but only after I had undergone a long spell of despising her. Still no Judge Murphy. Now the courtroom was hot and the air thick, and I was inhaling large blotches of air, holding them and exhaling very slowly, thinking that made it easier to breathe. When I began doubting that I could keep up that breathing pattern much longer, Judge Murphy took the bench and I stopped that exaggeration, telling myself that it would just be a few minutes before I was out of there. But he announced that he would take up preliminary matters first. Did counsel have anything that they wanted to discuss with the court? A bevy of defense attorneys stood, especially the Oakland lawyers, with complaints, questions and suggestions about the difficulty of obtaining the discovery and of communicating with their clients and the District Attorney.

They all had to be heard, especially since the courtroom was filled with media. On and on they went. Harder and harder it was becoming for me to breathe. And then, all of a sudden, I felt a sharp terrifying pain, unlike any I had ever felt before or since, at the top of my stomach just under my heart. I couldn't breathe. The pain paralyzed me. I was certain that I was having a heart attack, that I was dying. I had to get out of there. I had to get some air. Somehow I managed to rise and make my way to the aisle, doing all I could to hide my pain and fear. At the courtroom doors, I said to the guards, "I have to go to the bathroom. Please let me out."

"I'm sorry, sir, but the Judge has ordered that no one is to leave or enter the courtroom once the doors are locked until the court session is over."

"But I really have to go. Please. Believe me."

"Those are the Judge's orders, sir. You'd better take your seat again."

I knew I was going to die. The pain was excruciating. Still, I managed to get back to my seat, and then sat with my eyes closed, trying not to breathe, convinced that when I did, the pain increased. Finally Judge Murphy started calling the cases. By the time he called Arroyo's name, enough attorneys had appeared and requested a lengthy continuance that I simply stood and said, without looking down at the palm of my hand, "Ronald Ruiz appearing with and for the defendant Arroyo. We join in the previous requests for a continuance."

Then I sat and the pain seemed to subside, but there was still an ache in the hollow where it had been, and whenever I made a sudden movement, I was jolted with a reminder of that pain. But the pain was subsiding and gone by the time the court session was over, and when I reached the hallway, I could breathe easily again. I left the courthouse as quickly as I could, avoiding contact with anyone connected with the case. Once in the garage, I sat in my car shaken, as much as for what had just happened as for what was to come. One thing was certain; I couldn't breathe a word of this to anyone.

I couldn't return to my office. I didn't want my secretary to see the condition I was in. Every time I looked in the rear view mirror, there was strain and fear, and an ache remained where the pain had been. I drove to a nearby out-of-the-way park. There I sat in my car trying to fathom what had happened, fearing that my career as a lawyer had just ended. How could I ever set foot in a courtroom again? Had I just lost my livelihood? My daughter Phe had been diagnosed with a serious mental illness and Anna, my youngest, was just four. I had a big mortgage and a boatload of living expenses. After five, I drove to my office and sat at my desk in a stupor.

It was after 7:00 when I arrived home. When asked about the case, I said that nothing had happened other than that the case was continued for another two months. After dinner I said that I had work to do and sat at a desk with papers strewn all around me, waiting for her to go to bed. When she did I called Doctor Harvey Dondershine. He had helped me with Phe and I had consulted with him on several of my cases. He worked in his home late at night and it was not unusual for me to call him then.

"Harvey."

"Yes, Ron," in his soft, calm voice.

"I've got a problem."

"What kind of case is it?"

"No, this time it's me."

"Tell me."

I began awkwardly, hesitantly. When I'd pause, he'd say, "Go on," in his quiet voice. "Go on," he repeated several times until it all came pouring out. When I finished he said, "What you've described is a panic attack. You were having a panic attack."

"A panic attack? Harvey, it was more like a heart attack. The pain was right under my heart. It had nothing to do with my mind. I've never felt such physical pain. I couldn't breathe. I thought I was going to die. It took everything I had to stop from doubling over with pain."

"Those symptoms aren't unusual when a person is suffering from a panic attack."

"What's a panic attack?"

"It's a swelling of anxieties that build and build until they finally erupt, causing the kinds of physical ailments you're describing. It passes as soon as you leave the situation that brought it on. You seem perfectly fine now. Concerned, yes, but fine. From what you said there was pretty much a complete change in your condition once you left the courtroom."

"But Harvey, I need to keep practicing law. I'm only 56. How am I ever going to be able to go back into a courtroom, and especially that courtroom, and that case?"

"I think you'll be able to return to courtrooms. But let me refer you to a psychiatrist who routinely handles these types of cases."

"Harvey, you know what I think of psychotherapy. I really don't want to spend years with some psychiatrist wondering, as I sit there, who's the other psychiatrist that's dealing with *this* psychiatrist's problems."

"This man doesn't specialize in psychotherapy. He's the head of the Psychopharmacology Department at Stanford."

Two days later I was at Stanford. This doctor was a big, affable man in his late forties. I gave him a detailed account of what had happened. He listened carefully and then said, "I agree with Dr. Dondershine. You had a panic attack. I'm going to prescribe Xanax, and if you take it as prescribed, I believe that will take care of your problem."

I was dumbfounded: that simple, that minor? But my first words were, "And how many times am I going to see you from now on?"

"Not many. I'll see you again in two or three weeks to see how the medication is working, and then again in a month or so after that. That should be all, unless you feel you need to see me again."

His casual, off-handed approach had me baffled. I had experienced one of the most traumatic afternoons of my life and he was dealing with it as if it were an everyday occurrence. "How many of those pills do I have to take?"

"One, twice a day. And since you say you're in court most every day, I think you should take one in the morning before you go to court, and in the afternoon before you return to court."

Which I did for the following five years, taking a pill at the nearest water cooler a few minutes before the courtroom doors opened in the morning and again in the afternoon. Almost from the first day, I could feel the change. I slept better. I was calmer. A noticeable number of my daily fears and worries disappeared. I stopped making my secret notes before going to court. There was absolutely no reason why I couldn't expect to be able to identify myself and my client and the status of our case. Instead of fearing and dreading Arroyo's next court date, I welcomed its coming. I wished it would come sooner. I was ready for it.

But I often wondered what would have happened if those pills had been found on me at the metal detector. Most law enforcement officers had little respect for defense attorneys. They would have reveled in exposing me. And what would the court and the State Bar and my clients have thought of a defense attorney going into court under the influence of a prescription drug? Thankfully, it never came to that.

"The shed," as I called it, was an inexpensive but comfortable 8'x16' workspace structure that I had built on the Branciforte property. I chose a level spot on a hillside tucked away from the house. The structure itself was on cinder blocks. The outer walls were plywood, the inner walls fiberboard with plenty of fiberglass insulation in between. A 6'x6' window centered the front wall, under which I set my desk. The window faced the morning sun, a meadow, the green of a creekside below and a forested ridge above, beyond which was the Pacific Ocean. One side wall had a 4'x4' window that faced Loma Prieta, the highest peak in the Santa Cruz Mountains. One entered through a glass-framed door on the other side wall. Even on the darkest days, there was plenty of natural light. Stacked along the solid back wall would ultimately be 132 banker boxes of discovery. An electrical line had been run from the house and a single base board heater provided all the heat that was ever needed. I was to spend the next three years and nine months working there.

About the time "the shed" was completed, Chente and his codefendants were moved from San Quentin prison to San Jose and a specially renovated section of the old county jail on the third floor. He had been there a few days when I first visited him. The visit took place, as all of our visits would over the ensuing years, in one of three well-secured, 3'x6' cubicles with a chair on each side of a common wall. The upper portion of that wall was a thick, steel mesh through which we spoke. Chente seemed relaxed, upbeat and pleased to see me, which surprised me.

"What's up, Chente?"

"Oh, you know, just getting used to things here," but in a soft, pleasant voice.

"How is it back there?"

"Great. It's great, really."

"How so?'

"I haven't had it so good since I was in that federal joint 25 years ago."

"Really?"

"Yeah. They have us all back there in single cells, right next to each other and only behind bars. We can talk to each other all day and all night if we want. Everybody's allowed his own reading material and we can pass it around if we want. We can share our food. If somebody doesn't like something, he can pass it on to some other guy. We even have a TV, which for me isn't necessarily a good thing. The news and sports are fine but these fools be looking at that thing all day and all night. And most of that stuff isn't worth watching. Sometimes I make them turn it off. I can't concentrate, I can't read, I can't do my dictionary. But for me and where I've been, it doesn't get any better than this."

"It can't be that good."

"But you have no idea what Pelican Bay was like, and Corcoran before that was no picnic either."

"What was Pelican Bay like?"

"It was hell. Pure hell. It took some evil genius to think it up. It was all about breaking you. But they were very, very clever in the way they tried to do it. They had to be, because a lot of those guys in there had lawyers. I didn't have one, but a lot of them were still fighting their cases on appeal. And those lawyers would go into federal courts, not the state courts in those little out of the way towns where they've put all their prisons. No, those state courts won't do a damn thing for prisoners. Hell, they're part of the package too. They're not going to go against the prisons. Those are the main source of their town's money. So some of those lawyers took their clients' problems and some of the conditions we had in the SHU to federal courts where the judges have a lifetime job and don't have any ties with those small towns.

"But like I said, at the SHU in Pelican Bay, everything's set up to break you. They put you in pods up there. Those pods are little wings of 8'x10' single cells that jut out from a control center. Those cells have cameras that can see everything you do, day or night. Those pods are clean, spotless both inside and outside the cells. I never been in a cleaner place. But there aren't any windows, not one. So they have lights on all the time, everywhere. Good lights, strong lights. They never go off. So you never know if its day or night. And they keep the temperature in those pods at 70, always 70. Winter or summer, day or night, it's always 70. So you never know if it's winter or summer. You're always living in the same place with the same temperature and the same light. It's weird. You lose your sense of time. It messes with your mind.

"Then there's the silence. There's only one time when that place isn't silent and then you wish it was. You're in your cell for 23 hours a day and more like 24. Because your exercise hour can be taken away from you any time they want to. They'll always dream up some reason to do it. So you're in there with the silence, one man to a cell, completely shut off from the other cells and the walkways. So you're alone, always alone. It's not like here where the cells are open on one end, and you can talk to everybody down the line and pass things. Not there. Those cells in the pods are made of thick, sound-proof cement walls. About the only thing you can hear through that solid, steel door is the only sound you don't want to hear: guys breaking. There's a slit in that door so they can slide our food trays in and a peep hole for the guards. We're not allowed radios or TVs. Our beds are a mattress on a thick cement slab that comes out of the wall. Our toilet and our wash basin come out of the wall too. Nothing sticks out. No pipes, no tubing that we can take apart and use for other things, like making a shank or to rap on to send messages to other cells. They've thought of everything. So you're alone in silence in a place that never changes. And you never know if it's day or night or how much time has passed, an hour, a day, a winter or summer. It's hard to keep yourself together. The bastards are torturing you without laying a finger on you in the cleanest place and the most comfortable climate you can imagine.

"But some lawyer got a federal judge to say that they couldn't keep us in those cells for 24 hours a day. That they had to let you out of those 8'x10' cells for one hour a day to get some exercise. That turned out to be a joke because they got around that one too. What they did was they built what they call exercise yards on the back of each pod. That way they could take you to the end of the pod, open the door and you're in their exercise yard. And what an exercise yard it is. It's about half the size of a basketball court, all concrete and the walls go up 20 feet, straight up 20 feet. No one's ever gonna climb one of those. There's nothing in their exercise yards except the concrete floor and walls. There's no roof, except that the back end is covered with some sheet metal, 'cause it's always raining up there.

"When they did take me out for that hour, it was usually at night. Most of the time it was raining or there was fog. So I never saw much of the sky. What I saw was darkness. I liked that at first because it was a change from all the lights. But it was always cold out there and if it was raining, I'd end up huddling against the back wall to stay dry. 'Cause once you got wet, it was pretty miserable out there. That was their exercise yard.

"On top of that, the guards had another little game they played. They said that the exercise yard, that hour out of our cells, was a privilege, a privilege that could be lost by 'insubordination,' as they called it. What is 'insubordination?' Anything they wanted to make it. Cussing, slouching, the way you answered them. 'An attitude' was enough. Not leaving your cell or the exercise yard as quick as they wanted you to. Any of those things and more could make you lose your privilege for one, two or three or however many days they wanted. After a while, I just gave it up. I didn't want to be gamed with anymore. I didn't want to have anything more that they could take away from me. I was better off staying in my cell.

"But the toughest part came when guys started to break. Because then you knew for sure what they wanted to do to you, what they could do to you, and how easy it was for them to break you."

"Break you?"

"Drive you crazy. Make you lose it, go out of your mind. And then you've lost everything. So I fought it, struggled like hell to keep from going over the edge."

"How?"

"Exercises mainly and my dictionary. I had six books but the dictionary was the most important. I exercised every day, sometimes two, three, four, five times a day. But then I didn't know if it was the same day or night or what. And after a while, I didn't know if I had just exercised or not exercised or how long ago it was that I had exercised. See, that was their thing, there was no time, there was no yesterday or tomorrow or last week or next week. But no matter, if I felt myself slipping, if I felt myself getting close to that edge, I'd do more exercises, more burpees, four-count burpees, two-count burpees, sit ups, pushups, running in place, stretching, anything, until I didn't feel I was at the edge anymore."

"And your dictionary?"

"It kept my mind healthy. It gave my mind something to do every day other than think about the ugliness and hopelessness all around me."

"How?"

"I memorized 25 words every day."

"What words."

"I started with the letter 'a,' and have been working my way through ever since. It's a big dictionary, and every day I would take the next 25 words and repeat them to myself until I knew them. Then, using my other books, I would try to make sentences out of them, which weren't always right, I know. But it helped keep my mind straight, off the ugliness that I was living and breathing. And in the SHU you had to keep your mind straight.

"Because guys did start to break. It was the one thing you could hear through those steel doors, their screams. When that happened, you knew that what you were most afraid of, it happening to you, was happening close by. It was coming. It was getting closer and closer. And the guards just let them scream. Never tried to stop them. Just let them scream. And the more you tried not to hear them, to cover your ears, bury your ears, you could still hear them. And after so many hours or minutes or days, I didn't know. I had no way of knowing. After so much screaming without the guards doing anything, other guys started to break and they were screaming too. At times it seemed like the screaming would never end. But it did. I must have slept through some of it because at times I would wake and it was silent again. Finally, I got a copy of a court order from a judge in San Francisco saying that the guards had to put those guys somewhere else when they started screaming. That helped a lot."

He told me that during his three years in the SHU, he had one visit. That was in his first year and was with his sister, Lulu. She had traveled for 28 hours from southern California by bus, some 800 miles to Crescent City, California's northernmost town. There were few Mexicans there and she had great difficulty renting a room. She thought she looked and felt so strange that each time she asked to rent a room, she knew there would be none available for her. Some of the people said that they knew she was there to visit an inmate at the prison. At last, one woman took pity on her and said she'd rent her a room, but only if she paid in advance.

The next day, she took an expensive taxi ride for the final 12 miles to the prison. There she visited her brother, but only after waiting some two and a half hours and enduring several searches. The visit took place in a cubicle. The guards brought Arroyo to his side of the cubicle in leg irons, waist chains and cuffs. Lulu cried through a good part of the visit and never returned.

As Chente retold his SHU experiences, his voice had dropped and his look had changed. It was now a serious, quiet, faraway look. And as I sat across from him and listened to him and watched him, it was difficult not to admire him. During the course of our many conversations over the ensuing years, it would be impossible for me to listen to and watch Chente and not be filled with respect and admiration for his strength, self-discipline, intelligence and insight into himself and others. But always, if not at those moments, then certainly sometime soon after, I would remind myself who I was dealing with: the leader of a vicious gang that would stop at nothing to exact its will.

But there was something more that always weighed into my assessment of Chente. It arose out of a case in which I had been court-appointed to represent an 18-year-old youth who along with a 16-year-old had murdered another young man. Neither of the two culprits were strangers to the Juvenile Court system. Both had spent time in the California Youth Authority for criminal offenses. Upon release from the Youth Authority, the two had teamed up in Watsonville, California, a large farming community in which 90% of the farmworkers were illegal immigrants. They had little to do and less money to do it with. One day they decided that they wanted to visit friends in Sacramento, but they had no means of transportation. They had met a young farmworker who had managed to buy himself a nice car. They asked him if they could borrow his car to go to Sacramento. When he said no, they decided to take the car anyway.

They overpowered the young farmworker, bound and gagged him, and locked him in the trunk of his car.

They started for Sacramento, but once in the Santa Cruz Mountains, they stopped along a lonely road and knifed the farmworker to death, and dumped his body into a wooded ravine. Then they drove on to Sacramento for their reunion. Two weeks later, a jogger and his dog came up that mountain road. The dog must have picked up the dead body's scent because it wouldn't leave the spot where the body lay a few yards below the road. The jogger discovered the body and called the police. An all points bulletin was put out for the vehicle, and the two young murderers were apprehended in the car. The 16-year-old gave a complete confession and he was processed through the Juvenile Court system. My client, who at 18 under California law was considered an adult, was tried in the Superior Court where he was facing a first degree murder charge and potentially life in prison.

After two days in front of a jury, the prosecution's case was floundering. The prosecutor was poorly prepared. At the beginning of the third trial day, he offered to allow my client to plead guilty to a lesser manslaughter charge, which he did and was sentenced to six years in prison. After the sentence was pronounced, I visited with my client in the jail before he was sent off to prison. He was cocky, showed no remorse and was proud of the outcome. During that visit, he said something to me that I have never forgotten. He said, "You know, when you kill somebody, you feel like you're God. Because you've just taken a life and that's something not many people can or will do." My thoughts then were that he had already crossed an all important threshold with apparent ease. How much easier would it be to cross it a second time?

So to with Chente. There was always in my mind the fact that he had crossed that important threshold at *least* twice before with apparent ease. How much more likely was it that he would cross it again?

During the course of Chente's case, I made it a practice to visit him twice a week in the jail. Those visits averaged at least two hours. I would arrive at the jail by 7:00a.m. not only to avoid the morning commute but also to avoid conflicts with other attorneys wanting to use the three cubicles for visits with their clients. Sometimes it was necessary for me to visit with him more than twice a week.

It was during one of our first visits that Chente said something of note that he would repeat many times. I was explaining why I thought the case would take three years or longer to complete, when he interrupted me. "Look, take as long as you want, as long as you need, the longer the better. Every day that I'm here is another day that I'm not in the SHU. This is as good as it gets for me and I'll stay here as long as it takes. Believe me, I intend to see this case through to the end. I know there's a good chance that the jury will convict me, not for what I did but for who I am. Once they do that, I'm probably looking at the death penalty. I'm prepared for that. You see, I'm 46 right now and by the time the case is over, I'll be 50 or close to it. Those guys up there on Death Row with all their appeals and different lawyers are waiting more than 20 years before they execute them. Hell, by that time I'll be 70 or more. And you know what? The way I abused my body as a young man, I don't expect to live that long. And from what I hear, those guys up there on Death Row have it pretty damn good. Special visits, special food, good cells, radio and TV. Hell, that beats going back to the SHU, and that's where I'll go if I don't get the death penalty. So take your time.... Besides, Pinky and me have already talked it over and we're of the same mind."

Joseph "Pinky" Hernandez was another member of the *Nuestra Familia's* ruling *Mesa* and Chente's closest, most trusted friend. Chente was fond of saying that they were "road dogs," which I took to mean that not only had they done a lot of time in prison together, but that when they were out on the streets at the same time, they did many things together, good and bad. They had been cellmates at Corcoran prison before they were sent to Pelican Bay, where they were separated. The indictment said that Louie "Dumptruck" Chavez had left Pelican Bay armed with a "hit list" of people to be killed which had been issued by the ruling *Mesa*. Curiously, only two of the three *Mesa* members, Chente and Pinky, were named and indicted. The third member, Robert "Brown Bob" Viramontes was not mentioned in the indictment. According to the indictment, only Chente and Pinky were the members of the Mesa responsible for the six San Jose homicides.

Corcoran State Prison was opened in 1988 and is located 58 miles southwest of Fresno. Prior to the opening of Pelican Bay, it was the California Department of Corrections' maximum security prison. Chente was adamant that the guards there were sadistic animals. He said that inmates were segregated along color lines: brown, black and white. The three groups were bitter enemies and it was prison policy that they were to be kept apart at all times, especially in the prison yard which was used for exercise. On several occasions, the guards supposedly, inadvertently let a brown group into the prison yard while a black group was exercising there, and vice versa. Then the tower guards would wait for the melee to begin. Once it did, they opened fire, wounding many and killing some. Chente showed me multiple buckshot scars on his chest and arm which he said he received during one of the "inadvertent" mixings of brown and black inmates in the Corcoran prison yard.

Years later, I came across a Los Angeles Times article in August 1996 which said that during its eight-year existence, Corcoran prison guards had shot and killed more inmates than at any other prison in the country. The article went on to say that the guards and their supervisors staged fights between inmates during "gladiator days." In November 1996, CBS Evening News broadcast video footage of an inmate shot by guards at Corcoran in 1994. That prompted an F.B.I. investigation. In March 1997, CBS 60 Minutes discussed the 1994 death and the alleged cover up, and the alarming number of shootings at the prison. In February 1998, eight correctional officers and their supervisors were indicted on federal criminal civil rights charges brought by the United States Department of Justice in connection with the fights and the shootings that occurred at Corcoran. In June 2000, a Fresno jury acquitted all the defendants. Many of the 1700 Corcoran prison personnel live in Fresno and the Fresno Bee's headline reporting the acquittals read: ALL EIGHT CORCORAN GUARDS ACQUITTED: APPLAUSE ROCKS THE COURTROOM AFTER THE VERDICTS.

Whenever Chente spoke of his youth and his family, he always said of his mother, "I loved her very much. She was a good woman. She loved us and cared for us. But she had such a hard life. She deserved better." There was never an outright condemnation of his father, but the facts spoke for themselves. "He was tough, strict and he ruled with an iron hand. From the very beginning we did what he said. There was hell to pay if we didn't. There was never anything dumb or stupid about him. He knew how to get what he wanted and it seemed like he always got it. We were migrant farmworkers, and for most of the year we just followed the crops. Whatever needed picking or tending, we were there, me and my Mom and my sisters. But ours wasn't the only family my father took to those fields. He also took his other two families with us. You see, my father had three wives or three women or whatever you want to call them, and each wife had four or five kids. We all knew each other and he always managed to keep the three families close together when we were working. Even in the winter for those few months when there wasn't any work, he always settled the three families close together in some town so he could be with all of us. During the high season when we'd be in Earlimart. You know, that little town alongside highway 99 between Fresno and Delano? There was always a lot of grapes around there, a lot of work around there. Sometimes we could be there for a month and a half or more. But what I remember about Earlimart was that my father used to get us this little place that had three cabins on it with our own yard. The cabins were just a few feet apart. The three families were really together then, and each night he'd sleep in a different cabin with a different wife.

"We all worked in the fields together, except for my father. He'd make sure that we all got off to the fields in the morning, but he always stayed behind. He said there was a lot to do, a lot to take care of for 15 or 16 people working in those fields. Like buying food and water and camping supplies and making sure that we had some place to cook. And he'd say that he had to scout around to find out which ranches were paying the best and who had the best crops so that we could work there. He always did his buying in the nearest town, and because he bought so much stuff for all of us, people in those little towns knew him real well. And he spent a lot of time in those little towns, but he was always at our camp site at the end of the day waiting for us. Of course, once we were paid, the money went straight to him.

"We were all afraid of him. One thing he did to one of my sisters, I'll never forget. She was about 13 then but she was still wetting the bed and the little place we were sleeping in smelled pretty bad. He had been scolding her and hitting her and punishing her for years, but that hadn't done any good. She was still wetting the bed. He was still yelling at her after dinner one night and he had already hit her too. All of sudden he got real mad and he yelled at all of us, 'I want everybody around the table now!' Then he yelled at my sister, 'And you get on the table!' It was like she didn't know what he meant, so she just looked at him. 'I said get up on the table!' She started to get on the table but he said, 'No, I want you on the table without any clothes on!' She didn't know what to do. 'I said take them off! All off!' She got up on the table naked. 'Stand up!' She stood up. 'I want everybody here to remember how many times I've tried to make this girl stop peeing in bed. But she won't stop. She won't pay any attention to me. But I guarantee you that she'll pay attention to me from now on.' Then he lit a match and set it to my sister's pubic hairs. She didn't see him do that but when she felt the flame, she jumped, screamed, stomped on the table and tried to put the flame out with her fingers, burning them too. Then she was flat on the table screaming in pain. We just watched. There was nothing we could do, nothing we dared do. She lay on the table crying for a long time. But she never wet the bed again."

Of his service in the United States Army, Chente said, "I joined the Army when I was 17. I had planned on doing that for a long time. My main reason was to get my mother out of the hell she was living in. She was in no condition to be working in them fields anymore, and she didn't have much of a life being wife number three. The Vietnam war was going on then. Guys I knew were joining the Army. Seems like they were taking anybody and everybody. A lot of them were making their checks payable to their parents. When I joined, I told them to send my checks to my Mom. I was hoping to make her life a little better and help her get away from my father.

"They sent me to Vietnam. That wasn't something I was ready for. Lot of guys were getting killed and wounded over there. Lot of Mexicans and blacks. I'd never been out of the U.S. and sure as hell had never been halfway around the world with all those Asian people before.

"Everything was a big jumble over there. People going everywhere, being sent everywhere. They sent me to the jungle and that was pure hell. We were supposed to be fighting the Viet Cong but we never saw them. But they saw us alright, and fought us mostly at night. You couldn't sleep at night because the jungle was full of weird noises. You could even hear them talking, and that's when they came at us. They always seemed to know where we were and lot of guys were getting shot. It was hard to sleep in the daytime because we were always on alert. The tension was just too much. Lot of guys were on heroin and I started using it too. At first it calmed me. Then I started using it to take me and my mind out of there. I was one of the lucky ones. I didn't get killed or wounded. But I left Vietnam hooked on heroin.

"When I got back here, all I wanted to do was use. It made everything O.K. But money was always a problem. Once I got out of the Army, I started going to Mexico and smuggling marijuana across the border. I made some good money and it paid for my habit for a while. About the time I started thinking I had it made, I got busted at the border bringing some in. They sent me to a low level federal prison for two years. That was the first time I had been in jail and since then, I've always said, 'If that first time doesn't scare you, then you'll be back.' That was the first time for me and it didn't scare me and I've been back and back. The first day I got out of that federal prison, I was in the spoon by noon. I just couldn't stay away from the stuff. That's when my life of crime really began. Burglaries, robberies, scams, selling dope. You name it and I did it, and shot all that money into my arms. Four years later, I was in prison again, this time a state prison.

"That's when I got involved with the *Nuestra Familia*. Guys that I knew out on the streets were hooked up with the N.F. It was an easy choice. It wasn't just the protection, somebody covering your back. It also made doing the time easier. You weren't alone. You had friends. You were part of a family. It was a way of life. We did things together in there. We talked about things, planned things together. We lived better together in there. They taught me a lot. I was a hell of a better criminal when I got out three years later."

Released, Chente returned to the life he knew: burglaries, robberies, thefts, drug addiction, which this time landed him in a Salinas jail awaiting trial on a number of charges. It was there, in a dorm-like cell where he was housed with a number of other inmates, that a gruesome murder occurred.

Chente was reluctant to talk about it. "What's there to talk about? You've got all the reports there, don't you? They convicted me. What more do you need?"

"That case will probably come up during the trial. It's one of the things they'll use to put the death penalty on you. I need to know all I can about it."

"What's there to know about it that's not in the police reports?"

The police suspected that the murder was gang related. According to their reports, one night, a guard saw a body hanging from one of the cell girders. The man had been badly beaten before he was hanged, making his face grotesque. But all was quiet in the dorm-like cell. All the inmates were in their bunks purportedly asleep. No one had seen or heard anything. The police suspected it was the work of a prison gang that had gone after an errant gang member. The police report listed several suspected *Nuestra Familia* gang members who were living in the cell, one of whom was Vicente Arroyo. It was never clear what happened or how and why it happened, but Arroyo, along with several others, was convicted of murder and sentenced to prison.

Later, I provided Chente with copies of the police reports on a second homicide and asked him to review it so that we could discuss it. Paroled in 1981 after his Salinas murder conviction, Chente had moved to southern California in an apparent attempt to distance himself from his *norteño* brothers. Now in his mid-thirties, he had no formal education, no skills, and no work experience other than what he had acquired in prison and on the streets. It wasn't long before heroin was a welcomed visitor. Soon he was addicted again and began living with, "running with," a white female prostitute. The sale of her body was one source of their income. She had regular customers and at times Chente accompanied her, as a pimp would, for her protection. The more heroin they injected, the more heroin and the more money they needed. Money was always in short supply. One day, they hit upon a scheme that they felt would more than alleviate their immediate financial need. The woman was certain that one of her customers, an old man who lived alone in a trailer, had a large sum of money hidden there. Their plan was that once the woman had engaged the old man in sex, Arroyo would enter the trailer and force the old man to turn over the money. Chente waited outside for a few minutes after the woman entered the trailer before entering. When he did, he was armed with a brick. Rather than submit, the old man began struggling and screaming for help. Chente hit him several times on the head with the brick, crushing his skull and killing him. "I don't know how it came to that. I had no intention of killing him. I only wanted to scare him and make him turn over the money. But when he started struggling and screaming, I panicked and started hitting him on the head to quiet him. Before I knew it, he slumped over dead."

It was the prison sentence for the murder of the old man that Chente was serving when I met him in 1992.

There were several very good lawyers involved in the *Nuestra Familia* case, but none better than the lead prosecutor, Charles Constantinides. I first became acquainted with Charlie Constantinides in the early 1970's when he was a criminal defense attorney with an office in Palo Alto, a city located at the northern edge of Santa Clara County. In those days, felony cases arising in Palo Alto were first heard in the Palo Alto Municipal Court, and if the defendant was held to answer, the case was sent to the Superior Court in San Jose. Thus I did not see Charlie on a daily basis or all that frequently. But he was one of a handful of Palo Alto attorneys who appeared regularly in the Criminal Division of the Superior Court in San Jose. And he was the best. He had a distinct style in the courtroom that immediately caught my attention. He was of average height, of slender build with fine features and light brown, wavy hair. When he spoke, it was almost as if he were lecturing the judge and everyone around him. His tone was even, low-keyed and deliberate, but there was an arrogance to it, almost as if he were addressing people below him in stature and intelligence. He was obviously very bright and very well prepared. We were not close but knew each other well enough to exchange greetings and passing words. I had the impression that he frequently represented people involved in protest movements around Palo Alto and Stanford.

I lost track of Charlie when I went to work for the ALRB in 1975 through 1980. When I returned to San Jose, I had little or no contact with him and he remained out of my mind until the late 1980's, when much to my surprise, I learned that he had become a Santa Clara County Deputy District Attorney and was trying a highly publicized murder case in which the jury had returned the death penalty. I learned then too, not to my surprise, that Charlie had graduated from the prestigious Andover Academy, Princeton University and Stanford Law School.

There were two other prosecutors on the NF case: Kittie Constantinides and Eugene Castor. Kittie was a junior attorney in the District Attorney's Office who had been assigned to the case to do legal research. She and Charlie began dating and were married in 1994. Kittie wasn't nearly the seasoned, skilled trial attorney that Charlie was, but she was a very valuable addition to the prosecution's case. She gave Charlie what he lacked: people skills. She was warm, outgoing and spontaneous, everything that Charlie wasn't. She was approachable, something that Charlie, with his superior air, wasn't. And in a case involving 21 defendants, the prosecution had to be approachable. She also had a keen interest in people, in getting to know and understand them, which over the duration of the case became vastly important in scrutinizing the defendants and dealing with 150 prospective witnesses

Eugene Castor was an attorney in the California State Attorney General's Office, which had a keen interest in the activities of the prison gangs in the state prisons. He was the Attorney General's expert on prison gangs. I'm certain that he contributed much to the prosecution's case, but I had no dealings with him. He sat at counsel table with Charlie and Kittie during most of our court sessions, but said very little.

Once the NF defendants were housed in the Santa Clara County Jail, they were afforded the same visiting privileges afforded to all other inmates: two one-hour per week visits with people who had been cleared by the jail personnel for those visits. Those visits took place in cubicles on the first floor of the old jail. The cubicles were 3'x4' spaces separated by a base concrete wall with an upper plate glass window with a round, metal, centerpiece through which the inmates and their visitors could speak and be heard. It was common practice for the jail to tape record the visits of any inmate with visitors other than their attorneys, whenever it or any other law enforcement agency felt it advantageous. We advised our clients of the practice and indeed, every visit the NF defendants received over the next five years was tape recorded for the prosecution, with copies being provided to the defense attorneys a few weeks after the visits. What we did not know for some time was that not only were the visits being tape recorded at the jail, but they were also being simultaneously piped into the Constantinides' home as they occurred.

It had been almost 20 years since I had last seen Betsy Carr, last seen her glaring out at me with hate and scorn from the witness stand in Leroy Mims' trial. Some years after the murder of her husband, James Carr, she had married a German national and had gone to live with him in Germany for several years, traveling throughout Europe. Eventually, the marriage broke up and she returned to the United States. Back in San Jose, she became involved in liberal and feminist causes in the Bay Area. Her daughter was now a beautiful young woman who had become a professional model. Together they lived with Betsy's mother in her impressive Rose Garden home. Her father had drowned in the Pacific when she was a young girl and her Uncle Phil, a prominent San Jose attorney had become her surrogate father. San Jose attorney Dan Mayfield represented James "*Huevo*" Trujeque, another of the N.F. defendants. Unbeknownst to me, Betsy Carr was Mayfield's secretary during the first months of the case. After the defendants had been moved to San Jose, she had come to court one day to bring Mayfield some papers. Several days later, I received a phone call.

"Ron Ruiz, this is Betsy Carr. Remember me, James Carr's wife? I want you to know, before you find out from anyone else, that I went up to the jail two days ago to visit your client, Vicente Arroyo."

"What?"

"That's not all of it? I was Dan Mayfield's secretary at the time and when I told him what I had done, he fired me."

"Hold on, Betsy. I'm not getting any of this. What business do you have with my client? Who gave you the permission or the right to go into the jail and see him?"

"It's not about rights or business. The last time you were in court with Arroyo, I had to take some papers to Dan. After I gave the papers to Dan, I sat there for a while, curious. Then I saw Arroyo and I couldn't take my eyes off him. I fell in love with him then and there. I'm head over heels in love with him and I'm going to continue to see him and no one can stop me. So I think we'd better talk about it."

I didn't know what to make of it and I didn't know what had been said during that visit, but I did know that I had to talk to Chente before I did anything else. "I need to talk to my client, Betsy. I'll get back to you after I've done that."

I drove to San Jose and the jail. "Chente, I understand you had a visit the day before yesterday."

"Yeah. Who was that crazy, fucking woman? How did you find out?"

"She called me and told me."

"Who is that bitch anyway? Do you know her? Who put her up to it?"

"I know her. I've known her for 20 years. Aside from what she claims, I have no idea why she came up here."

"Is she a plant? Does the District Attorney think they can get me to confess to her? Or is she just a nut?"

I told him about Betsy's politics and her marriage to and the murder of James Carr, George Jackson's cellmate at San Quentin. I told him that Dan Mayfield was an avowed leftist and he wouldn't have hired her as his secretary if she was anything but one too. No, I didn't think she was any part of a police or prosecution plant. I also said that she was a member of a prominent San Jose family and that her aunt was the mayor of San Jose.

He mulled over what I said and said, "Then she's crazy."

"She might be weird, but she's not crazy."

"Then why'd she come and see me?"

"She told me that she had gone into court the last time we were there and had seen you and had fallen in love with you."

"Aw, come on, you believe that? She said that same shit to me."

"I don't know. It's possible. You're a pretty strong personality, Chente. But what I want to know is what you said to her?"

"Come on. I haven't had a woman around me for years. It's been so long, I've almost forgot what it was like. The only woman that visited me for years was my sister Lulu, and a couple of times when I was at Corcoran, she brought my daughter with her. But that's the only contact I've had with women."

"What did you say to her?"

"Not much. She took me by surprise. I couldn't believe what she was saying."

"Like I've told you, everything you said to her or any visitor is being recorded. So what did you say to her?'

"Not much. Just like, who are you? What do you want? Get out of here and leave me alone."

"Well, she says that she loves you and she's going to keep coming to see you and that nobody can stop her."

"Yeah, I know. She kept saying that. She's not ugly or anything like that. In fact she looked damn good. I'm sure she could get a man out there on the streets if she wanted to. Wouldn't have much trouble. She seemed intelligent. You know what I mean, educated, smart. So, I'm thinking, what the hell is this woman up to?"

"You can refuse her visit, Chente. You can stay in your cell and refuse to come out. You can tell the guards that you don't want a visit from her and that will end it."

"What do you think?"

"It's up to you, entirely up to you. You know they'll be recording everything you say. But if you don't say anything about the case or the gang, I don't see how it can hurt you. But it's up to you. Let her come in a time or two more to see what she's up to. Or just refuse the visit."

A week later, I had a copy of their tape recorded first jail visit. Chente's amazement was clear. "Who are you woman! What do you want!"

The recording devices in those cubicles were of top quality, designed to pick up any sound, any whisper. I could hear Betsy's deep breathing.

"I said, who are you and what do you want!"

More heavy breathing.

"Look woman, I don't know who you are or what you want. But you're not getting anything out of me. I don't have time for this."

More heavy breathing and then in a low, controlled deliberate voice she said, "I saw you in court the other day and I fell in love with you."

"What! Who are you? Why did you come here? Who sent you?"

"My name is Betsy Carr. Nobody sent me. I came because I wanted to, because I fell in love with you."

"So what do you want from me?"

"I want to make you love me. I'm going to make you love me."

"Are you crazy?"

"No."

That was the beginning of twice weekly jail visits that would go on for three and a half years.

I met with Betsy Carr a few days later in a coffee shop. It had been twenty years since I had last seen her. Someone had once said to me, "Funny how we can see so much more clearly how other people have aged than we can see the aging in ourselves." My, how Betsy had changed. Long gone was that school girl look. She was now 40 and a little heavier, not fat, but fuller and an attractive woman. She wore no make-up. She didn't need any. Her complexion was a smooth olive. She was spunky and youthful. Only the fine creases at the edge of her hazel eyes spoke of her years. Her long brown hair was well-groomed and had a natural look that I thought was important to her.

She was upbeat and gracious, which took me by surprise, almost as if the brutal murder of James Carr had never happened. It took only a few sentences for me to see how articulate and bright she was. There was a child-like openness to her. There was nothing to hide, nothing to hide behind. She spoke of her life style, of her trips to San Francisco for concerts and movies and causes. She was very pro-choice and active in women's rights issues. She was concerned with the plight of the poor. She read extensively: novels, historical works, Eastern philosophy. And she meditated. She spoke openly of her relationships with men. Some years after Carr's murder, she had met and married a German national and had gone to Germany to live with him. He was a rigid man, too rigid for her, and she eventually left him and returned to the United States. There had been other men in her life since then, men she had dated and lived with briefly. She was still dating. There was a very nice, well-educated, older man who was very interested in her, but she did not feel the same about him.

But when she saw Chente, she knew that he was the man she wanted. This was the man for her and she was very much in love with him. As Dan Mayfield's secretary, she had to have known that he was the leader of the infamous *Nuestra Familia* prison gang. She never mentioned that. She said simply that when she saw him, sat watching him, she saw and felt his strength and knew that he was the man for her.

When she finished talking, she said, "Do you have any objection to my continuing to visit with him?"

I felt as if I had been set up. "Why do you ask?"

"Because you're his lawyer and you could put a stop to it."

"Could I?"

"If you wanted to, I suppose."

"It's entirely up to Arroyo. He was concerned that you might have been sent there by the District Attorney or the police."

"Do you think that? Do you think I could do that to him or anyone?"

The look on her face was convincing. "No."

"Then you have no objection?"

"It's totally up to Arroyo. If he wants to see you, he'll see you."

In multiple defendant cases, there were always divergent interests on the defense side. Who was the most culpable or more culpable and who was less or not at all culpable? Who had the most or least to lose? Who was going to testify and how would that defendant's testimony incriminate or exonerate the other defendants? Most importantly, which of the defendants would turn on the others and enter into a plea bargain with the prosecution to save his own neck and inculpate the others. Mix into that the fact that each defendant had a separate lawyer, and each of those lawyers had egos, different levels of ability and work ethics, along with different fears and feelings of inadequacies, and there was bound to be contentiousness on the defense side. Putting that into perspective, most multiple defendant cases had two or three codefendants, sometimes as many as four or five. In the *Nuestra Familia* case there were 21 codefendants.

About three months into the case, I received a call from Betty, Judge Murphy's clerk. "Ron, Judge Murphy would like to see you in his chambers tomorrow morning at 11:00."

"Do you know what this is about, Betty?" Fully aware that even if she did know, she wouldn't tell me.

"Not really, but he expects to see you here at 11:00."

The next morning, I was outside Judge Murphy's chambers a full five minutes before 11:00. Then, most likely at 11:00 exactly, the judge's bailiff opened the chamber doors and said, "The judge will see you now, Mr. Ruiz."

Kevin Murphy was in his late forties then and still very well preserved. At six foot, he appeared to be very trim, even in his black robe. There was a pleasantness to his face that belied his toughness. He was a handsome man with dark wavy hair over a smooth complexion and sharp, fine features. He was soft-spoken, courteous and appeared to be mild mannered, although the scores of defendants that he had sent to prison would never attest to that. His dark eyes were on you when you were speaking or when he was speaking to you, watching. It was not a harsh look or stare, but rather polite and even deferential, but watching, gauging all the while.

"Good morning, Mr. Ruiz. Come in. Please come in and have a seat," in his pleasant, polite manner. We had known each other for many years and in private he called me Ron, but in anything that had a judicial appearance, it was Mr. Ruiz. And looking at one of the two chairs in front of his desk, this meeting had a judicial air to it. Because seated in that chair was Dan Mayfield, James Trujeque's attorney. I nodded to Dan and took a seat.

"Mr. Ruiz, Mr. Mayfield has brought to my attention a matter that I believe warrants discussion before he proceeds any further with it. Mr. Mayfield."

"Your Honor, I've had to deal with a matter in my office that's caused me considerable turmoil and discomfort. Not long ago, I discovered that my former personal secretary, Betsy Carr, had become romantically involved with Mr. Ruiz's client, Vicente Arroyo. Obviously, I had to fire her. But I'm concerned that my client's right of confidentiality has been violated and I have no idea how much privileged information she's turned over to Mr. Arroyo or to Mr. Ruiz, whom she has known for some time. I believe that I'm entitled to an explanation from Mr. Ruiz before I take any further action in this matter."

"Wait a minute! Wait a minute. I don't appreciate threats whether they're veiled or stark. Let Mr. Mayfield take whatever action he wants. I have no idea what he's talking about, but let him proceed. He doesn't frighten me in the least."

"Calm down, Mr. Ruiz. I think Mr. Mayfield has a valid concern here and I'd like to hear whatever you might have to say on the matter."

"He may have a valid concern, Your Honor, but he shouldn't start by threatening me."

"I didn't perceive any threats here, Mr. Ruiz, but I'd like to hear what you have to say on this matter."

"Your Honor, I know absolutely nothing about the visits between Mr. Mayfield's ex-secretary and my client other than what I've heard on the tape recordings the jail has made of their visits and what my client has told me. Mr. Arroyo was taken by complete surprise, as was I, when Ms. Carr appeared in the jail for her first visit. He demanded to know who she was and what she wanted. He asked her to leave, but she wouldn't leave and instead said that she had come to see him because she had fallen in love with him the very first time she saw him in court. Since then she has visited him twice more. There are tape recordings of those visits as well. Not once has there been any mention or discussion of Mr. Arroyo's or Mr. Trujeque's case. Not a word. I believe she's also written to him twice. All of those defendants' incoming and outgoing mail is opened, read and copied by the jail personnel. Copies of those letters are being made available to the defense attorneys. I have read copies of those letters. There's not a single reference to the *Nuestra Familia* case. I can provide the court with copies of the relevant tape recordings and the letters, if the court wishes."

"Mr. Mayfield."

"Well, Your Honor, it's my understanding that Mr. Ruiz has known Betsy Carr for more than 20 years, which was not known to me when I hired her, but then, there was no need to inquire into that relationship two years ago. Now however, after working on this case with me for some time, this old friend or acquaintance of Mr. Ruiz begins visiting Mr. Arroyo, whose interests in this case may be diametrically opposed to those of my client. I fired her, but I'd like to know what's going on here."

"Mr. Ruiz."

"Your Honor, Betsy Carr is hardly a friend of mine. I met her briefly more than 20 years ago when I attended two meetings at her mother's house where she was then living. The next time I saw her, or had any contact with her whatsoever, was two years later when I cross-examined her on behalf of a client who was charged with murdering her husband. Needless to say, she was not very happy with me then and I have had absolutely no contact with her since."

"Anything further, gentlemen?"

"No, Your honor."

"No, Your honor."

"Well, if either of you wish, I'll have the District Attorney furnish me with copies of the recordings and letters that have been mentioned here. But I see no need for that now. I must say to you, Mr. Mayfield, that I don't believe that there's been any sort of misconduct on Mr. Ruiz's part, or by his client, nor any breach of Mr. Trujeque's confidentiality privilege. And unless there is something else that you want me to consider, that will be all."

"How many times has she been up to see you now?"

"Five."

"Neither of you talks about the case, right?'

"No, she doesn't and I never will."

"Why is she doing this?"

"I don't know. She keeps saying she loves me, but who the hell knows. I'll just have to wait and see on that one."

"Are you going to keep on seeing her?"

"Well for now, I don't see how it can hurt me. I haven't had a woman around me for a long, long time. My sister's seen me six or seven times over the past ten years and twice she brought my daughter with her. But that's not the same thing and wouldn't be even if she was coming every week. This is a different kind of thing. This woman says she wants to be with me."

"What's she like?"

"She's smart. I mean intelligent. She's read a lot and seems to know a lot about a lot of different things. Her mind's quick and sharp. She doesn't miss much. When I told her that I like to read too, she said that she'd send me some books. She asked me what I like to read and I told her that I wanted to read about the history of Mexico. Yesterday she said she'd mailed me two books on the history of Mexico. I haven't got them yet and I'm not holding my breath. But we'll see."

"So you're going to keep on seeing her?"

"Yeah. Why not? I like having her around, until she gives me some reason not to. We talk about things, things happening in the world outside these bars. We talk about ideas and beliefs, things I can't talk about with most of the guys in here. Besides, she put ten bucks on my books the other day. I know ten bucks might not seem like a lot to you, but those ten bucks are more than I've had on my books for the past three years. Now when the comissary comes around, I can buy me a couple of candy bars or a packet of soup or some chocolate milk. It's been a hell of a long time since I've been able to do that and, believe me, it feels good."

Besides the six counts of murder and the enhancing prior felony convictions, the indictment also charged additional felony violations ranging from attempted murder to robbery, intimidating witnesses, and multiple drug offenses. Under a sweeping conspiracy theory, many of the defendants were criminally liable for acts they were in no way directly involved in. As a result, all of the discovery pertaining to one defendant was provided to all the other defendants. Which meant that the banker boxes of discovery continued to pile up, inundating me with a mountain of material that first had to be sorted out, then read and understood, then compared and related to other pieces of discovery, all before the preparation of a defense could begin. Most of the defense attorneys felt it would be three years before we got to trial. In the meantime, our courtroom work was at a minimum. We appeared in court at most once every six weeks. Those hearings dealt primarily with scheduling matters, attempts by the court to set dates and deadlines for future motions, progress reports by the prosecution regarding the existence and delivery of more discovery, complaints by defense counsel about the discovery, and various complaints about the custodial conditions of the defendants, some of which were set for a further hearing.

The banker boxes kept arriving. There was no end to them. Thousands and thousands of type-written pages. Hundreds of tape recordings. Thousands of pages of hand-written letters and responses. It seemed as if by the time I had gotten through one banker box, two more arrived. Judge Murphy acknowledged the enormity of the discovery when he set the defendants' motions to dismiss the indictment pursuant to penal Code 995/997 for hearing. Under existing court rules at the time, all 995 motions had to be set for hearing within 60 days of a defendant's arraignment in the Superior Court. In this case, because of the enormity of the discovery, a year and six months would elapse between the defendants' arraignments and the hearing date: November 30, 1993.

The indictment had originally charged 21 defendants. One defendant had never been apprehended. The remaining 20 were in custody. Thirteen of the defendants faced the death penalty, and nine were charged with multiple murders. By early 1993, some of the accused began accepting plea bargains from the District Attorney and were sentenced to prison. By November 30, 1993, 10 of the original 21 suspects had pleaded guilty to various charges and had been sentenced to prison and/or had agreed to become witnesses for the prosecution.

About eight months into the case, Chente said to me during one of our morning visits, "There's something going on here that I don't like."

"Like what?"

"You know how they've got all of us up here in this separate part of the third floor, except for Cripple Jerry who's down next to the infirmary because he can't walk?"

"Yeah."

"Well, something's going on with Lucky."

"Like what?"

"A couple of weeks ago, they started pulling him out for visits. But some of the guys down there on visits said they hadn't seen him down there. Then they started pulling him for visits when there were no visits scheduled. He said they were taking him to the infirmary because he had these bad headaches. Then the night before last, they pulled him and he ain't been back since."

"He hasn't been back?"

"No, and he didn't look sick to me. Unless I've missed my guess, he's turned."

"Lucky Shelton turned? How could that be? He's the worst of the bunch, a cold-blooded, serial killer. How could he turn?"

"You tell me."

Ronald "Lucky" Shelton was the gang member, the indictment said, that had been hand-picked by Vicente Arroyo and Pinky Hernandez in April 1990 to lead the San Jose regiment and to carry out the execution "hit list" that they had sent to him. Shelton was a 31-year-old ex-con, the son of a Mexican mother and an Irish father, who was attending San Jose City College when he took over the local NF gang. After I had been in the *Nuestra Familia* case for a few months, it was Ronald "Lucky" Shelton that I paid the closest attention to whenever the defendants were brought into court. In my mind, he was the key to Chente's case. If Chente had never known Lucky before the San Quentin bus ride, and more and more I was beginning to believe him, then how could he have hand-picked him to lead the San Jose regiment? Then too, Lucky had boasted to other gang members that he liked killing people, that he got a "rush" when he did it. The indictment seemed to corroborate this: he had been at the scene of four of the six murders and had fired one of the guns that had been used. None of this was apparent by looking at him. He was a handsome, light-skinned, clean-cut, young man who wore horn-rimmed glasses and was easily the best looking of the bunch.

I was in a funk when I left the jail that morning. What Lucky could gain by turning was to avoid the death penalty. But why would the District Attorney, Charlie Constantinides specifically, be willing to give a cold-blooded, serial killer a life sentence in exchange for his testimony? The only rational explanation taunted me. More than anything, Charlie wanted a death penalty for Chente and Pinky Hernandez, the leaders of the gang. With Lucky's testimony, he had an air-tight case against Chente. Chente could tell a jury as many times as he wanted that he hadn't known Lucky but any jury would be only too ready to believe Lucky's testimony that it was Chente, the two-time murderer and leader of the gang, who had hand-picked him and ordered him down the path of killing people. If anyone deserved the death penalty, it was Ronald "Lucky" Shelton. But that wasn't what the prosecution wanted.

I had had some experience with informants and codefendants who had turned on their former colleagues. During their testimony, I especially despised them. They had sold themselves to save their necks. They had willingly, willfully participated in criminal activity and now were using that activity for profit a second time. Nor did I have much regard for prosecutors that used them. It was bought testimony. Juries, on the other hand, seemed to hold their testimony in high esteem. It seemed to fascinate them, to hear from other-world participants about the inner workings of criminal acts. It mattered not how much jurors were reminded by defense attorneys that this was tainted, purchased testimony, because they inevitably found the other defendants guilty.

In fact those witnesses knew beforehand exactly what the prosecutors wanted them to say to the juries. They had usually been questioned by the police for hours before they turned, then again as they turned, and again after they turned. Then again by the prosecutors' investigators, and finally by the prosecutors themselves before they testified. They had entered into a bargain to save their lives or years of freedom before they took that witness stand and were determined to keep their end of the bargain. But life being what it is, later in my career I found myself encouraging, pleading, with a client to turn in order to save his life.

As long as prisons and jails use inmates they call trustees to do menial or clerical tasks, and as long as inmates can peer out of their bars and see what is going on around them, there is very little that can remain secret within those walls.

"He's turned," Chente said a few days later. "There's no doubt about it. He hasn't been back and the word is that they have him down on the second floor right below us."

"What's he gonna tell them?"

"Whatever they want to hear."

"That you hand-picked him? That you ordered him to do those killings?"

"What do you think?"

A few days later, "He's down there alright and the guys right above him are yelling down on him, giving him hell."

"Like what?"

"That he's a fucking snitch, a *puto*, an asshole, everything."

"Can he hear them?"

"Yeah, he can hear them. They're not letting up. The word is that it's driving him crazy. That he's yelling and screaming to the guards to get him out of there."

Days later.

"He's gone. The word is that he's not in this jail anymore. But no one knows where they've got him."

Neither he nor his attorney was present at the next scheduled court session. I had listened to tape recordings of jail visits Lucky had. There were only a few and there had been no indication that he was turning. I had read the few letters he had written before he turned, but there was nothing there to lead me to believe that he was even thinking of turning. After he was moved from the jail's third floor, he wrote two letters to his family. Both mentioned that he had found God and one said that he would like to see a psychiatrist. At that court hearing, Charlie Constantinides informed the defense attorneys that Lucky had agreed to testify for the prosecution. When I asked Charlie for copies of any statements that Lucky had made to them, he said that the discussions thus far had been informal and that nothing had been reduced to writing. Charlie was no fool.

On November 30, 1993, the defense attorneys argued their motions to have the indictment dismissed on the grounds that there had been insufficient evidence presented to the grand jury to hold their clients to answer to the charges. At the heart of the indictment was the conspiracy charge. The culpability of many of the defendants hung on that charge. On the basis of the conspiracy charge, Chente and Pinky were being held liable for six murders and a number of other felonies that they had allegedly ordered from their prison cells. I joined in the motions, although at the time I didn't believe that there was any hope that the indictment would be set aside. On its face, I felt that the testimony presented to the grand jury was sufficient to hold the defendants to answer. But that testimony had not been contested, had not been subject to cross-examination or contradicted by other independent evidence. That would only come at the trial. Judge Murphy took the motions under submission and two weeks later, as everyone expected, denied them.

On December 7, 1993, Herminio Serna, one of the defendants in the *Nuestra Familia* was arraigned on a second grand jury indictment for murder. This time Serna was charged with the robbery and murder on July 14, 1991, of Esteban Guzman, whom he allegedly shot and killed in the Guzman home. The indictment further alleged that Serna, upon conviction, would be subject to the death penalty because he had killed Guzman while lying in wait as part of a criminal street gang. Serna had been charged in the first indictment with the killing of Marcos Baca on July 26, 1991, and the murder of Sheila Apodaca on August 28, 1991. Despite the fact that the Guzman murder took place within twelve days of the Baca homicide and 34 days of the Apodaca slaying, there was no mention of Vicente Arroyo or Pinky Hernandez in the second indictment.

Eight days later, Charlie Constantinides publically announced that Ronald "Lucky" Shelton and Jerry "Cripple" Salazar had pleaded guilty to four San Jose murders with the understanding that if they were to tell everything they knew about the *Nuestra Familia* prison gang and testify truthfully against the remaining defendants, they would receive life sentences. Shelton pleaded guilty to the murders of Tony Herrera, Larry Valles, Sheila Apodaca and Raymond Perez. Salazar admitted to taking part in the murders of Apodaca and Perez. Shelton would be eligible for parole in 2059 and Salazar in 2025. Those plea bargains brought the number of defendants awaiting trial to nine, although one, Martin Serna had never been apprehended and was still at large. It was also noted that law enforcement authorities were still investigating whether the September 27, 1993, shooting death of Paul Anthony Farfan was connected to the gang.

I had known Charlie Constantinides for many years and though we were never close, I knew that we had shared many of the same experiences when he was a defense attorney. Despite his arrogant, petulant, supercilious air, I admired his ability as a lawyer and in the end, I actually liked him. Perversely, I enjoyed needling him with snide remarks whenever we passed in the court-house halls and were relatively alone. It was always worth the arrogant sneer or smirk he gave me. One day early on in the case, I stopped him and asked, "Charlie, why in the hell did you become a District Attorney? Why'd you stop being one of us? Why'd you sell out?" He looked at me with those keen hazel eyes as a sardonic, superior smile spread across his face. "I'll tell you why, Ron. I got sick and tired of having my head bashed in by jurors year after year." Then he left, completely self-satisfied.

Not long after the public announcement of Lucky's turning, I said to Charlie in one of the courthouse hallways, "Hey Charlie, why is it that before Lucky turned, we were getting a fair share of his letters? Since then, we've only gotten two letters, one asking to see a psychiatrist."

He gave me a contemptuous sneer and said, "Has it ever occurred to you that Lucky may have stopped writing letters?"

"Did you have anything to do with that, Charlie?" unable to resist.

He walked away with a "Hmpf."

It was the case's second winter and Betsy Carr was still taking up Chente's visiting allotment of two, one-hour visits per week. Betsy had proven her mettle and commitment that first winter. Those visits were had in one of two cu-bicles in the old jail, five mornings a week. Visitors were allowed into the jail at 8:00a.m. each weekday morning to sign up for daily visits on a first come, first serve basis, although preference was sometimes given to out-of-town visitors who phoned in and made reservations. During the first winter, there were more N.F. defendants in custody than there were available weekly visiting slots. The visitors were almost entirely women who had come to see their men. Because of the limited visiting slots, women began arriving as early as 6:00a.m. in the morning, and sat or lay on the front steps of the new jail, waiting for the doors to open. As winter arrived and the mornings became dark and cold, the women brought blankets to warm themselves as they waited. Almost without excep-tion, they were Mexican women. Two days a week, the exception was Betsy Carr who was known to arrive with her blankets even before 6:00a.m. to see her man. Nothing or no one was going to prevent Betsy from seeing her man. Except when Chente's sister and daughter phoned from southern California for a reservation, which Betsy didn't especially like but said she understood. It was an entirely different matter when Gloria, an old girlfriend from Fresno, phoned in for a reservation visit with Chente.

What these women endured to see their men for two hours a week impressed me greatly. Especially when I compared their situation to that at the women's jail in Milpitas. There, the women were also allowed two, one-hour visits per week. But there, the visitors were primarily women: mothers, sisters, friends, and daughters. Rare was the husband or boyfriend or any male visitor.

From time to time, I would ask Chente about Betsy and her visits. It always brought a smile to his face. "Oh, she's fine. Kind of crazy. I mean, she's out there, you know. But I enjoy seeing her. She gives me a lot."

For my part, I listened to the tape recordings of their visits intently. There was a give and take, a banter in their conversations that fascinated me. Betsy with that full, clear, high-spirited voice. Chente with his low, growling, sometimes grunting responses. She led the way, always full of news, ideas, questions and suggestions. He would mull over what she said. Then his answers would come, slow, deliberate and often well thought out. Hers was a world of books and ideas; his of everyday living, cunning and survival. And yet there was a mesh, a yin and yang, a supplementing of thoughts and ideas. Each was feeding the other with newness. I never felt that either had the upper hand. Instead there was a remarkable balance, each willing to accept and learn from a world they had never known. They laughed a lot, they teased each other. Time flew by. At the end of each visit, you could hear a guard in the background, "Time's up, Ma'am. Time's up, Ms. Carr."

She sent him books, mostly historical works, a few novels and even some eastern philosophy. He read them and they talked about them. His questions were good, his observations keen. She loved prodding him, prompting, refuting him. Now he watched the evening news with interest and had access to the local paper. There was always something to talk about, never enough time. Then there were her letters, concise, beautifully written letters that could also take him into another world.

He told her that his sister and daughter were planning to visit. She called me wanting to know what I knew about the visit. I told her I was making arrangements for them to stay at a motel near the jail. She wanted to meet them. Could I help with that? I said I would. She met them and they loved her. Betsy made sure of that. Compared to them and the women she mingled with twice a week on the jail steps, Betsy was from a very privileged class. And yet she had gained entry into their hearts.

Gloria was a different matter. "Ron," Betsy said over the phone, "can you tell me who this Gloria witch-bitch is? I was on those steps at 5:30 this morning only to be told at 8:00 that this Gloria woman from Fresno had already made a reservation for the visit. Who is she?"

"Gloria who?"

"Gloria, Chente's visitor this morning."

"I have no idea. I don't know any Gloria."

My first words to Chente the next morning were, "Who in the hell is Gloria?"

"Who told you about Gloria? Betsy?"

I nodded.

A big, self-satisfied grin appeared on his face. "Was she pissed?"

"Really pissed."

He laughed loud and hard.

"Who is she?"

"She's an old girlfriend of mine from Fresno that I haven't had anything to do with for years."

"What's she doing up here?"

"Beats the hell out of me. They pulled me for a visit yesterday morning. I just thought it was Betsy. They took me downstairs. I opened the door and there on the other side of the glass was Gloria. Surprised the shit out of me."

"How'd she get here?"

"I imagine she drove."

"That's not what I mean."

"She said she read about my case in the paper and called my sister, Lulu, who told her where I was and what she had to do to get a clearance to see me. And there she was."

"You didn't talk about the case, did you?"

"Oh, hell no. I don't even talk about it with Betsy."

"Is she coming back?"

"She says she is."

"Oh, God."

A few days later.

"Has Betsy been up?"

"Yeah, she came up yesterday."

"What did she have to say about Gloria?"

"Not a word."

"Nothing?"

"Nothing."

"What'd you say?"

"Nothing."

"You didn't say anything?"

"Nope."

"Why not?"

"If she doesn't want to talk about it, why should I talk about it?"

"Come on, Chente, the woman's hurting. Don't play with her."

"She didn't seem to be hurting to me."

"Well, I can tell you for sure that she didn't like it."

"Then she ought to say something about it and not act like it didn't happen."

"She's waiting for you to tell her, to explain it."

"I don't have anything to explain. I didn't have anything to do with that woman coming up here."

"Tell her that."

"I don't have to tell her anything."

"You've got a good thing going with her, Chente. Don't blow it."

He didn't answer, which ended the discussion. But the recording of his next visit with Betsy was telling. He stumbled into Gloria's visit and awkwardly began explaining that he had nothing to do with her visiting him. Betsy cut him short. "Well, Chente, if you want to see her more than me, that's entirely up to you." Gloria visited Chente once more, but not again.

In our visits, he began bemoaning the gang members' lack of education. "They don't read and they can't write. They speak their broken-down version of English from the streets. They know nothing about their own heritage, so they've got nothing to be proud of. Shit, most of those youngsters can't even speak Spanish. They don't fit into either world, any world, except their own."

It wasn't long before education and self-discipline became his mantra. His body and the size of the cells he had lived in for years clearly said that he had long been obsessed with self discipline. He made 4:30a.m.exercises for himself and his codefendants mandatory in the specially modified cell block of the county jail. From his cell he called out and led the counts, which the others repeated from their cells: sit-ups, push-ups, burpees, four count burpees and much more, all in those 8'x10' cells. Those pre-dawn cadences made the guards wary. And if I arrived early enough for my morning visits, I could still see the sweat that had poured out of that massive body and had soaked through the red jump suit. But to Chente's frustration, that form of self-discipline did not lead to learning. "When are they gonna start using their minds too?" he would say.

Then came the ruminations. He would wander off in some of our visits and say that there would come a time when there would be enough self-discipline and self-respect on the part of gang members out on the streets that bank accounts could be opened and money gained from robberies, drug sales and taxes imposed on drug dealers deposited in them. In time, with those funds legitimate businesses could be established: bakeries, auto repair shops, dry cleaners, barber shops. All of which would be run by gang members. The profits of those businesses would be used to create more businesses, until the gang members had a legitimate means of supporting themselves and their families and began encouraging their children to educate themselves.

As more and more of the gang members pleaded guilty to various plea bargains, Chente became annoyed and even angry in some cases. "Chumps! Wanna play, but don't wanna pay," he'd mutter in contempt. When Shelton pleaded guilty to four murders in exchange for briefings, testimony and a life sentence, he was furious. "That son of a bitch out-smarted everybody. Guys are going down left and right for the murders he ordered and did, and some of us are gonna get the death penalty for them, and he walks away with a life sentence, not in Pelican Bay but in some special protective custody. Pretty slick." Jerry Salazar's plea didn't bother him, at least not then. "That crippled's got it tough enough. I don't know the guy, I never knew him, never heard of him until we got here. He wasn't even a gang member. He was a Structure member. You know, one of those little wannbe guys running around in the streets. He doesn't know anything about the gang or even about us up here because they've always kept him downstairs by the infirmary 'cause he can't walk. There's not much he could tell them. And the two murders he copped out to, Lucky was behind them, so they don't really need him to testify about anything. But it's probably better for him to get out of that little cell they had him in anyway, so he can get in a place where he can wheel around in his wheelchair.

"And let me remind you, just 'for the record' as you lawyers like to say, I'm not copping out to nothing, not a damn thing. Twenty-five years on Death Row has to be a hell of a lot better than life in the SHU. Pinky feels the same way. We didn't do a goddamn thing and they're gonna have to come and get us."

Nor did he have to remind me that I was going to try a death penalty case in which there was little hope of avoiding the death penalty. Any jury would definitely be inclined to exterminate the leader of this gang, no matter what the evidence showed. Still, I couldn't disagree with Chente's logic: he'd be far better off on Death Row than in the SHU for the rest of his life. But I wasn't looking forward to a six month or longer trial. The only consolation I had was that I believed that the prosecution was going to have problems proving that Chente and Pinky had actually smuggled out orders for the specific murders and other felonies with which they were charged from their cells in the SHU at Pelican Bay. The necessity of getting Judge Murphy to sign a discovery order allowing me to photograph the SHU unit was nagging me.

About four months after Shelton and Salazar officially turned, Charlie Constantinides approached me in one of the courthouse halls and said, "I think we should talk." We went off to a less busy hallway, and as we walked, I wondered what Charlie had to talk to me about, probably a bit flattered that he had singled me out because up to that point, it was always us, the defense attorneys, who were seeking him out and never the reverse. When I looked at him, he was peering out into the distance with that elitist look of his. Charlie always needed to appear as if he was in control of every situation. When he turned to me he said, "I've talked to George (George Kennedy was then the District Attorney of Santa Clara County) and people in the Attorney General's Office, and they're in agreement that if Arroyo were to plead guilty to a first degree murder charge we would agree to a life sentence."

I was stunned. That awesome burden of a sure-loser death penalty trial was being lifted off my shoulders. All I could manage was, "Which one?"

"That's not important. We can decide which one later. All we have to know now is whether he'll accept the offer of a life sentence in exchange for a guilty plea to a first degree murder."

"That's all?'

"Yes. He won't have to give us any information about the gang or testify in any trial."

I was so pleased, so relieved, that I didn't dare ask Charlie why they were doing this, although I should have. I was tongue-tied.

Charlie finally said, "I've got to get back into court. Get back to me on this, will you?"

"Sure, Charlie," and he was gone.

I stood there for a few moments more, thrilled. The dreaded trial had passed. Then reality set in. Chente would never plead guilty to any murder charge. Then I was depressed.

I saw Chente the next morning and though Charlie's offer was uppermost in my mind, it was well into the two-hour visit before I could reveal it. When I did tell him, his big, dark face contorted with rage. I had never seen him so angry. He breathed hard, looked from side to side, and then said, "Tell that son of a bitch to go fuck himself! Do you hear me? Tell that asshole to go fuck himself!"

"Don't get pissed-off at me, Chente," I said defensively. "The law says that I have to relay any offer the D.A. makes to you, and that's what I'm doing."

"I'm not pissed-off at you! But make sure you tell that asshole that I said that he can go fuck himself!"

I put off calling Charlie for a few days, but then I saw him at the courthouse. Rather, we saw each other at a distance and he started towards me. As much as I didn't want to finalize my trying that death penalty case, in those seconds as he moved toward me, I remember the flash of joy I felt in what I was about to tell old Charlie.

"Did you get a chance to talk to Arroyo about our offer?"

"Yeah."

"What'd he say?"

"He told me to tell you that you could go fuck yourself."

Charlie turned beet-red and stood there for several seconds before he said, "O.K." and turned and left. I was gloating. That supercilious son of a bitch deserved it. Once again reality set in. There was going to be hell to pay for this and I was going to be on the receiving end of some of it. There was no way I could have then anticipated how much more hell.

Two months later, on July 14, 1994, I received a call from Betty, "Ron, Judge Murphy wants you here in court at 1:30. There've been some new charges filed against your client, Mr. Arroyo."

"What new charges?"

"I don't know. The Judge just wants you here at 1:30."

When I entered that courtroom that afternoon a few minutes before 1:30, Chente was already seated, chained and cuffed in the jury box. Seated next to him was Carlos Mendoza, a codefendant in the N.F. case, and next to him, Louis Oliverez, an individual I had never seen before. They too were chained and cuffed. Seated across the courtroom, chained and cuffed was Mendoza's wife, Deborah, also unknown to me.

When I approached Chente, he said, "What's this all about?"

"I don't know. Maybe you can tell me?"

"Hell, I don't know what I'm doing here and I sure as hell don't know the guy sitting next to Carlos or that woman over there. You sure you don't know anything about this?"

"Chente, I have no idea what this is all about."

Within minutes we did. Judge Murphy read from another grand jury indictment accusing Chente of yet another murder as Charlie Constantinides sat across from me gloating. The indictment said that while in custody at the San Jose jail, Chente had order the killing of Paul Farfan. The order was said to have been passed on to Carlos Mendoza who then conveyed it to his wife, Deborah, during one of their jail visits. Thereafter on September 23, 1993, Louis Oliverez and Adam Caris, who was still at large, had shot and killed Farfan in San Jose's Watson Park. For a second time, an indictment sought the death penalty against Vicente Arroyo.

When Judge Murphy stopped reading, Chente and I looked at each other in disbelief. Then Judge Murphy left and Chente asked me, and I asked him, what was this all about? Before either of us could answer, the deputies were leading him and his codefendants back to the holding cell. I sat there numb, holding a copy of the new indictment and another thousand pages of grand jury testimony.

I left the courthouse battered and felt that way the rest of the day. How much longer was this going to go on? How much more of this could I take? How many more years of Chente and his cases was I facing? Even if I were successful in the first death penalty case, which I doubted, there would be a second death penalty case to try. And I was very much aware of cases in which the prosecution, after obtaining one death penalty verdict against a defendant, and being fearful of being overturned on appeal, had gone on with a second death penalty trial. Four more years? Five?

I didn't sleep much that night and I was up long before dawn. Scanning the grand jury transcript, I saw that Jerry "Cripple Jerry" Salazar was the prosecution's chief witness. He had testified that Chente had ordered the Farfan murder because Farfan had been skimming drug profits from gang partners. Salazar said that Chente had gotten his order out through fellow gang member Carlos Mendoza, and his wife Deborah. The San Jose Mercury News corroborated my reading. The article said that when word got back to Arroyo that Farfan was holding back profits from drug sales that belonged to the gang, Arroyo got angry and it was Arroyo who gave the "green light" to kill Farfan. "Arroyo could still run things in the jail. That's the whole process. It's based on communication, on getting things out," quoting Salazar's testimony.

When I got to the jail, I asked Chente, "Who's Paul Farfan?"

"I don't know. I've never seen him, heard of him, talked to him or had anything to do with the guy. And I sure as hell didn't send out any order to kill him. What the hell is this all about?"

"I don't know. If what you just told me about Farfan is true, then all I can make of it is that Charlie's trying to get at us for the way we handled his offer."

"I don't care how many cases he puts on me, I'm not gonna plead guilty to nothing."

"I know that. But he's probably thinking it's one way to pressure you into taking the deal. What I don't understand is why they didn't charge Pinky too. He's part of the Mesa.... I guess the one they really want is you, Chente."

"I don't care what they want. I'm not pleading guilty to nothing."

"I'm not asking you to."

"Did you look at those transcripts?"

"I did, but I didn't get very far. There's a thousand pages there. But you know who one of their main witnesses is?"

"Who?"

"Jerry Salazar."

"Cripple Jerrry?"

"Yeah."

"Are you kidding me?"

"No."

"What the hell does that little punk know about anything? He's never been a gang member. I've never dealt with him. Since we came here, he's always been locked up down there on the second floor all by himself. He's never been up here with us. How in the hell would he know anything about what goes on up here?"

"I don't know. I have no idea." All of a sudden I felt very tired. None of it made any sense. Chente was claiming that not only did he not know any of the victims but also none of the perpetrators in two death penalty cases, and yet he was the prosecution's principal target in both cases. We lapsed into silence until I said, "What does Carlos say?"

"He says they're full of shit. That he never gave his wife any message from me and especially no message to kill this Farfan guy."

"I don't know what to make of it."

"What makes it weirder is that Carlos and Cripple Jerry were best friends, road dogs. They were family, almost family. Carlos' brother is married to Jerry's mother and Carlos says that he was always at their house, that he practically lived there."

"So why would Cripple Jerry turn on Carlos?"

"Well remember what Cripple Jerry's lawyer said after Cripple Jerry copped-out and turned?"

"Not really."

"Yeah we talked about it. It was in the paper."

"I don't remember. What did he say?"

"He said that Cripple Jerry probably would never be out on the streets again. That Cripple Jerry knew that, but that he just wanted to escape the death penalty."

"So?"

"Well think about it. People will do and say anything to avoid death. Right?'

When I left the jail that morning, one thing was clearer than ever. I was much more concerned about losing the death penalty trials than Chente was. The first trial was looming on the horizon and I still wasn't prepared to go to trial. Now I had a second death penalty case sitting on my desk. My only option was to concentrate on the first, far more serious case involving six murders and ignore the second case for the time being. Once the first trial was over, I would put off the second trial for as long as possible by telling the court that I hadn't had sufficient time to prepare that case for trial.

Meanwhile, Betsy Carr was continuing to add another dimension to the scenario. She had been unfailing in her devotion to Chente. She visited him twice weekly, no matter how early she had to get out of bed or what the weather was like. She was careful to accommodate his sister's and daughter's visits, graciously ceding her time to them the two or three times a year that they came up from southern California. She showered them with attention when they came. That was money in the bank. They loved her and they sang her praises to Chente not only in their visits, but in their letters to him as well. How fortunate he was to have her, how could he ever hope to do better, was the constant cry.

Her visits, all still tape recorded, were upbeat, filled with positive ideas, discussions and suggestions. And there was always the spontaneous, in the middle of his sentences or hers or during a momentary silence, "I love you, Chente, I love you. Do you know that I love you?" Not infrequently those words would make him pause, reset himself, even if he never answered or seldom acknowledged them. "I love you, Chente. Do you know that I love you?"

She left him money, not large amounts, whenever she could, but enough for him to buy soups and chocolate milk and candy from the jail commissary that passed by the cells. A purchasing power that he had seldom had during his many years in prison. She continued sending books, mostly historical works and now a biography or two. The letters came, one usually after each visit, all read and copied by the jailers who sent copies to the District Attorney, who made and sent copies to all the defense attorneys, who made and gave copies to all their clients. Betsy had a beautiful script. Her letters were not long. Each paragraph was concise, to the point, and loving.

Sometime in early 1995, Betsy created quite a sensation with one of her letters which reached the hands of its normal numerous recipients and probably then some. Because in this letter to Chente, she enclosed a nude photo of herself. In the colored photograph, Betsy was sitting on the floor, cross-legged in a yoga position in front of what appeared to be an Eastern religion altar. Her hands were folded in front of her and her look was austere. She had a full supple figure and the photo captured most of it.

Another of the defense attorneys called me. "Ron have you seen the photo that Betsy Carr has sent your client in one of her letters? It's in the latest box of discovery."

"No, I haven't."

"I think you'd better have a look at it, the sooner the better."

When I saw the photo, I was astounded. Jesus, Betsy! I thought. What now!

I was at the jail the next morning. "Did you get the photo Betsy sent you?"

"What photo?"

"The one where she's all naked."

"Yeah, I got that one."

"What the hell is wrong with her? Doesn't she have any sense at all?"

"Calm down. Calm down."

"What do you mean calm down? Every guard and deputy in this jail must have a copy of that photo by now. And every one of your cell mates will have one, if they don't already have one now."

"So what? What harm does that do to the case?"

"That's not the point, Chente."

"Yes, it is. That's exactly the point. That picture doesn't hurt me or bother me and I don't care who has it or gets it. That woman loves me and she sent me that picture to show me what's mine to enjoy. Only mine. If all those other guys want to beat their meat to it, then let them. The bottom line is that it's mine, not theirs, and every one of them knows it. Let them suffer"

Once Chente rejected Charlie's offer to plead guilty to a life sentence, the line of communication between us and the prosecution froze. Whenever I'd see Charlie in the hallways or in court, he'd ignore me or do his best to avoid speaking to me. Gregarious Kittie would still smile and say "Hi," but little more. Eugene Castor never had much to say to me before and even less then. Their message was clear. There was no time to waste; I'd better be ready for trial.

I filed an extensive motion for discovery which would allow me to photograph Pelican Bay's SHU in detail. The thrust of the motion was that in order to prepare a proper defense for my client, I had to be permitted to photograph the high security area in which he had been imprisoned at the time he allegedly sent out his "hit list" so that I could demonstrate to a jury how improbable that was. To my knowledge, few people outside of law enforcement had been allowed inside the SHU and no one had been permitted to photograph it. Judge Murphy signed the order and I immediately made preparations to photograph the SHU.

My son, Stefan, was by then an accomplished, professional photographer. His resume was impressive. He agreed to go with me to Pelican Bay and photograph the SHU. In late September 1994, we flew to Crescent City and then drove to Pelican Bay State Prison eleven miles from the Oregon border.

The SHU was pretty much as Chente had described it, but being there added a different dimension to it for me. He had mentioned the rain, but I had no idea how much it rained in that northern coastal corner of California. California has been called the Golden State, and I had always assumed that was because of the golden dry grass that covers its hills and unirrigated fields eight months out of the year. The winter rains of December, January and February bring green to those hills and fields. By September and October, the grass and the brush are at their driest, inviting acres of wildfires each year. There was no sign of dryness as we left the Crescent City airport and headed toward the prison. In fact, many of the house roofs were covered with a thick, verdant growth of moss. I had never before seen moss growing on California roofs. Forests, trees, streams abounded; nothing was golden.

About half an hour later, we came upon an immense clearing. Trees had been cut back everywhere. In the distance, I could see the two and three-story, grey, concrete buildings that were the hallmark of California's newer prisons, and the giant 20-foot cyclone fence which encompassed them and the gun towers. I had seen aerial photos of the SHU and it appeared to be a number of earthen mounds on one end of the prison. I could see none of those as we approached.

Prison officials were expecting us. Judge Murphy had directed the District Attorney to apprise the prison authorities of his order and to ask them to facilitate it. We were greeted by a captain and two guards in an administration building. They were polite but cool. After we identified ourselves, I tried to hand the captain a copy of the Judge's order but he said, "That won't be necessary. I already have one." They searched Stefan's camera bag and then the captain informed us that he would be accompanying us throughout our entire visit. He led us through a maze of halls, buildings and walkways until we were there. Without a word from him, I knew we were in the SHU. The circular, glass encased, space-age, control center looked like something out of Star Trek. Three or four guards sat inside monitoring screens and control panels. No other guards were in sight, nor did I see any other than the captain during the entire time we were there. Everything appeared to be run electronically.

There was an eerie silence to the place. I had been in the cell blocks of several jails and prisons, and there had never been an absence of sound. As I looked around at the cells, I could see the reason for the silence. Every cell had a steel door that was shut tight. There were no open-bar cells. This particular pod, as each of the earthen mounds were called, was the one in which Chente had been housed. It reminded me of a small basketball arena. Wings were set perpendicularly to the control center. Each wing had two tiers; each tier had eight to ten cells; each cell was sealed off from everything and anything outside it. The tiers themselves were low-slung. The pod's ceiling was less than 20 feet high. Everything except for the glass in the control center was made of steel and concrete. There were no windows. The entire pod was well-lighted with artificial light that, as Chente had described, was constant. As I stood there, I tried to imagine living with the same artificial light day after day, night after night, month after month, year after year. The pod was antiseptically clean, not a smudge, stain, crack anywhere. On the wall was a large, clock-like thermometer whose needle pointed to 70, always 70, eternally 70. The air was stale.

Stefan and I had talked about what I hoped to show the jurors, and he set right to work, painstakingly, with the captain watching and sometimes taking notes. It would have been clear to anyone what my intention was. I asked to see and we were taken to what had been Chente's cell. It was located on the upper tier of one of the wings. No one was housed there then and it was as bare as bare could be. Eight by ten feet of concrete with a concrete slab upon which a mattress had once laid protruding from one wall, a stainless steel commode and wash basin protruding from the opposite wall, and nothing else. The cell itself had the same artificial light and the same stale air. Inside the cell, there wasn't a hint of an outside sound anywhere. Stefan took a number of photos of the cell and the steel door. When we left, I was convinced that it would have been impossible for Chente to have smuggled a "hit list" out of that cell.

One of the prosecution's theories was that SHU inmates smuggled messages out of the pod when they used the pod library. Inmates could be granted permission to use the law library, especially if their cases were on appeal. According to the prosecution's theory, inmates left messages concealed for other inmates to retrieve and pass along. We were taken to a small room separate and apart from the cells. Here there was an abundance of glass which allowed a guard to watch an inmate on the other side of the glass take and use a book from shelves which contained state and federal statutes and case reports. And watch too when he replaced a text on a shelf. Stefan took photos from every conceivable angle on both sides of the glass. I wondered how Chente could have apprised another inmate that he was going to the law library where he would leave a "hit list" for him in a particular one of many books, and then how the second inmate could retrieve it unseen.

Legally, inmates were to be allowed out of their cells to exercise for one hour a day, and an exercise yard had been constructed at the rear of this pod. Entry into it was through another steel door. It was smaller than half a basketball court and had nothing in it. The floor was of concrete, as were the four 20-foot walls that rose straight up to an open sky. A third of that opening had a covering. But even on that September afternoon, considered to be the driest month in California, the exercise yard was cold, wet, dark and dank. The walls were water-stained and streaked. I saw no electrical lighting. What must it have been like to have been brought out there on those coastal nights to exercise?

I left Pelican Bay glad that I had gone. With the photos and the "hit list" theory, I felt I had something to talk about in the trial. But that feeling never overcame the awful foreboding I had that no jury would ever be able to look past the fact that Vicente Arroyo was the leader of the *Nuestra Familia*.

Chente and Pinky remained close friends throughout the three years and nine months that they were in the Santa Clara County jail together. Pinky came up often in our conversations. "Pinky said...I told Pinky...Pinky thinks...Pinky asked...." Once Lucky turned, Chente seldom raised the names of any of the other codefendants. Like Chente, it had been years since Pinky had had a relationship with a woman. Like Chente, Pinky had a daughter who during the time he was in the local jail must have been 15 to 19 years old. Every defense attorney received copies of every letter written and received by all the incarcerated codefendants. I read the letters Pinky had sent to and received from his daughter. His were loving, caring letters filled with parental advice and safeguards against problems and dangers adolescents faced; some smacked of love letters.

Chente had talked about Betsy with Pinky, who was well-suited to see the effect that she was having on him. More than a year after Betsy had been visiting Chente, Pinky told Chente that he wished he had a girlfriend too. The refrain must have continued and even swelled, because after several months, Chente told me that his family was trying to make arrangements to have a woman visit Pinky and become a friend, a pen pal, and perhaps more. Still later, Chente told me that those arrangements had been made and that Pinky was excited about the prospect. Pinky was in good physical condition. A few inches taller than Chente, more slender in build but muscular too, light skinned with black wavy hair, he could very well have been attractive to women.

I took an interest in the scheduled visit, and after it, I asked Chente, "How did Pinky's visit with that woman go?"

"Not so good."

"Why?"

"He's not saying. He doesn't want to talk about it."

I listened to the jail's recording of that visit which arrived some time later. The visit was awkward and nervous from the beginning. There were several false starts, half sentences and jumbled words on both sides until the woman gave her name, told Pinky where she lived and who she knew in his family. Pinky blurted out, "I'm Pinky." Then there was another long pause until Pinky exclaimed, "Do you like to fuck?...Do you like to fuck?" There was nothing more on the recording and the woman never returned.

The cold war between the prosecution and me continued. Other than the required written material that passed between us, there was no communication. The first trial date had been set for late 1995, but as that date neared, it was clear that none of the defense counsel were ready for trial. Judge Murphy granted what he said would be the final continuance and set the new trial date for the second Monday of June, 1996. There would be no further continuances, he repeated several times. We were going to trial.

By March of 1996, as the trial date neared, there was a distinct change in the tone of Chente and Betsy's visits. For the first time, some of the visits were marked with periods of tension and irascibility. The closer the trial date came, the longer those periods lasted. Betsy was not as sanguine as Chente about the increasing possibility of a death penalty verdict. Death was death no matter how many times Chente said that inmates on Death Row were not being put to death for 20 or 25 years or longer. Betsy couldn't seem to get past the death word itself. That may have contributed to her asking one question over and over again as the trial neared.

"Do you love me, Chente? I love you. Do you love me?"

"Love you? What does that have to do with anything?"

"Do you love me?"

"I don't know what you're talking about."

"Do you love me?"

"I don't know what you mean by 'love.'"

"Yes, you do. It's what I've felt for you for years now. What I've shown you in so many ways."

"I care about you. You know that. I like and respect you. You know that too. But this 'love' business. Why do I have to use that word?"

"Because I want you to. Do you love me?"

"Let's stop this right now. You know how I feel about you. That should be enough. That's plenty. We've got to stop playing these word games and taking all this time out of our visits."

Chente wouldn't tell her. Betsy persisted, but he wouldn't say it, wouldn't voice the word.

Then in the final weeks, Betsy added another request. "Chente, I want you to marry me."

"What! You've got to be kidding. You've got to be out of your mind. What the hell are you talking about, woman?"

"I want you to marry me, that's all."

"Marry you? Why? What do we get out of that? I'm probably going to spend the rest of my life in prison. What good will getting married do? What will it accomplish?"

"We'll be together."

"Together! How in the hell can we be together when you're out there and I'm in here?"

"We'll be one, Chente. You and me. Man and wife."

"Woman, I don't understand you."

And so it went in those final weeks. Meanwhile, I had gotten ready for trial. I could now say to myself that if and when a death penalty verdict came, it would not be because I had not adequately prepared our defense.

Then some eleven days before the trial was to begin, I saw Spencer Strellis, who was representing Carlos Mendoza, in the jail as I was leaving. Strellis was a competent, veteran Oakland defense attorney, who had litigated many high profile homicide and death penalty cases.

"Hold on, Ron, I need to talk to you for a minute."

We moved off to the side. "You ready for trial?" he asked.

"Yeah."

"Still not talking to Charlie and Kittie?"

"No. And they're not talking to me either."

"I think you should talk to them."

"About what?'

"Well, I was talking to Kittie yesterday and the sense that I was getting is that they don't want to try Arroyo."

"Oh, they've already played that game with me. Cop Arroyo to a homicide and they'll drop the death penalty."

"No, the impression I got was that they'll go well below the death penalty and don't need a homicide."

"Are you serious?"

"Yeah, I'm serious. Don't be an idiot. Go talk to them."

I was filled with doubt. But Strellis had been around a long time. He knew prosecutors. I called Kittie, not Charlie. She said, "Charles and I (she always called him 'Charles') would like to talk to you about Arroyo's case. We don't have much time. Can you come up here today?"

I was in the District Attorney's Office in a matter of minutes. Charlie was more cordial than I had ever known him to be; arrogant still, but cordial. It was as if I had never told him that Chente had said that he should go fuck himself. There was no posturing, no games, no reasons (fabricated or otherwise) given for their offer, which was clearly and succinctly laid out by him. "Arroyo can plead guilty to any one of the felonies, not the homicides, in the indictment that he chooses, and we'll drop all the other counts against him. He only has eight years to serve on his present sentence. We will stipulate that whatever time the judge gives him on the felony he chooses to plead to will run concurrent with the term that he's already serving. Which means that he'll be out of prison, if he behaves himself, in eight years. Less with good time."

I was wild with excitement as I tried to parse my way through several thoughts that were banging around in my head. "Will he have to testify against the others?"

"We really don't need him," Charlie said. "But I'm going to have to talk about that with George and Castor. I don't think he'll have to. We can talk about that later though."

"Will he have to debrief?"

"Yes, we'll want him to debrief fully and truthfully."

"Will he have to go back to Pelican Bay and the SHU to serve out the rest of his sentence?"

"We've thought about that..."

"Charlie," I blurted out, "his life won't be worth a dime if he debriefs and doesn't get protective custody."

"I agree. If he debriefs fully and truthfully, we'll see to it that he's placed in a protective custody setting where he can't be hurt."

"So he won't go back to the SHU?"

"No."

"Great. But it may take me a couple of days to talk to him."

"We understand. But get back to us as soon as you can. We don't have a heck of a lot of time before the trial date."

"I will." I was about to leave when it occurred to me that we still had the Farfan case to deal with. "What about the Farfan case? What happens to that?"

"If he cooperates with us fully and truthfully, we'll dismiss it as to him."

I had nothing more to say, nothing more to ask. I was so overwhelmed with their offer that I left immediately, afraid that they might change their minds. Once outside the building, I took stock. Pinky and his first lawyer had come to a parting of the ways. For some time they had not been communicating and Judge Murphy had finally allowed the first lawyer to withdraw from the case and appointed another lawyer to represent Pinky. But that had only been recently and the second lawyer was years away from being prepared to go to trial. Which meant that Chente was about to go to trial with only six codefendants. My guess was that Charlie and Kittie had concluded that Chente could not have smuggled the "hit list" out of the SHU and/or if a "hit list" had been smuggled out, it did not bear any resemblance to the names of the six people who had been murdered or the felonies committed. As to the Farfan dismissal, my guess was that they had decided that Jerry Salazar, their principal witness, did not have enough first-hand knowledge to convict Chente.

But as had been my experience in Chente's case, my exaltation because of the new offer was short-lived. Reality set-in. Chente would never plead guilty to anything under those conditions. He might have pled guilty to a lesser in-nocuous charge. But subject himself to debriefing, expose and incriminate un-told others? No, he would never do that. Chente's identity, his status in life, his self-worth, were based on being the leader of the *Nuestra Familia* prison gang. He was a strong, intelligent man; perhaps more than anything he was a proud man, and very proud of being the leader of that gang. That position had to be the pinnacle of whatever success he had had in life. He cherished it. Now to ask him to become an informant, a rat, the lowest possible form of being in the eyes of himself and the gang, and to stand alongside Lucky and Salazar and the other rats, would be asking too much. Nor could I assure him that he wouldn't have to testify in court against the remaining defendants and become a public rat. No, he would never plead guilty to anything under those conditions. As high as I had felt but minutes before, I then felt lower, it seemed, than I had ever felt in dealing with his case.

I was then still in close proximity to the jail. I could have talked to Chente in a matter of minutes. That was the last thing I wanted to do then. I had to find another way. I had to talk to Betsy. I called her. There was no answer. I called her many times throughout the day. No answer. I finally reached her early in the evening. I told her about the offer. I said I knew Chente wouldn't accept it but, I told her, he had to accept it.

"Betsy, as sure as I'm sitting here, those other six guys are going to get convicted. They're going to get the death penalty. Believe me. My biggest fear is that, regardless of what the evidence shows, Chente will go down with those other six. The jury's not gonna like the *Nuestra Familia*. He's the leader. All those other guys are younger than him, some young enough to be his sons. That jury will think that he's responsible, that he brought them to this point. But for him, the others wouldn't have done what they did. So more than any of them, he should pay. Now more than ever, I'm convinced that he had absolutely nothing to do with any of this. You've got to help me, Betsy. You've got to help Chente help himself."

"How?"

"Betsy, more than anyone, I think that *you* can help him."

"How? What do you want me to do?"

"Tomorrow morning, I'm going to go see him early, before 7:00. I'm going to tell him about the offer. He's going to get angry, pissed-off, pissed-off at me, say there's no fucking way he's going to plead guilty to anything. I'll try to reason with him, explain why he really doesn't have a choice. I hope he doesn't walk out on me. But that's not important. What's important is that you see him tomorrow morning too, after me. Make your visit for the last available one in the morning. That way he will have had time to cool down, to think about everything."

"What do you want me to say?"

"What do I want you to say...? I want you to tell him he has to take the offer. You've got to look past all his macho crap. He loves you, Betsy. He does. He may not want to admit it or bring himself to say it, but he does. He loves you, Betsy. He knows what you've given him. You've probably been the biggest positive force in his life. He needs you more than ever now. Don't hold back, Betsy. If you want a life with him, this is the only way you'll get it."

"You say he'll be out of prison in eight years?"

"Six with good time. You've already been with him three years. Six isn't that much longer."

"Will he go back to Pelican Bay for those six years? That's very far away."

"No, they'll put him in protective custody somewhere nearby if he debriefs fully and truthfully."

"Debriefs?"

"Tells them what he knows about the Nuestra Familia gang."

"I'll be there tomorrow morning after you. I'll do everything I can."

"Thank you, Betsy."

"No, no. Thank you. But will he know that we've talked?"

"If he asks me, I'll have to tell him. If he doesn't, I won't say anything. But you'll have to tell him that I called and told you about the offer. But you shouldn't say anything more about our conversation other than I told you about the offer. I won't tell him anything more than that too. Are you O.K. with that?"

"Yes."

He was already sitting behind his side of the metal mesh when I entered the cubicle the following morning. He watched me warily as I put my things down, as if he knew. Or was it me? He said, "What's up?" those big black eyes riveted on me. How could he have known? I avoided his eyes, busying myself trying to find a pen knowing full well where it was. When I knew I had better look at him, I did, and said, "Chente, something big's come up."

"What?" he said, watching me carefully.

"The D.A. has offered to drop everything, both cases, if you'll plead guilty to one felony, any felony. You pick it and everything else goes away."

"What?" His brow was furrowed, his eyes distrusting.

"The death penalties are dropped, the life sentences are dropped. All you have to do is plead guilty to one felony and the time you get for that will run concurrent with the sentence you're serving now. You can be out on the streets in six years with good time."

"Wait a minute, wait a minute. Explain this to me. How did all this happen?"

"I really don't know what happened or how it came about."

"What do you mean you don't know? You're up here telling me all this. You must have talked to them."

"I haven't been talking to them. You know that. But yesterday when I was leaving the jail, Carlos Mendoza's lawyer told me that I should talk to them because he had the impression that they wanted to cut you a good deal."

"Why?"

"My guess is that now they're convinced that there's no way you could have smuggled a 'hit list' out of the SHU, and even if you did, you couldn't have put the names of the people that were killed on that 'hit list' because you didn't know them or couldn't have known them."

"So you talked to them?"

"Yes I did and that's the offer they made me."

"And I don't have to testify in court for them?"

"They said they didn't think they needed you to."

"But they didn't say that I didn't have to?"

"No, but they were leaning against it and we're going to talk about it some more."

"What else?"

"They said that you would have to debrief, tell them everything you know about the *Nuestra Familia*."

He bit his lower lip, put his head down, resting it on the outside of his hands and then began shaking his head back and forth, stopped, looked up at me and said, "I can't do that." He wasn't angry. Rather, he was thoughtful, sad and low-voiced. "I can't do that, "he repeated several times.

"Chente, we've talked about this many times, too many times. Regardless of what the evidence is, that jury's not going to like the N.F. and they're not going to like you, its leader. They're going to want to hold you responsible for everything that's happened. You could get the death penalty. It's too big a risk to take. Until now I could understand you thinking that the death penalty on Death Row is better than a life sentence in the SHU. But that's not what we're talking about now, Chente. We're talking about six years and you're out on the streets."

"I can't do it," he said, looking away. "I would be going against everything I stand for and believe. I would be going against myself. To turn on all those guys is not something I could live with. I've preached against it. I've preached brotherhood. I've hated every punk that's turned, and now I'd be turning. I can't do it."

We sat in silence. Though I had nothing more to say, nothing more I could think of to say, I couldn't leave, I didn't want to leave. I didn't want to return to that world in which I would have to face Charlie and Kittie and tell them no.

After a while he said, "What about Pinky?"

"What do you mean, what about Pinky?"

"What's gonna happen to him?"

"Chente, Pinky's not going to go to trial for two or three years yet. Pinky's in nobody's sights now. He has nothing to do with this."

"Have they made him an offer too?"

"Pinky's new lawyer's just been in the case a few months. It'll be years before he'll be in a position to talk deals with the D.A."

More silence.

Five, ten minutes later, he said with a mocking look on his face, "How could you ask me to plead guilty to something I didn't do. I was in the SHU in 1991 and 1992, how could I have committed a felony here in San Jose when I was two or three hundred miles away?"

"Don't play with me, Chente. I'm not asking you to do something that's morally wrong. You could plead 'no contest.' That would be enough. It's a way out of this nightmare. That's all it is, a way out."

We sat again without a word for I don't know how much longer. Until he dropped his hands flat on the shelf on his side of the screen and said with finality, "I'm sorry, I can't do it.'

"I'm sorry too," I said and left.

I talked to Betsy late that afternoon. "Did you see him?"

"Yes, of course."

"How was he?"

"Torn. He's going through a lot right now."

"Was he angry? Was he pissed off at me?"

"No, no. When I first saw him, he asked me if I knew. I told him yes, that you had called and told me. That was the only time your name came up. It's more like he's tormented, like he doesn't know which way to turn. It's heavy on his mind. I don't think he's been able to do anything but think about it."

"He wasn't indecisive with me. All he said to me was that he couldn't do it. He said it a number of times, as if he had no other choice, no other options."

"He said that at first to me, but only at first. The longer we were together, the clearer it was to me that he didn't know what to do."

"What did you tell him?"

"I told him it was his life and his decision, but it was really about us. I told him that now, for the first time, it really seemed that we could have a life together. In six years he could be a free man, free to let us spend the rest of our lives together. He didn't put me off the way he can whenever I start talking about our relationship. This time he was stumped, struck by the reality of what could be. I told him that I loved him more than anything in the world and that he had to know that. I asked him, 'Do you love me, Chente? Do you love me?' He looked at me but this time he didn't scoff or ridicule me or try to change the subject like he usually does. He just looked. It wasn't a stare. It was more like he was trying to find the answer somewhere in me. I let him look, I let him search. I knew he wouldn't answer no, not then. But how long would it take for yes?

"I had his full attention then, so I said, 'I want you to marry me, Chente.' That broke his spell. He said something like, 'Are you kidding?' And I said no, that I was very serious. I told him that I heard that if we were married before he went back to prison, we could have conjugal visits, and that I had heard of women that had followed their husbands to some of the prisons, and had actually set up their residence in the small towns near the prisons so that, besides the conjugal visits, they could visit their husbands every day. He was staring at me again. It was like he was trying to sort everything out. I'm not as pessimistic as you, Ron. He just might do it."

I met with Charlie and Kittie the next day. I told them that Chente would not plead to anything unless he was assured that he would not have to testify in court against any N.F. gang members. They said they had cleared that with George and Castor and assured me that he would not be called as a witness, but that he would have to debrief fully and truthfully. I told them I was going to see Chente on the weekend and that I would get back to them on Monday.

Betsy saw Chente again before I did. She called me after the visit. The excitement in her voice told me before she could articulate, "He's going to do it! He's going to do it! He said that he loves me and that he's going to marry me! Please make that part of the bargain too."

Chente was in a subdued, reflective mood when I saw him. "I'm gonna take the deal. I'm gonna do it. I talked to Pinky. We had a long talk. I told him what I was going to do and why I was going to do it. He said, 'Do what you have to do, Chente.' I think he understood. I'm going to marry Betsy. I hope you can arrange that with the judge."

I called Charlie and told him, adding as a condition the marriage in court after Chente's plea had been entered. He said he thought it could be done and would talk to Judge Murphy. I didn't doubt for a moment that the marriage would happen. I guess because, rightly or wrongly, I have always felt that Kittie played a much bigger role in the resolution of Chente's case than would ever be known. For years as the defendants' visits in the jail were being recorded, they were also being simultaneously piped into Charlie and Kittie's home. Sometime later, Kittie was quoted as saying that she had come to know more about the lives of the gang members than she did about her best friends. I'm sure she had watched and appreciated with great interest the change that Betsy Carr had brought about in Chente's life.

Although the impending marriage was only a few days away, word of it spread quickly through the upper echelons of San Jose's society. Uncle Phil, Betsy's surrogate father, and Aunt Susan, the mayor of San Jose, were shocked and not at all pleased. So much so that arrangements were made to have the San Jose Police Chief visit Betsy at her home and apprise her of the threats and dangers from the gang world that she was exposing herself to by marrying Chente.

But Betsy was not to be dissuaded. The marriage took place in Judge Murphy's courtroom after Chente pleaded no contest to a 1991 robbery in San Jose and was sentenced to eight years in prison to be served concurrently with his then existing prison sentence. Then Judge Murphy left the courtroom and, for reasons I have never known, Presiding Judge Jack Komar entered the courtroom. Judge Komar said that he would perform the marriage and asked that the bride and groom and the maid of honor and the best man stand. Betsy had been seated directly behind us in the first row of the spectators' section. She rose and moved as close to her husband-to-be as the railing separating them permitted. Chente rose and moved back in his leg irons as close as he could to the railing. Christy Conroy Lucio, my investigator and someone who had been an immense help to me in the case, rose and stood next to Betsy as the maid of honor, and I stood next to Chente as his best man. Judge Komar recited the marriage vows which Betsy and Chente nervously repeated and accepted. Then they were pronounced man and wife. A few awkward moments of silence followed before Christy whispered to me, "Ron, ask the Judge to let them kiss." I made a brief request and there was more silence in that courtroom packed with armed deputies guarding the man who up to that point had been thought of by many as one of the most heinous criminals to appear in that courthouse. Judge Komar blinked, thought and finally said, "Alright, one kiss, but a brief one please." Chente turned and Betsy leaned over the railing and put her arms around her chained and cuffed husband and kissed him.

This was a happy beginning. Chente was immediately transported to an unknown destination by the local and state authorities. It was several days before Betsy and I were told that he was being housed in the Protective Housing Unit at the Corcoran State Prison some 50 miles southwest of Fresno. The Protective Housing Unit holds up to 47 inmates who require "extraordinary protection" from other inmates. Housed in the PHU at the time of Chente's arrival were, among others, Juan Corona who in 1971 was convicted of murdering 25 people; Charles Manson, the head of the infamous Manson Family; and Sirhan Sirhan, the convicted assassin of Senator Robert F. Kennedy.

In the months that followed, I talked to Betsy on the telephone several times. She was always up beat no matter how difficult things might have become for her. She was still living with her mother, but whatever source of income she might have previously had, no longer existed. She had taken a clerical job with a non-profit organization that, while low-paying, gave her the flexibility to visit

Chente as often as she could. She didn't have a car, so she took a Greyhound bus from San Jose to Fresno. From Fresno, she took a rural bus that left irregularly and infrequently for the small town of Corcoran. She and Chente had been granted conjugal visits, so she bought and took as many provisions as she could on the buses to make the two day visits as special as possible. She said she loved Chente more than ever and was happy to have this time with him. After a few months, Betsy no longer called me. But for several years, she would leave a bouquet of handpicked roses at my office on my birthday, telling the receptionist only, "These are for Mr. Ruiz. He'll know who they're from."

Three months after Chente was sentenced, Charlie asked that I meet with him, Kittie and Chente and prison officials at the PHU in Corcoran. They apparently wanted to satisfy themselves and/or the prison officials that Chente had debriefed fully and truthfully. I drove to Corcoran curious about the PHU and some of its inmates. The PHU was not what I expected. Unlike Pelican Bay's SHU with its earthen mounds off to one side of the general population buildings, Corcoran's PHU was a small concrete building squarely inside the main prison, but completely sealed off by a high cyclone fence with electronic security wiring atop it. The PHU building was a miniature replica of the buildings surrounding it. Inside the front of the building was a 100'x100' open plot of ground that was the inmates' yard. When I asked him about some of the other inmates, he said that Sirhan Sirhan kept to himself, that Corona was weird, and that Manson was crazy, that he walked around the yard endlessly.

When Charlie and Kittie arrived, I was struck by the relationship they now had with Chente. They were like old friends, warm and casual. But then I thought that they must have had a lot of contact with him in the debriefing process that had taken place over the many days since I had last seen him. The meeting took place within a small office inside the PHU. I had advised Chente beforehand to answer everything openly and completely. He said that he had already told them everything he knew about the N.F., and was convinced that none of it was anything they didn't already know. A prison captain did most of the questioning and Chente's answers were forthright and complete. The session was short, well under an hour. When it was over Chente and I shook hands and that short bear of a man hugged me and said goodbye. It was the last time I was to see Chente.

Four months later, Charlie and Kittie began trying the case against four N.F. gang members who, aside from Pinky Hernandez, were the last remaining defendants of the original 21 charged in the first indictment. All the others had reached a plea bargain agreement with the District Attorney and had been sentenced or had sentences pending. Once the trial was underway, Kittie called me with an unusual request. She asked me to visit Pinky in the jail and try to persuade him to accept a plea bargain they were offering him. The request was unusual in two respects. First, Pinky was already represented by an attorney and, without that attorney's permission, there was no way I could speak to him. Second, Charlie and Kittie were now willing to let Pinky plead no contest to a single misdemeanor charge in return for which they would drop all the other charges against him. Kittie said that Pinky's attorney had tried to have him accept their offer of a misdemeanor plea with no success, and was willing to let me talk to him. They thought that because of my relationship with Chente, Pinky's closest friend, he might more willingly accept my advice. I agreed to try, thinking it was foolish for Pinky to risk going to trial on six murder charges that carried the death penalty and an assortment of felonies when he could dispose of the matter with a misdemeanor guilty plea.

This time I went up to the jail on behalf of the District Attorney. It's amazing what kind of treatment one receives from the jail personnel, as well as the increased amount of access you are allowed to have with an inmate then. The sergeant in charge greeted me with open arms and personally led me back to Pinky's cell, not the visiting cubicle that I, Chente and Pinky too had used for years. Standing on one side of the open-bar cell, I looked down at Pinky who was lying in his bunk. It struck me as bizarre that Pinky was the only inmate left in these series of cells, in this specially modified cell block for the *Nuestra Familia* gang members.

"Pinky," I said.

Looking up, getting up, he said, "Ron, what are you doing here? How's Chente?"

"He's fine."

"Where's he at?"

"I can't get into that."

"That's O.K. I understand. But what are you doing up here?"

He was at the bars then. We were inches apart. "Pinky, your lawyer said I could talk to you. I came up here to see if I could convince you that it's in your best interest to take the deal the D.A.'s offering you."

Despite the pages of criminal records Pinky had, he looked hurt, as if I had offended him. "I can't do that."

"Why not?"

"Because I didn't do anything and I'd be pleading guilty to something I didn't do. Believe me, I had nothing to do with this fucking mess."

"Pinky, you may be 100% right, but do you understand what you're risking by going to trial? And the D.A.'s not asking you to testify or debrief."

"I can't do it. It's not right." His look was filled with self-righteousness.

"Pinky, we're talking about a misdemeanor, about a disturbing the peace, a trespass, a petty theft. That's nothing."

"I can't. I can't. I can't."

On and on I went, each time faced with a refusal, until I began to feel that I was preying on Pinky, that I was trying to get him to do something he didn't want to do for my sake, my ego, not for his sake. I left then and called Kittie and told her that Pinky wouldn't accept their offer. Later, I remembered how many times Chente and Pinky must have talked the matter through and were convinced that it would be far better for them to go to Death Row rather than return to Pelican Bay's SHU.

The case against Pinky was ultimately dismissed. Bobby Lopez, James Trujeque and Herminio Serna were convicted of multiple murders and received the death penalty. Eddie Vargas was convicted of murder and received a life in prison sentence.

The further away I got from the *Nuestra Familia* case, the clearer it became to me that the District Attorney had no case against Chente and Pinky. The satisfaction I had initially received from the result in Chente's case was very likely self-deception. Would Charlie and Kittie not have treated Chente as they did Pinky, if he had refused their offer? To give Chente and Pinky what they gave them meant that at some point, Charlie and Kittie had come to the conclusion, and had to admit, that they had been lied to, duped, deceived from the beginning of the case and on through several years by their informants, Louie "Dump Truck" Chavez, Ronald "Lucky" Shelton, and Jerry "Cripple" Salazar. All the hullabaloo that had appeared in the media for years about Chente and Pinky, their ruling mesa and their "hit list" was nothing more than lies. And life being what it is, the man most deserving of the death penalty, the serial killer, Ronald "Lucky" Shelton, got away with murder.

Several years later, I heard that Betsy and Chente had divorced. Then I heard that Chente had been released from prison on parole. Not long ago, I heard that Chente had married a school teacher and is living somewhere in California.

In January 1999, the Santa Cruz County Board of Supervisors appointed me the District Attorney of Santa Cruz County, filling a vacancy created when the former District Attorney became a Superior Court Judge. I held that office until I was defeated in the November 2000 general election. Those two years were a harrowing experience, but I have never regretted them because they gave me an opportunity to see and experience law enforcement and politics as I would never have had otherwise.

In September 2001, I began working on an independent contract basis as a deputy Public Defender for San Mateo County. After years of office overhead and a daily suit and tie, it was a refreshing change. I had no office to speak of and the only time I wore a suit and tie then was when I was in trial. I tried several cases over the two years I was there until I suffered a bout of global amnesia, and my doctor advised me in November, 2003 that, "Unless your next case is a walk in the park, I wouldn't go on with it if I were you." That evening, after 33 years, I retired from the practice of law.

Acknowledgements

My thanks and appreciation to Jan McClellan, Renick McClellan, Leigh Stowell, and Jay Amberg for their time, comments, and interest in helping with this project.